Insider's Guide To Government Benefits

TABLE OF CONTENTS

Chapter 8

Chapter 9

Chapter 10

Chapter 11

Chapter 12

INTRODUCTION

I *nsider's Guide To Government Benefits* lists sources of grants and other financial help that can benefit you and your company. Since there are so many resources, it would be impossible for you to find out about all of them. The extensive list of sources- including cash grants, private grants, and government aid- each have their own qualifications. Although not everyone qualifies for each grant, you can write directly to the source to find out if you qualify.

There are many opportunities to obtain cash grants and other types of financial aid. Remember *Insider's Guide To Government Benefits* provides lots of information, you choose the sources that you can qualify for. Here are a few of the topics covered in the book:

1. Grants for Education
2. Business loans, SBA loans and sources
3. Housing grants, rental help
4. Doing business with the government
5. Government grants
6. Financial help for the needy
7. Help for the handicapped
8. Government subsidies, financial aid for crime insurance, money for the artist
9. Mortgage loans for land, mobile homes
10 . Inside information on bank loans

There is a variety of programs and opportunities which can help you and your business. Simply go through the book and pick out the programs or grants you want to apply for. Send a letter asking for details and qualifications.   In our Free Bonus section we have outlined procedure for obtaining signature loans and establishing credit. You'll discover how easy it is to establish your credit and get a signature loan.

We have tried to provide you with updated addresses for each of the different sources. However, addresses (even government agency addresses) do change. If you come across an address that has changed or no longer exists we would appreciate knowing about it. Please write a letter to the address below:

> Book Changes
> The Editor
> Keystone Publishing
> P.O. Box 51488
> Ontario, CA 91761

Chapter 1
HOW TO GET IN ON A FEDERAL LOTTERY

I f you enter one of these relatively unknown federal lotteries, you have a chance to obtain a permit that entitles you to drill for oil or gas on the land you are leasing. If you win, you pay a low rental fee of $1 per year for the first five years (then $3 per year thereafter) to lease land on which you can drill for oil and gas.

HOW TO ENTER THE DRAWINGS:

These drawings, which are held monthly at a central government office in Wyoming, allow randomly selected winners to lease tracts of land owned by the federal government to drill for oil and gas. The winners cannot build a house on the land or do anything else to the government property.

"Many tracts offered are in the Western states where most of the public land is located. These are the states of Alaska, Arizona, California, Colorado, Idaho, Montana, Nevada, New Mexico, Utah and Wyoming. Occasionally tracts in Washington, Oregon, Alabama, Arkansas, Florida, Louisiana, Michigan, Mississippi and Ohio are offered," according to a federal government report.

Listed at the end of this booklet is a selection of the lands that are offered by state offices of the Bureau of Land Management. Tracts of land from 10 to 10,240 acres are available from these lotteries. Contact these state offices to find out what land is up for auction in the months of February, April, June, August, October and December.

When you enter the lottery, list only the particular property you wish to purchase. You will be competing with others for this same piece of valuable land.

HOW TO FILE FOR THE LOTTERY

Five free applications can be obtained by contacting the Bureau of Land Management offices listed at the end of this chapter. The Government Printing Office has additional applications if you need them. Indicated on the form will be the deposit that is required to bid on each piece of land. You send this completed form to the central address listed on the form. At this Wyoming office, the federal government decides who gets the drilling rights.

WHEN YOU WIN A TRACT

Major oil companies will want your land if they believe it has considerable value. You will be offered either a lump cash payment or you will receive royalty benefits, depending on how much oil is found on the land; either way the oil companies will reimburse you, so remember to bargain for the best deal.

Contact both large and small oil companies if none asks to purchase your land. You can return your land after one year if no one buys it, and you will be charged only for the filing fee.

Unless huge amounts of gas or oil are drilled, your lease to the land lasts 10 years. Many people put in bids for land they hope will be profitable for them, but this is a lottery and anyone is eligible to strike it rich.

State Offices of the United States Department of the Interior, Bureau of Land Management

States east of the Mississippi River, plus Iowa, Minnesota, Missouri, Arkansas, Louisiana and Wisconsin.

Alaska

701 C Street, Box 13
Anchorage, AK 99513

Arizona
3707 North 7th Street
Phoenix, AZ 85014

Eastern States Office
7450 Boston Blvd
Springfield, VA 22304

Idaho
3380 Americana Terrace
Boise, ID 83706

Montana, North Dakota, and
South Dakota
222 North 32nd Street
P.O. Box 30157
Billings, MT 59107

Nevada
Federal Building, Room 3008
300 Booth Street
Reno, NV 89520

California
Federal Building,
Room E-2841
2800 Cottage Way
Sacramento, CA 95825

Colorado and Kansas

2020 Arapahoe Street
Denver, CO 80205

New Mexico, Oklahoma,
and Texas
Joseph Montoya Federal Building
P.O. Box 1449
Santa Fe, NM 87501

Oregon and Washington
829 N.E. Multnomah Street
P.O. Box 2965
Portland, OR 97208

Utah
University Club Building
136 East South Temple
Salt Lake City, UT 84111

Wyoming and Nebraska
2515 Warren Avenue
P.O. Box 1828
Cheyenne, WY 82003

I n this day and age, when everyone is dying to talk about what
they do for a living and rarely is

Chapter 2
GETTING SOMEONE TO HELP YOU

one given the chance to share that information, large bureaucracies and impersonal organizations can work to your advantage. An expert can be found on any topic providing you make an average of seven telephone calls to find that expert.

The Value Of Experts

With so much information to absorb, experts can be your key to understanding the necessities. Although computers have helped to disseminate some of this information, they fail to contain information from non-traditional sources, such as buried documents of government agencies. Another problem with computers is that their databases do not hold the most current information. Most publishers have long lead times before any material gets to print.

Another serious problem with computers, is that because of their ability to store large quantities of data, there is even more information for a person to absorb. For example, if you were to access a major database on a subject like poverty, you are more than likely to be confronted with more than 750 citations. Do you have time to read all of these articles, some of them being useless?

The answer to such predicaments is to find an expert who specializes is poverty issues. Yes, one does exist and will have already read all of those 750 articles and more. This expert will also help you with your information needs by telling you what will be in the literature in the near future, because he or she will probably be reviewing forthcoming articles and books. These government bureaucrats know every fact and figure right off the top of their heads, or they know where to find it, and it can be yours for the mere price of a telephone call.

Getting An Expert To Talk

There are certain tactics, however, that you must be aware of when dealing with the experts. You must be able to treat the expert with the kind of respect that will persuade him or her to come forth with your information needs. Although most individuals feel important when you need their knowledge, belittling the importance of the subject or creating a negative environment that makes the expert uncomfortable, will not help you in your search for the answers. Just remember to be polite and that a government bureaucrat is not obligated to assist you. He or she will always receive the same amount of pay whether you get your answers or not.

Telephone Tips

To keep you from losing your call when trying to find an expert, keep the following guidelines in mind. Although most of them are common sense, when you begin to feel stressed, they will help.

1) Introduce Yourself Cheerfully: Your introduction will set the tone for the entire interview. Be cordial and enthusiastic, and give the person the feeling that this isn't just another phone call, but a chance for that person to provide great assistance.

2) Be Open And Candid: If you expect the person to be candid and open with the information you need, then you should expect to do the same. No one will help you if you are evasive or deceitful.

3) Be Optimistic: Having a positive attitude when speaking to someone will go a long way. Your confidence will show if you call and say "you probably aren't the person that I am looking for." So always have a positive attitude.

4) Be Humble And Courteous: Never question a person's authority. If you do that person will feel that you are being rude and will not want to help you. So be polite.

5) Be Concise: Be as clear as possible when explaining what you need. A long-winded explanation may bore the recipient of your phone call, so communicate your needs concisely. It will increase your chances of getting the information that you need.

6) Don't Be A "Gimme": You must always consider the other person's feelings and time. Don't say "give me this" or "give me that." You hurt your chances of getting some help.

7) Be Complimentary: Remember the old adage "Flattery will get you everywhere," and it's true. Compliment the person on his or her expertise or insight. That makes the person feel more important and not to mention, will get you going to where you want to be.

8) Be Conversational: When you do find your expert, don't over-whelm him or her with questions. You may scare the individual into giving you the wrong information. First mention a few irrelevant topics to make the person feel comfortable. Being social puts you on a friendly basis and will make the expert feel like he just isn't being used, but is actually a human being.

9) Return The Favor: You may find that you have information that may be beneficial to the expert as well. Share your information or even call back later during your research with information the expert may find interesting.

10) Send Thank You Notes: A short note showing your appreciation will ensure that your source will be just as cooperative to other infor-mation-seekers, as he was to you. And will provide assurance that you can rely on that source in the future.

Tips On Applying For Money

The following guidelines are meant to give money seekers, advice and encouragement when applying for money. Keep them in mind always, and you may find cash in your pockets.

1) Don't Always Believe A Negative Answer: If you ever call a government office to ask about a particular money program, and they say that no programs of that nature exist, don't believe them. Not every gov-ernment employee knows everything. In fact, you can expect to get your answer from only 50% of the people that you ask. The same people who are even responsible for administering money programs. Sometimes the program that you are seeking may have been consolidated with other programs under a new name. To help you find that program, ask the fol-lowing questions;

- Did such a program ever exist?
- What happened to the program?
- Are there any similar programs?
- Can I get a descriptive listing of all your current money programs?
- What other programs might offer money in similar areas?

Asking the government employee probing questions like these, will help you find the program you are looking for. And if that individual still can't give you the answers, ask to speak to someone else.

2) Apply To More Than One Program: There is no rule that says you can't apply to more than one program. Some applications don't even ask you if you are receiving money from anywhere else. Although you may not be able to accept the money from all the departments that approve your application, you increase your chances of getting any money at all.

3) Don't Be Discouraged If You Think You Are Not Eligible: If you find out that you are not eligible for a specific program because of some requirement that was changed in the criteria, don't be discouraged. There are so many programs that the government offers, that you will probably find one that you qualify for. Just ask.

4) Talk To Those Who Give The Money: Before you fill out any applications, it is a good idea to review the forms with the program directors. This will help you to tailor your answers on the application in your favor, and provide the government with information that meets their expectations.

5) Give Them What They Want: Even though a question on the application may not seem logical to you, give the government the answer that they are looking for. It doesn't help you to get angry and fight, because most likely the government will not change the question.

6) Starting Small Or Big? : Depending on the program, you will need to be careful in saying how much money you need. Be sure you understand the maximum amount and the average amount of money given to applicants. You can ask the program office to give you this information.

7) Try Again: Never give up! If your application is rejected, it may have been a minor error on you part or even the government's. Find out why your application was not approved and either try again next year or try a different program. Some programs will turn you down just to see if you are serious about your project, so be persistent.

8) When The Bureaucracy Is Stuck, Use Your Representative: If you have found that the bureaucracy is having a problem with handling your paperwork in a prompt fashion, call your U.S. Senator or Congressperson to help give them a push. Remember, though, to use this as a last resort.

9) Don't Overlook State Programs: State agencies many times, can offer you the same assistance that the federal financial programs can. So check them out. If you are looking for real estate programs, look under "Real Estate Ventures" or if you are looking for business money programs, they are listed under "State Money and Help for Your Business."

Chapter 3
LOANS AND GRANTS
FOR EDUCATION

M ore than $17 billion in financial aid is available for students each year, according to the College Board Scholarship Service. Although you don't have to be poor to receive aid, you have to prove you need it.

Most students receive different types of financial aid. Grants (aid given without condition of return), loans and work-study programs are available. Many institutions offer grants, aids and work-study loans based on demonstrated need, not on past or present family income.

Demonstrated need is the difference between what an education actually costs and how much a family can legitimately contribute toward a student's education. To qualify, fill out all aid forms at the college of your choice.

TYPES OF LOANS & GRANTS

The U. S. Department of Education offers several student financial aid programs. Many are grants which do not have to be repaid.

PELL GRANTS

Pell Grants are awards to help undergraduates pay for their education after high school. For many students these grants provide a "foundation" of financial aid, to which aid from other federal and non-federal sources may be added. Unlike loans, grants don't have to be paid back.

1) Pell Grants are:

Free gifts--thus, no repayment

For undergraduates only

For part-time or full-time students

Usually limited to 5 full years of study

HOW MUCH MONEY CAN YOU GET?

You must submit all three parts of your Student Aid Report (SAR) to your school, which will then credit your award to your account, pay you directly or use a combination of these methods.

SUPPLEMENTAL EDUCATIONAL OPPORTUNITY GRANTS

A Supplemental Educational Opportunity Grant (SEOG) is an award to help you pay for your education after high school. It is for undergraduate students with exceptional financial need (priority is given to Pell Grant recipients). The grant does not have to be paid back.

Free gifts--thus, no repayment

For undergraduates only

A campus-based program

Awarded based on need and availability of funds

HOW MUCH?

You can obtain up to $4,000 per year, depending on your need, the availability of SEOG funds at your school and the amount of additional aid you are receiving.

HOW TO APPLY?

Different schools set different deadlines. Deadlines are usually early in each calendar year, so apply as soon as possible. Find out what the deadlines are by checking with the financial aid administrator at your school.

PERKINS LOANS

The National Direct Student Loan has been renamed the Perkins loan as a memorial to Carl D. Perkins, the late chairman of the House Education and Labor Committee, for his support of public education and desire for a program of direct federal loans to students. The Perkins loan is a low-interest (five percent) loan to help you pay for your education after high school. These loans are for both undergraduate and graduate students and are offered through a school's financial aid office. Check with your school financial administrator to determine if your school takes part in the Perkins loan program.

Must be repaid. Loans:

> Are for undergraduate and graduate students

> Are offered through a campus-based program

> Are based on need and availability of funds

How Much Can I Get?

Depending on your financial need, the availability of Perkins loan funds at your school and the amount of additional aid you are receiving, you may borrow up to--

- •$4,500, if you're enrolled in a vocational program or have completed less than two years of a program leading to a bachelor's degree.
- •$9,000, if you're an undergraduate student who has already completed two years of study toward a bachelor's degree and has achieved third-year status.
- •$18,000 for graduate or professional study.

When Do I Apply?

Each school usually has a deadline early in the calendar year, so apply as soon as possible.

Can I Receive a Perkins Loan if I'm a Part-Time Student?

Perhaps. Perkins loans are often available to part-time and sometimes less than part-time students.

GOVERNMENT STUDENT LOANS

A Guaranteed Student Loan (GSL) is a low-interest loan offered by a lender such as a bank, credit union or savings and loan association to help you pay for your education after high school. These loans are insured by the guarantee agency in your state and reinsured by the federal government.

For new borrowers who take out a loan before July 1, 1988, the interest rate is eight percent. For new borrowers who seek loans for periods of enrollment beginning on or after July 1, 1988, the interest rate is eight percent for the first four years of repayment and 10 percent thereafter. For students who currently have a seven or nine percent GSL, the interest rate on additional GSL's will continue to be seven or nine percent.

Guaranteed Student Loan borrowers must:

>Repay their loans

>Be undergraduate or graduate students

>Be enrolled at least part time

>Apply for a Pell Grant

How Much Can I Borrow?

Depending on your need, you may borrow up to--

- $2,625 per year, if you're a first- or second-year under graduate student.
- $4,000 per year, if you have completed two years of study and achieved junior status.
- $7,500 per year, if you're a graduate student.

The total outstanding GSL debt allowable is $17,250. The total for graduate or professional study is $54,750, including any GSL loans made at the undergraduate level. You can't borrow more than the cost of education at your school, minus any other financial aid you receive. Remember, all GSL applicants must show financial need, and in some cases, the amount of need may limit the size of the GSL.

When Should I Apply?

You should begin looking for a lender as soon as you are accepted by your school. After you submit your application to a lender and the lender agrees to make the loan, it usually takes four to six weeks to get your loan approved by the guarantee agency. Consequently, allow yourself as much time as possible to complete the application process.

PLUS LOANS-SUPPLEMENTAL LOANS

PLUS loans are for parent borrowers; SLS's are for students. Both loans provide additional funds for educational expenses and are offered by a lender such as a bank, credit union or savings and loan association. Before July 1, 1987, interest rates on PLUS loans ranged from 9 to 14 percent, depending on when the loan was made. The interest rate for each loan is shown on the promissory note to be signed by the borrower when the loan is made.

SLS and PLUS loans disbursed on or after July 1, 1987 will have an interest rate which is adjusted each year. For the 1987-88 award year, the interest rate was 10.27 percent. The interest rate for the 1988-89 award year will be determined in June 1988.

Who Can Get a Loan, and How Much Can They Borrow?

* PLUS enables parents to borrow up to $4,000 per year, to a total of $20,000, for each child who is enrolled at least part-time and is a dependent student.

* Under SLS, graduate students and independent undergraduates may borrow up to $4,000 per year, to a total of $20,000. This amount is in addition to the GSL limits.

How Does a Borrower Apply?

The same way as for a GSL. Unlike GSL borrowers, however, PLUS and SLS borrowers do not have to show need. They may have to undergo a credit analysis, though.

Is there any charge to make a PLUS loan or an SLS?

The guarantee agency in your state may charge an insurance premium of up to three percent of the loan principal. This premium must be deducted proportionately from each loan disbursement made to you. There is no origination fee for these loans.

What are the repayment and deferment conditions?

SLS and PLUS borrowers must begin repaying interest within 60 days after the loan is disbursed, unless the lender agrees to let the interest accumulate until the deferment ends.

SLS borrowers get the same deferments as GSL borrowers. However, under SLS, the deferments apply only to loan principal. PLUS deferments are much more limited and apply only to principal. For more information about specific repayment and deferment conditions for SLS and PLUS loans, contact your financial aid administrator, lender or the guarantee agency in your state.

I'm Having Trouble Finding a Lender. What Should I Do?

Contact your state guarantee agency. It is the best source of information on the GSL, PLUS and SLS programs in your state.

Banks and other lenders take part voluntarily in these programs and lend out their own money. While the Department of Education encourages lenders to provide student loans, it can't dictate the policies of a lending institution as long as those policies don't discriminate based on the applicant's race, religion, national origin, sex, age, marital status, handicap or financial situation.

What are the rights and responsibilities of a PLUS or SLS borrower?

Many of the rights and responsibilities of GSL borrowers also apply to PLUS and SLS borrowers. Lenders will also inform you of any refinancing options available when you take out a loan. If you have a GSL, PLUS or SLS and need to borrow again, contact your first lender to make future refinancing easier.

COLLEGE WORK STUDY

The College Work-Study (CWS) Program provides jobs for undergraduate and graduate students who need financial aid. CWS offers an opportunity to earn money for your educational expenses.

College Work-Study:

Provides jobs, so you can earn money for school

Is for undergraduate and graduate students

Is a campus-based program

Awards jobs based on need and availability of funds

HOW MUCH CAN YOU MAKE?

Your pay will be at least the current federal minimum wage, but also may be related to the type and difficulty of the work.

Your total CWS award depends on your need, the amount of money your school has for this program, and the amount of aid you receive from other programs.

If you're an undergraduate, you will be paid by the hour. If you're a graduate student, you may be paid hourly or receive a salary. No CWS student may be paid by commission or fee. You will be paid at least once a month.

Are College Work-Study Jobs On-Campus or Off-Campus?

Both. If you work on-campus, you'll work for your school. If you work off-campus, your job will usually involve work that is in the public interest. Your employer will usually be a private or public non-profit organization, or a local, state or federal agency. However, some schools may have agreements with private-sector employers for CWS jobs.

Is employment based on need and availability of funds?

No. Your school sets your work schedule. In arranging a job and assigning work hours, your class schedule, health and academic progress will be considered. Remember, the amount you earn can't exceed your total CWS award.

I'm Going to School Part-Time. Can I Get a CWS Job?

Possibly. A school may use a portion of its CWS funds for part-time and less than part-time students. To find out your school's policy on this matter, contact the financial aid administrator.

How Will I Know if I'm Going to Get a CWS Job?

You will receive a list of the amount and kinds of financial aid available, including information about CWS employment. In addition to the specified loans and grants listed above, there are several types of aid offered by individual states. Listed below are the names and addresses of the state agencies which offer these programs. Contact your school financial aid administrator to obtain further and more up-to-date information.

PRIVATE SUPPORT FOR EDUCATION

Bank of America-Giannini Foundation
Bank of America Center, Department 3246
Box 37000
San Francisco, CA 94137
(415) 953-0932

Information: Research fellowships for California medical students.

University of California

Information: Grants available for Jewish orphans interested in aeronautical engineering.

CONNECTICUT

The Balso Foundation

c/o The Ball & Socket Manufacturing Company

493 West Main Street

Cheshire, CT 06410

(203) 272-5361

Information: Scholarships given to high school seniors and college undergrads in the Cheshire area.

Undergraduate Scholarship

P.O. Box 2170

Yale Station

New Haven, CT 06520

Information: Scholarships for undergraduates studying at Yale.

ILLINOIS

The Aurora Foundation

111 W. Downer Place, Suite 312

Aurora, IL 60507

(312) 896-7800

Information: Loans and scholarships for students living in the Aurora area.

INDIANA

Babcock Memorial Scholarship Fund

c/o Bank One of Indianapolis N.A.

101 Monument Circle

Indianapolis, IN 46277

(317) 639-8145

Information: Scholarships for graduates of Rochester High School only.

Baber Foundation, Inc.
535 S. Broadway
Peru, IN 46970
(317) 437-7526
Information: Loans for graduates of Miami County high schools only.

MASSACHUSETTS
Kimball Endowment
Financial Aid Office
Amherst College
P.O. Box 2207
Amherst, MA 01002 (413) 542-2296
Information: Grant is need-based for students of Amherst College.

Colman Trust
c/o Boston Safe Deposit & Trust Company
One Boston Place
Boston, MA 02106
(617) 722-7341
Information: Grants given to artists living in the New England area

Pennoyer, Downer, Ellis and Floyd Grants
Harvard Financial Aid Office
312 Byerly Hall
8 Garden Street
Cambridge, MA 02138
(617) 495-1581

MISSOURI
Barber Scholarship Trust
P.O. Box 938
Hannibal, MO 63401

Information: Scholarships for graduating seniors in Marion County and Pike County, Illinois.

Ayres Trust
c/o First National Bank of Kansas City
14 W. Tenth Street
Kansas City, MO 64105
(816) 234-7481
Information: Scholarships & awards for theological and medical training

MISSISSIPPI
Biglane Foundation
P.O. Box 966
Natchez, MS 39120
Information: Scholarships for residents of Natchez only.

NORTH CAROLINA
Gatling Grant
North Carolina State University
P.O. Box 7302
Raleigh, NC 27695-7302
(919) 737-2421
Information: You qualify for this scholarship if your name is Gatling.

NEW HAMPSHIRE
The Barker Foundation Inc.
P.O. Box 328
Nashua, NH 03061
(603) 889-1763
Information: Scholarships given based on need and academic performance.

Berry Trust Fund
c/o George Findell, Jr.

P.O. Box 2036

Rochester, NH 03867

(603) 332-1670

Information: Scholarships for male students attending college in Strafford County, NH

NEW JERSEY

Bergen Foundation

765 Broad Street

Newark, NJ 07102-3717

(201) 829-7111

Information: Financial aid for music students living in New Jersey

NEW YORK

The Bagby Foundation for the Musical Arts

501 Fifth Avenue

New York, NY 10017

(212) 986-6094

Information: Music study grants given based on talent and need

OHIO

Beta Theta Fraternity Founders Fund

208 E. High Street

P.O. Box 111

Oxford, OH 45056

(513) 523-7591

Information: Scholarships for members of Beta Theta Pi fraternities in U.S.

UTAH

Bamberger and John Ernest

Bamberger Memorial Foundation

1201 Walker Center

Salt Lake City, UT 84111

(801) 364-2045

Information: Scholarships for Utah undergraduate medical students.

CALIFORNIA

Barco Employees Educational Trust

c/o Michael C. Ferguson

2168 Shattuck Avenue, No. 300

Berkeley, CA 94704

(415) 548-9005

Information: Scholarships to employees of Barco and their descendants

Whitelight Foundation

703 Hilcrest

Beverly Hills, CA 90210

Information: Grants for established classical musicians living in Southern Calif.

Borrego Springs Educational Scholarship Committee

P.O. Box 59

Borrego Springs, CA 92004

(619) 767-5314

Information: Loans & Scholarships to graduating seniors of Borrego Springs high schools

Gemco Charitable and Scholarship Fund

6565 Knott Avenue

Buena Park, CA 90620

(714)739-6351

Information: Scholarships to high school seniors in California communities

Disney Foundation

500 South Buena Vista Street

Burbank, CA 91521

(213) 840-1000

Information: Scholarships to children of Walt Disney Productions and its affiliates

Corti Family Agricultural Fund

c/o Wells Fargo Bank, Trust Department

618 East Shaw Avenue

Fresno, CA 93710

(209) 442-6232

Information: Scholarships for graduates of Kern County, CA, high schools interested in agriculture-related careers.

Carnation Company Scholarships Foundation

5045 Wilshire Boulevard

Los Angeles, CA 90036

(213) 932-6282

Information: College scholarships for relatives of Carnation Co. employees

Stacey Testamentary Trust

c/o Security Pacific National Bank

P.O. Box 3189 Terminal Annex

Los Angeles, CA 90051

Information: Awards to artists whose work is devoted to Western culture

Grubb Oakland Scottish Rite Scholarship Foundation

1367 Lakeside Drive

Oakland, CA 94612

Information: Scholarships to students wishing to study in Central & Northern California

Boye Scholarship Trust

c/o Wells Fargo Bank

400 Capitol Mall

Sacramento, CA 95814

Information: Scholarships to residents of Sacramento County who are pursuing careers in agriculture

Grotefend Scholarship Fund
c/o Wells Fargo Bank Trust Department
400 Capital Mall
Sacramento, CA 95814
(916) 244-4600

Information: Scholarships to students who attended high school in Shasta County and are in need

BankAmerica Foundation
c/o Bank of America Center
Dept. 3246, P.O. Box 37000
San Francisco, CA 94137
(415) 953-3175

Information: Scholarships to BankAmerica employees and their children.

Brandt Scholarship Fund
c/o Wells Fargo Bank, N.A. -- Trust Tax Division
343 Sansome Street, Third Floor
San Francisco, CA 94163

Information: Scholarships to graduating seniors of high schools in the southern San Joaquin Valley.

Wilbur Foundation
P.O. Box B-B
Santa Barbara, CA 93102
(805) 962-0011

Information: Fellowships, grants and support for persons interested in humane literature.

COLORADO
Flatirons Foundation, The
P.O. Box 2088

Aspen, CO 81611

(303) 925-2094

Information: Scholarships for students who have attended Aspen High School

CONNECTICUT

Amax Foundation, Inc.

Amax Center

Greenwich, CT 06836

Information: Scholarships for children of Amax employees only

DELAWARE

Beneficial Foundation, Inc.

1100 Carr Road

P.O. Box 911

Wilmington, DE 19899

(302) 798-0800

Information: Scholarships for children of employees of Beneficial Foundation's affiliated corporations.

FLORIDA

Dettman Foundation Inc.

108 Southeast Eighth Avenue

Fort Lauderdale, FL 33301

(305) 525-6102

Information: Scholarships for employees of Personnel Pool of America

GEORGIA

Brightwell School Inc.

254 Oakland Avenue

Athens, GA 30606

(404) 543-6450

Information: Scholarships for unmarried or divorced students under 30 who resided in the Maxeys, GA, area for at least six months prior to scholarship date.

ILLINOIS

The Cultural Society Inc.

P.O.Box 1374

Bridgeview, IL 60455

(312) 371-6429

Information: Welfare assistance to needy Muslims.

INDIANA

Central Newspapers Foundation

307 North Pennsylvania St.

Indianapolis, IN 46204

Information: Scholarships for children of employees employed continuously with Central Newspapers Inc.'s affiliated companies.

IOWA

Collins Trust, No. 2

c/o Lyon County State Bank

Rock Rapids, IA 51246

(714) 427-2581

Information: Scholarships for individuals who pursue college education.

KANSAS

Borton-Ryder Memorial Trust

Bank IV Emporia, N.A.

P.O. Box 1048

Emporia, KS 66801-1048

Information: Scholarships for students in the Emporia area who wish to study medicine.

KENTUCKY

Young Memorial Fund

c/o Owensboro National Bank, Trust Department

230 Frederica Street

Owensboro, KY 42301

Information: Scholarships for students in Owensboro, Davies and McClean counties, KY, school districts.

MAINE

Gould Point Sebago Scholarship Fund

Point Sebago

RR 1, Box 712

Casco, ME 04015

(207) 655-7948

Information: Scholarships for employees and their children who work at Point Sebago, as well as graduates of Lake Region HS in Naples, ME, and Windham HS in Windham, ME.

MARYLAND

The Easton Fund Inc.

c/o Mercantile-Safe Deposit & Trust Company

Two Hopkins Plaza

Baltimore, MD 21201

Information: Assistance to women 60 or older & residents of Baltimore

MASSACHUSETTS

Boston Globe Foundation

The Boston Globe Building

Boston, MA 02107

(617) 929-2895

Information: Scholarships for employees of Affiliated Publications, its subsidiaries, their families, and residents of the metropolitan Boston area.

MICHIGAN

Gerber Companies Foundation

c/o Gerber Products Company

445 State St.

Fremont, MI 49412

(616) 928-2224

Information: College scholarships for employees of Gerber products.

MISSISSIPPI

Feild Co-Operative Association Inc.

P.O. Box 5054

Jackson, MS 39216

(601) 939-9295

Information: Educational loans and students loans to Mississippi residents who are college juniors & seniors or graduate & professional students.

MISSOURI

Block Foundation

4410 Main Street

Kansas City, MO 64111

(816) 932-8424

Information: Scholarships to children of employees of H & R Block.

NEW HAMPSHIRE

Young Trust

c/o BankEast Trust Company

2 Wall Street

Manchester, NH 03105

(603) 335-1534

Information: Scholarships to needy residents of Strafford County who have completed at least one year of college.

NEW JERSEY

Grupe Foundation Inc.

22 Old Short Hills Road

Livingston, NJ 07039

(201) 740-1919

Information: Medical, nursing and paramedical scholarships to residents of Bergen, Essex and Hudson counties, NJ.

NEW YORK

Braverman Foundation, Inc.

1609 Avenue J

Brooklyn, NY 11230

(718) 377-4466

Information: Scholarships to graduates of the Yeshiva of Flatbush Joel Braverman High School only. Grants are for one year of study in Israel.

NORTH CAROLINA

Giles Foundation

736 Hempstead Place

Charlotte, NC 28207

Information: Scholarships to descendants of employees of Carauster Industries and its subsidiaries.

NORTH DAKOTA

Brown Trust

112 Bismarck, ND 58501

(701) 223-5916

Information: Student loans to residents of North Dakota.

OHIO

Austin Powder Foundation

c/o Austin Powder Company

3690 Orange Place

Cleveland, OH 44122

Information: Scholarships to children of employees who have worked at least 10 weeks for five seasons at Austin Powder Company.

OKLAHOMA

Educational Fund for Children of Phillips Petroleum Company Employees

180 Plaza Building

Bartlesville, OK 74004

(918) 661-4087

Information: Scholarships for high school seniors who are children of employees of Phillips Petroleum Company.

OREGON

Bohemia Foundation

2280 Oakmont Way

Eugene, OR 97401

Information: Scholarships to college students who are employees of Bohemia.

PENNSYLVANIA

Blank Scholarship Fund

c/o Jeffrey Blank

300 Jenkintown Commons

Jenkintown, PA 19046

Information: Scholarships to children of employees of Continental Bank, Philadelphia.

SOUTH CAROLINA

Bailey Foundation

P.O. Box 1276

Clinton, SC 29325

(803) 833-6830

Information: Loans & scholarships to children of employees of Clinton Mills Inc. or its subsidiaries.

TEXAS

Caston Foundation Inc.

c/o Navarro College

Corsicana, TX 75110

(214) 874-6503

Information: Scholarships for residents of Navarro, TX & surrounding area who wish to attend Navarro College.

VERMONT

Faught Memorial Scholarship Trust

Bellows Falls Trust Company

P.O. Box 399

Bellows Falls, VT 05101

(802) 463-4524

Information: Scholarships to graduates of Bellows Falls Union High School, District 27, VT.

VIRGINIA

Virginia S. Grim Educational Fund

c/o First National Bank Trust Department

P.O. Box 1301

McLean, VA 22101-1340

(703) 667-2000

Information: Educational loans to students in the Winchester, VA area.

WASHINGTON

Schiff Foundation

c/o Bank of California, N.A.

State Educational Agencies

Information: Educational Grants to 11th and 12th graders in DC public high schools.

ALABAMA

Alabama Commission on Higher Education

1 Court Square, Suite 221

Montgomery, Alabama 36197-0001

GSL, PLUS, SLS and State Aid: (205)269-2700

ALASKA

Alaska Commission on Post-secondary Education

400 Willoughby Avenue, Box FP

Juneau, Alaska 99811

GSL, PLUS, SLS and State Aid: (907)465-2854

ARIZONA
State Aid:
Commision for Post-secondary Education
3030 North Central Avenue, Suite 1407
Phoenix, Arizona 85012
(602)255-3109

ARKANSAS
GSL, PLUS, SLS:
STUDENT GUARANTEE PROGRAM
FOUNDATION OF ARKANSAS
219 SOUTH VICTORY
LITTLE ROCK, ARKANSAS 72201-1884
(501)371-1441

CALIFORNIA
California Student Aid Commission
P.O. Box 945625
Sacramento, California 94245-0625
GSL, PLUS, SLS: (916)323-0435
State Aid:
P.O. Box 942845
Sacramento, California 04245-0845
(916)445-0880

COLORADO
GSL, PLUS, SLS:
Colorado Guaranteed Student Loan Program
11990 Grant, Suite 500
North Glenn, Colorado 80233
(303)450-9333
State Aid:
Colorado Commission on Higher Education
Colorado Heritage Center

1300 Broadway, 2nd Floor
Denver, Colorado 80203
(303)866-2723

CONNECTICUT
State Aid:
Connecticut Department of Higher Education
61 Woodland Station
Hartford, Connecticut 06105-2391
(203)566-2618

DELAWARE
Delaware Higher Education Loan Program
Carvel State Office Building
820 North French Street, 4th Floor
Wilmington, Delaware 19801
GSL, PLUS, SLS:
(302)571-6055
State Aid: (302)571-3240

FLORIDA
Office of Student Financial Assistance
Department of Education
Knott Building
Tallahassee, Florida 32399
GSL, PLUS, SLS:
(904)488-8093
State Aid: (904)488-6181

GEORGIA
Georgia Student Finance Commission
2082 East Exchange Place, Suite 200
Tucker, Georgia 30084
GSL, PLUS, SLS: (404)493-5468 State Aid: (404)493-5444

HAWAII

GSL, PLUS, SLS
Hawaii Education Loan Program
P.O. Box 22187
Honolulu, Hawaii 96822-0187
(808)536-3731
State Aid:
State Post-secondary Education COM.
209 Bachman Hall
University of Hawaii
2444 Dole Street
Honolulu, Hawaii 96822
(808)948-8213

IDAHO

GSL, PLUS, SLS:
Student Loan Fund of Idaho Inc.
Processing Center
P.O. Box 730
Fruitland, Idaho 83619
(208)452-4058
State Aid:
Office of State Board of Education
650 West State Street, Room 307
Boise, Idaho 83720
(208)334-2270

ILLINOIS

Illinois State Scholarship Commission
106 Wilmot Road
Deerfield, Illinois 60015
GSL, PLUS, SLS and State Aid: (312)948-8550

INDIANA
State Student Assistance Commission of Indiana
150W. Market Street, #500
Indianapolis, IN 46204-2811
GSL, PLUS, SLS: (317)232-2366
State Aid: (317)232-2351

IOWA
Iowa College Aid Commission
201 Jewett Building
9th and Grand Avenue
Des Moines, Iowa 50309
GSL, PLUS, SLS: (515)281-4890
State Aid: (515)281-3501

KANSAS
GSL, PLUS, SLS:
Higher Education Assistance Foundation
6800 College Blvd., Suite 600
Overland Park, Kansas 66211-1532
(913)345-1300
State Aid:
Kansas Board of Regents
Suite 609, Capitol Tower
400 SW 8th
Topeka, Kansas 66603
(913)296-3517

KENTUCKY
Kentucky Higher Education Assistance Authority
1050 U.S. 127 South
Frankfurt, Kentucky 40601
GSL, PLUS, SLS and State Aid: (502)564-7990

LOUISIANA
Governor's Special Commission on Education Services
P.O. Box 44127, Capital Station
Baton Rouge, Louisiana 70804
GSL, PLUS, SLS and State Aid: (504)342-9415

MAINE
Maine Department of Educational and Cultural Services
Division of Higher Education Services
State House Station 119
Augusta, Maine 04333
GSL, PLUS, SLS and State Aid: (207)289-2183

MARYLAND
GSL, PLUS, SLS:
Maryland Higher Education Loan Corporation
2100 Guilford Avenue, Room 305
Baltimore, Maryland 21218
(301)333-6555
State Aid:
Maryland State Scholarship Board
2100 Guilford Avenue, 2nd Floor, Room 207
Baltimore, Maryland 21218
(301)333-6420

MASSACHUSETTS
GSL, PLUS, SLS:
Massachusetts Higher Education Assistance Corporation
Berkeley Place
330 Stuart Street
Boston, Massachusetts 02116
(617)426-9434

MICHIGAN
GSL, PLUS, SLS:
Michigan Department of Education
Guaranteed Student Loan Program
Box 30047
Lansing, Michigan 48909
(517)373-0760
State Aid:
Michigan Department of Education
P.O. Box 30008
Lansing, Michigan 48909
(517)373-3394

MINNESOTA
GSL, PLUS, SLS:
Higher Education Assistance Foundation
85 7th Place East, Suite 500
St. Paul, Minnesota 55101-2173
(612)296-3974
State Aid:
Minnesota Higher Education Coordinating Board
Capitol Square, Suite 400
550 Cedar Street
St. Paul, Minnesota 55101
(612)296-3974

MISSISSIPPI
GSL, PLUS, SLS:
Mississippi Guaranteed Student Loan Agency
3825 Ridgewood Road
P.O. Box 342
Jackson, Mississippi 39211-6463
(601)982-6663
State Aid:

Mississippi Post-secondary Education Financial Assistance
Board
P.O. Box 2336
Jackson, Mississippi 39225-2336
(601)982-6570

MISSOURI
Coordinating Board for Higher Education
P.O. Box 1438
Jefferson City, Missouri 65102
GSL, PLUS, SLS and State Aid: (314)751-3940

MONTANA
Montana University System
33 South Last Chance Gulch
Helena, Montana 59620-3104
GSL, PLUS, SLS and State Aid: (406)444-6594

NEBRASKA
GSL, PLUS, SLS:
Higher Education Assistance Foundation
Cornhusker Bank Building
11th and Cornhusker Highway, Suite 304
Lincoln, Nebraska 68521
(402)476-9129
State Aid:
Nebraska Coordinating Commission for Post-secondary
Education
P.O. Box 95005
Lincoln, Nebraska 68509-5005
(402)471-2847

NEVADA
GSL, PLUS, SLS:

NGSLP Nevada State Department of Education
400 West King Street, Capitol Complex
Carson City, Nevada 89710
(702)885-5914
State Aid:
Student Financial Aid Services
University of Nevada-Reno, Room 200 TSSC
Reno, Nevada 89557-0072
(702)784-4666

NEW HAMPSHIRE
GSL, PLUS, SLS:
New Hampshire Higher Education Assistance Foundation
P.O. Box 877
Concord, New Hampshire 03302
(603)225-6612
State Aid:
New Hampshire Post-secondary Education Commission
2 and one-half Beacon Street
Concord, New Hampshire 03301
(603)271-2555

NEW JERSEY
GSL, PLUS, SLS:
New Jersey Higher Education Assistance Authority,
C.N. 543
Trenton, New Jersey 08625
(609)588-3200
State Aid:
Department of Higher Education
Office of Student Assistance
4 Quakerbridge Plaza, C.N. 540
Trenton, New Jersey 08625
1-800-792-8670

NEW MEXICO
GSL, PLUS, SLS:
New Mexico Educational Assistance Foundation
P.O. Box 27020
Albuquerque, New Mexico 87125-7020
(505)345-3371
State Aid:
Commission on Higher Education
1068 Cerrillos Road
Sante Fe, New Mexico 87501-4295
(505)827-8300

NEW YORK
New York State Higher Education Services Corporation
99 Washington Avenue
Albany, New York 12255
GSL, PLUS, SLS: (518)473-1574
State Aid: (518)474-5642

NORTH CAROLINA
North Carolina State Education Assistance Authority
P.O. Box 2688
Chapel Hill, North Carolina 27515-2688
GSL, PLUS, SLS and State Aid: (919)549-8614

NORTH DAKOTA
GSL, PLUS, SLS:
Bank of North Dakota
Student Loan Department
P.O. Box No. 5509
Bismarck, North Dakota 58502-5509
(701)224-5600
State Aid:
North Dakota Student Financial Assistance Program

10th Floor, State Capitol
Bismarck, North Dakota 58505-0154
(701)224-4114

OHIO
GSL, PLUS, SLS:
Ohio Student Loan Commission
P.O. Box 16610
Columbus, Ohio 43266-0610
(614)466-3091
State Aid:
Ohio Board of Regents
Student Assistance Office
3600 State Office Tower
30 East Broad Street
Columbus, Ohio 43216
(614)466-7420

OKLAHOMA
Oklahoma State
Regents for Higher Education
500 Education Building
State Capitol Complex
Oklahoma City, Oklahoma 73105
GSL, PLUS, SLS: (405)521-8262
State Aid: (405)525-8180

OREGON
Oregon State Scholarship Commission
1445 Willamette Street
Eugene, Oregon 97401
1-800-452-8807 (within Oregon)
GSL, PLUS, SLS:
(503)686-3200   State Aid: (503)686-4166

PENNSYLVANIA
Pennsylvania Higher Education Assistance Agency
660 Boas Street
Harrisburg, Pennsylvania 17102
GSL, PLUS, SLS: 1-800-692-7392
State Aid: 1-800-692-7435

RHODE ISLAND
Rhode Island Higher Education Assistance Authority
560 Jefferson Boulevard
Warwick, Rhode Island 02886
GSL, PLUS, SLS: (401)277-2050
Out of State Toll-Free #: 1-800-922-9855

SOUTH CAROLINA
GSL, PLUS, SLS:
South Carolina Student Loan Corporation
Interstate Center, Suite 210
P.O. Box 21487
Columbia, South Carolina 29221
(803)798-0916
State Aid:
Higher Education Tuition Grants Agency
411 Keenan Building, Box 12159
Columbia, South Carolina 29211
(803)734-1200

SOUTH DAKOTA
GSL, PLUS, SLS:
Education Assistance Corporation
115 First Avenue, SW
Aberdeen, South Dakota 57401
(605)773-3134

TENNESSEE

Tennessee Student Assistance Corporation

400 James Robertson Parkway, Suite 1950, Parkway Tower

Nashville, Tennessee 37219-5097

GSL, PLUS, SLS and State Aid:

(within TN: 1-800-342-1663); Rest of the United States: (615)741-1346

TEXAS

GSL, PLUS, SLS:

Texas Guaranteed Student Loan Corporation

P.O. Box 15996

Austin, Texas 78761

(512)835-1900

State Aid:

Texas Higher Education Coordinating Board, Texas College and University System

P.O. Box 12788

Austin, Texas 78711

(512)462-6400

UTAH

GSL, PLUS, SLS:

Loan Servicing Corp. of Utah

P.O. Box 30802

Salt Lake City, Utah

84130-0802

(801)363-9151

State Aid:

Utah State Board of Regents

3 Triad Center, Suite 550

335 West North Temple

Salt Lake City, Utah

84180-1205   (801)538-5247

VERMONT

Vermont Student Assistance Corporation
Champlain Mill
P.O. Box 2000
Winooski, Vermont 05404-2000
GSL, PLUS, SLS and State Aid: (within VT: (1-800-642-3177); Rest of the United States: (802)655-9602

VIRGINIA

GSL, PLUS, SLS: State Education Assistance Authority
6 North Sixth Street, Suite 300
Richmond, Virginia 23219
(804)786-2035
State Aid:
State Council of Higher Education for Virginia
James Monroe Building
101 N. 14th Street
Richmond, Virginia 23219
(804)225-2141

WASHINGTON

GSL, PLUS, SLS:
Washington Student Loan Guarantee Association
500 Colman Building
811 First Avenue
Seattle, Washington 98104
(206)625-1030
State Aid:
Higher Education Coordinating Board
908 East Fifth Avenue
Olympia, Washington 98504
Attn: Financial Aid Office
(206)753-3571

WEST VIRGINIA

GLS, PLUS, SLS:

Higher Education Assistance Foundation

Higher Education Loan Program of West Virginia Inc.

P.O. Box 591

Charleston, West Virginia 25322

(304)345-7211

State Aid:

West Virginia Board of Regents

P.O. Box 4007

Charleston, West Virginia 25364

(304)347-1211

WISCONSIN

GSL, PLUS, SLS:

Wisconsin Higher Education Corporation

2401 International Lane

Madison, Wisconsin 53704

(608)246-1800

State Aid:

Wisconsin Higher Educational Aids Board

P.O. Box 7885

Madison, Wisconsin 53707

(608)267-2206

WYOMING

GSL, PLUS, SLS:

Higher Education Assistance Foundation

American National Bank Building

1912 Capitol Ave., Suite 320

Cheyenne, Wyoming 82001

(307)635-3259

State Aid:

Wyoming Community College Commission

2301 Central Avenue
Barrett Building, 3rd Floor
Cheyenne, Wyoming 82002
(307)777-7763

AMERICAN SAMOA

GSL, PLUS, SLS:
Pacific Islands Educational Loan Program
United Student Aid Funds Inc.
1314 South King Street, Suite 961
Honolulu, Hawaii 96814
(808)536-3731
State Aid:
American Samoa Community College
P.O. Box 2609
Pago Pago, American Samoa 96799
(684)699-9155

NORTHERN MARIANA ISLANDS

GSL, PLUS, SLS: See American Samoa
State Aid:
Northern Mariana College Board of Regents
P.O. Box 1250
Saipan, CM 96950
(Saipan) 670-7542

FEDERATED STATES OF MICRONESIA; MARSHALL ISLANDS REPUBLIC OF PALAU

GSL, PLUS, SLS: See American Samoa
State Aid:
Community College of Micronesia
P.O. Box 159
Kolonia, Ponape, F.S.M. 96941
(Ponape) 480 or 479

VIRGIN ISLANDS
Virgin Islands Board of Education
P.O. Box 11900
St. Thomas, Virgin Islands 00801
GSL, PLUS, SLS and State Aid: (809)774-4546

USUF, INC
United Student Aid Funds Processing Center
P.O. Box 50827
Indianapolis, Indiana 46250
(800) 382-4506 (within IN)
(800) 824-7044 (rest of United States)

GUAM
GSL, PLUS, SLS: See American Samoa
State Aid:
University of Guam
UOG Station
Mangilao, Guam 96913
(671)734-2921

PUERTO RICO
GSL, PLUS, SLS:
Higher Education Assistance Corporation
P.O. Box 42001
Minillas Station
San Juan, Puerto Rico 00940-2001
(809)758-3356/3328
State Aid:
Council on Higher Education
Box F-UPR Station
San Juan, Puerto Rico 00931
(809)758-3356/3328

> # Chapter 4
> # Cash And Grants
> # For The Needy

ALABAMA

Middleton Fund
P.O. Box 2527
Mobile, AL 36601

Information: Grants or 4% loans are available to pay the hospital bills of Mobile County, AL residents.

The Dixon Foundation
1625 Financial Center
Birmingham, AL 35203
(205) 252-2828

Qualifications: Must be resident of Alabama
Grant Amount: Average grant $200 - $2500
Purpose: For prescription medications and health supplies.
Contact: Carol Dixon - Write letter.

Cambodian Association of Mobile
box 160812
Mobile, Al 36616
(205) 957-2096

Qualifications: Must be Cambodian immigrant who is a resident of Alabama.
Grant Amount: N/A

Purpose: To help pay for health services.
Contact: Sanh Suon - Write letter.

Kate Kinloch Middleton Fund
P.O. Drawer 2527
Mobile, AL 36601

Qualifications: Residents of Mobile County
Grant Amount: $81 - $8,094
Purpose: Help with medical expenses.
Contact: Joan Sapp - Write Letter, interview required.

La Nelle Robson Foundation
25612 E. J. Robson Blvd.
Sun Lakes, AL 35248

Qualifications: Must be resident of Alabama
Grant Amount: $145,000 for 15 grants
Purpose: To pay for medical expenses and higher education.
Contact: Steven S. Robson - Write letter.

McWane Foundation
P O Box 43327
Birmingham, AL 35243

Qualifications: Must be resident of Alabama
Grant Amount: $373,400
Purpose: To pay for medical expenses.
Contact: J. R. McMahan - write letter.

The William H. and Kate F. Stockham Foundation Inc.
c/o Stockham Valves and Fittings Inc..
4000 North Tenth Ave
P O Box 10326
Birmingham, AL 35202

Qualifications: For former and present employees who are residents of southeastern states.

Grant Amount: $225 - $3,500
Purpose: For education and general living expenses
Contact: Richard J. Stockham, Jr.

ARIZONA
Jewish Family and Children's Service
2033 North Seventh St.
Phoenix, AZ 85006
(602) 257-1904

Qualifications: Residents of Arizona who are immigrants or refugees.
Grant Amount: N/A
Purpose: To help with general living expenses.
Contact: Patricia M. Brouard - Write letter.

Lorraine Mulberger Foundation, Inc.
c/0 Burch & Cracciolo
702 East Osborn
Phoenix, AZ 85014
(602) 274-7611

Qualifications: For Arizona residents
Grant Amount: $300 - $3,436 (eleven grants   awarded)
Purpose: For people who can demonstrate financial need.
Contact: Andrew Abraham - Formal Application

The Wallace Foundation
3370 North Hayden Road
Suite 123-287
Scottsdale, AZ 85251
(602) 962-4059

Qualifications: Residents of Arizona
Grant Amount: $184,530 for 28 grants
Purpose: To help with general living expenses
Contact: Nancy Shaw - Write letter

ARKANSAS

Arkansas Department of Human Services

Refugee Resettlement Program

P O Box 1437

Little Rock, AR 72203

(501) 682-8263

Qualifications: For refugees and immigrants who are residents of Arkansas.

Grant Amount: N/A

Purpose: To help with medical and living expenses.

Contact: Walt Patterson - Write letter.

Lyon Foundation, Inc.

65th and Scott Hamilton Dr

Little Rock, AR 72204

Application Address:

P O box 4408

Little Rock, AR 72214

Qualifications: Residents of Arkansas

Grant Amount: $35,730

Purpose: For those who demonstrate financial need.

Contact: Ralph Cotham - Write letter and include personal backround.

CALIFORNIA

All Culture Friendship Center Refugee and Immigration Services

5250 Santa Monica Blvd

Los Angeles, CA 90029

(213) 66700489

Qualifications: For immigrants and refugees who are residents of California.

Grant Amount: N/A

Purpose: To help with living expenses and provides educational and social services.

Contact: N/A

Arrillaga Foundation
2560 Mission College Blvd
Room 101
Santa Clara, CA 95050
(408) 980-0130

Qualifications: Resident of California
Grant Amount: $364,255 for 40 grants
Purpose: For help with living and educational expenses.
Contact: John Arrillaga - Write letter

Avery-Fuller Children's Center
251 Kearney Street
San Francisco, CA 94108
(415) 930-8292

Information: Financial aid to help disabled & handicapped children in living in the counties of San Francisco, Alameda, Contra Costa, San Mateo, and Marin.

William Babcock Memorial Endowment
305 San Anselmo Ave Suite 219
San Anselmo, CA 94960
(415) 453-0901

Qualifications: For residents of Marin County.
Grant Amount: $407,020 for 480 grants.
Purpose: To help pay medical and surgical expenses.
Contact: Alelia Gillin - Call, Formal Application.

Brotman Foundation of California
c/o Robert D. Harford
433 North Camden Dr., No. 600
Beverly Hills, CA 90210
(213) 271-2910

Qualifications: For child welfare and residents of California.
Grant Amount: $302,200 for 36 grants.
Purpose: To help pay medical expenses.

Contact: MIchael B. Sherman - Write letter.

California Department of Social Services
Office of Refugee Services
744 P Street
Sacramento, CA 95814

Qualifications: Grants for immigrants and refugees who are residents of California.

Grant Amount: N/A

Purpose: To help pay for resettlement expenses.

Contact: Walter Barnes - Write for guidelines.

Cambodian Association of America
602 Pacific Ave
Long Beach, CA 90802
(213) 432-5849

Qualifications: For Southeast Asian immigrants and refugees who are residents of California.

Grant Amount: N/A

Purpose: For living expenses and integration.

Contact: Nil Hul - Write or Call.

Catholic Social Service Refugee Resettlement Project
5890 Newman Ct
Sacramento, CA 95819

Qualifications: Residents of Sacramento who are refugees.

Grant Amount: N/A

Purpose: To help pay resettlement expenses, also provide other social services.

Contact: Cau Lao - Write or Call.

Clinica Monsigneur Oscar A. Romero
2675 West Olympic Blvd.
Los Angeles, CA 90006
(213) 389-0288

Qualifications: Must be resident of California who is a Central American or Caribbean immigrant.

Grant Amount: N/A

Purpose: For help with living expenses. Educational, Cultural, and other social services are available.

Contact: Ana Zeledon - Write letter.

Coalition for Immigrant and Refugee Rights and Services

2111 Mission St.

San Francisco, CA 94110

(415) 626-2360

Qualifications: Must be resident of San Francisco who is an immigrant or refugee.

Grant Amount: N/A

Purpose: To help pay medical expenses. Legal and other social services are available.

Contact: Emily Goldfarb - Write letter.

Ebell of Los Angeles Rest Cottage Associates

743 South Lucerne Blvd

Los Angeles, CA 90005

Qualifications: Residents of Los Angeles.

Grant Amount: $90,000 for 3 grants of $30,000 each.

Purpose: To help pay medical expenses.

Contact: Alberta Burke - Write letter.

Myrtle V. Fitchen

Charitable Trust

380 Eddy Street

San Francisco, CA 94102

(415) 558-4161

Qualifications: For elderly residents of San Francisco County.

Grant Amount: $2,400 - $10,000

Purpose: To help pay for health expenses.

Contact: Richard Livingtston - Write letter.

German Ladies Benevolent Society

P O Box 27101

San Francisco, CA 94127

(415) 391-9947

Qualifications: For women and children of German heritage who are residents of San Francisco.

Grant Amount: $83,813

Purpose: To help those who can demonstrate financial need.

Contact: Inge Byrnes - Write for guidelines.

Clorinda Giannini Memorial Benefit Fund

P O Box 37121

San Francisco, CA 94127

Application Address:

Bank of America

Bank of America Center

San Francisco, CA 94101

(415) 622-4915

Qualifications: For employees of Bank of America **Grant Amount:** $20,699 for 25 grants.

Purpose: To help those in financial need due to injury or other emergency.

Contact: Susana Morales - Write letter.

Hattie Givens Testamentary Trust

1017 West 18th St

Merced, CA 95340

(209) 722-7429

Application Address:

1810 M Street

Merced, CA 95340

Qualifications: For residents of California.

Grant Amount: $9,150 for 3 grants.

Purpose: For help with health expenses.

Contact: Trustees - Formal Application.

The Goodman Foundation
700 South Flower St
Los Angles, CA 90017-4101
Qualifications: For residents of Los Angeles.
Grant Amount: $136,240 for 82 grants.
Purpose: To help with health expenses.
Contact: Lawrence M. Goodman, Jr. - Write letter.

Good Samaritan Community Center
1292 Portrero Ave
San Francisco, CA 94110
(415) 824-3500
Qualifications: For Central American and Caribbean refugees who are residents of San Francisco.
Grant Amount: N/A
Purpose: Grants and cultural programs.
Contact: Will Wauters - Write or call.

Hmong Council
4670 East Butler Ave
Fresno, CA 93702
(209) 456-1220
Qualifications: For Southeast Asian immigrants and refugees who are residents of Fresno.
Grant Amount: N/A
Purpose: To help pay living, medical, and legal expenses.
Contact: Phen Vue - Write for information.

Hoefer Family Foundation
100 Pine St. Fifth floor.
San Francisco, CA 94111
(415) 342-7111

Qualifications: For residents of California.

Grant Amount: 66 grants ranging from $20 - $10,000.

Purpose: To help pay for living and higher education expenses.

Contact: Alan Hoefer - Write letter.

International Institute of Los Angleses Refugee Relocation and Placement Program

164 West Valley Blvd.

San Gabriel, CA 91776

(818) 307-1084

Qualifications: For immigrants and refugees who are residents of California.

Grant Amount: N/A

Purpose: To help pay general living and medical expenses.

Contact: Thongsy Chen - Write or call.

International Institute of San Francisco

2209 Van Ness Ave

San Francisco, Ca 94109

(415) 673-1720

Qualifications: For immigrants or refugees who are resident of California.

Grant Amount: N/A

Purpose: To help pay living expenses.

Contact: Don Eiten - Write or call.

John Percival and Mary C. Jefferson Endowment Fund

114 East De La Guerra

Santa Barbara, CA 93102

(805) 963-8822

Qualifications: For residents of Santa Barbara.

Grant Amount: 29 grants $106 - $6,500.

Purpose: To pay medical, dental, and living expenses.

Contact: Patricia M. Brouard - Write letter.

The Trustees of Ivan V. Koulaieff Educational Fund
651 11th Ave
San Francisco, CA 94118

Qualifications: Russian Immigrants.

Grant Amount: 27 grants $100 - $43,200

Contact: W.W. Granitow - Write letter and proposal.

Loa Family Community
855 West 15th Street
Merced, CA 95340
(209) 384-7384

Qualifications: Southeastern Asian immigrants or refugees who are residents of California.

Grant Amount: N/A

Purpose: Emergency aid for living and medical expenses. Legal assistance and educational programs also available.

Contact: Houa Yang - Write or call.

New Horizons Foundation
700 South Flower St Suite 1122
Los Angeles, CA 90017-4160
(213) 626-4481

Qualifications: Christian Scientists over 65 who live in Los Angeles.

Grant Amount: 11 grants $200 - $6,000

Purpose: To help those in financial need.

Contact: C. Grant Gifford - Call or write.

Peninsula Community Foundation
1700 South El Camino Real, No. 300
San Mateo, CA 94402-3049
(415) 358-9817

Qualifications: Must be resident of San Mateo County or northern Santa Clara County.

Grant Amount: 161 grants given - $50 - $100

Purpose: To provide emergency assistance.

Contact: John D. Taylor - Write letter and proposal.

Pfaffinger Foundation
Times Mirror Square
Los Angeles, CA 90053
(213) 237-5743

Qualifications: For current and former employees of Times Mirror company.

Grant Amount:$1,000 - $10,000

Purpose: To help those in financial need.

Contact: James C. Kelly - Submit proposal between July and September.

Charles E. Saak Trust
c/o Wells Fargo Bank
2222 West Shaw Ave Suite 11
Fresno, CA 93711
(209) 442-6230

Qualifications: Disadvantaged residents under 21 of Poplar, California area.

Grant Amount: 170 grants for $67 - $960.

Purpose: To help pay for higher education and dental and emergency medical costs.

Contact: Wells Fargo Bank, N.A.

Virginia Scatena Memorial Fund
for San Francisco School Teachers
c/o Bank of America, N.A.
555 California Street
Seventeenth Floor
San Francisco, CA 94104

Qualifications: Retired San Francisco public school teachers who are sick or in financial need.

Grant Amount: 4 grants for $2,400 - 12,000

Purpose: To help with general living expenses.

Contact: Walter M Baird - Write letter.

The Sonoma County Foundation
1260 North Dutton Ave Suite 280
Santa Rosa, CA 95401
Qualifications: Must be resident of Sonoma County.
Grant Amount: $10,000 for 10 grants.
Purpose: To help with education and living expenses.
Contact: Virginia Hubbell - Write letter.

Sunnyvale Community Services
810 West McKinley Ave
Sunnyvale, CA 94086
(408) 738-4321
Qualifications: Must be a resident of California who is a refugee or immigrant.
Grant Amount: N/A
Purpose: For help with emergency expenses. Social services provided.
Contact: Janet Gundrum - Write letter.

Vietnamese Community of Orange County
3701 West McFadden Ave Suite M
Santa Ana, CA 92704
Qualifications: Southeast Asian immigrants and refugees for are residents of Orange County.
Grant Amount: N/A
Purpose: To help with living expenses. Social services provided.
Contact: Tuong Njuyen - Write letter.

Winnett Foundation
c/o Bullocks Executive Offices
800 South Hope St.
Los Angeles, CA 90017-4684
Qualifications: Residents of California.
Grant Amount: 22 grants for $2,229 - $5,279.
Purpose: To help those in financial need and to help with medical expenses.

Contact: N/A - Formal application.

COLORADO
Cochems Trust
c/o Colorado National Bank of Denver
P.O. Box 5168
Denver, CO 80217
Information: Relief fund for needy or indigent doctors in Colorado.

Colorado Masons Benevolent Fund Association
1770 Sherman Street
Denver, CO 80111
Application Address:
1130 Panorama Drive
Colorado Springs, CO 80904
(719) 471-9589

Qualifications: Masonic lodge members and their families.
Grant Amount: $592,994 for grants..
Purpose: To help those in financial need.
Contact: Local lodge in Colorado.

Colorado Refugee and Immigrant Services Program
190 East Ninth Ave Room 390
Denver, CO 80203
(303) 863-8211

Qualifications: For immigrants and refugees who are residents of Colorado.
Grant Amount: N/A
Purpose: To help with living expenses. Social services are provided.
Contact: Laurel Bagan - Write or call.

Fort Collins Area Community Foundation
215 West Oak St. Suite 102
Fort Collins, CO 80521
(303) 224-3462

Qualifications: Residents of Lamimer and Weld counties.

Grant Amount: 75 grants for $1,000 - 5,000.

Purpose: To help those in financial need.

Contact: Diane M Hogerty - Write letter and proposal. Deadline - February 1, May 1, August 1, and November 1.

A. V. Hunter Trust, Inc.

633 Seventeenth St. Suite1780

Denver, CO. 80202

(303) 292-2048

Qualifications: For residents of Colorado.

Grant Amount: $58,757 in grants given.

Purpose: To help with medical expenses and for those in financial need.

Contact: Sharon Holt - Formal application and interview required. Social worker must apply for recipient.

Henry W. Stoddard Trust

P O Box 1365

Arvada, CO 80001

Application Address:

7910 Ralston Rd. Suite 1

Arvada, CO 80001-1365

Qualifications: For caretakers of handicapped children.

Grant Amount: $1,000 for 67 grants.

Purpose: To help the children and caretaker.

Contact: Wallis L. Cambell - Write letter.

CONNECTICUT

Charitable Society in Hartford

c/o Connecticut National Bank

777 Main Street

Hartford, CT 06115

(203) 275-8200

Information: Grants to persons in the Hartford area who need necessities.

Marion Isabelle Coe Fund
c/o Colonial Bank & Trust Co.
P O Box 2210
Waterbury, CT 06722

Qualifications: For residents of Goshen, Litchfield, Morris and Warren.
Grant Amount: $100 per month.
Purpose: To help with living, transportation, and medical expenses.
Contact: Mrs. Speers - Write letter.

Connecticut Department of Human Resources
State Refugee Coordinator
1049 Asylum Ave
Hartford, CT 06115
(203) 566-4329

Qualifications: Connecticut residents who are refugees.
Grant Amount: N/A
Purpose: To help with resettlement. Social services provided.
Contact: Elliot Ginsberg - Write or call.

James Crocker Testamentary Trust
P O Box 1045
Canaan, CT 06018

Qualifications: For residents of Winchester.
Grant Amount: 9 grants given $70 - $450.
Purpose: To help those in financial need.
Contact: Kevin F. Nelligan - Write letter.

The de Kay Foundation
c/o Manufacturers Hanover Trust Company
600 Fifth Ave.
New York, NY 10020
(212) 957-1668

Qualifications: Elderly residents of New York, New Jersey, and Connecticut.

Grant Amount: 83 grants given - $1,000 - $5,000.

Purpose: To help with medical expenses and to help those in financial need.

Contact: Lloyd Saltus, II - Write letter.

Larrabee Fund Association
c/o Connecticut National Bank
777 Main St.
Hartford, CT 06115
(203)728-2664

Qualifications: Female residents of Hartford.

Grant Amount: $203,285 for grants.

Purpose: For those in financial need.

Contact: N/A - Write letter.

W. J. Munson Foundation
c/o Colonial Bank & Trust Co.
P O Box 2210
Watertown, CT 06722
(203) 574-4575
Application Address:
71 Scott Rd.
Watertown, CT 06795

Qualifications: For residents of Watertown.

Grant Amount: 172 grants for $4 - $1,563.

Purpose: To help with medical expenses.

Contact: William H. Eppenhimer - Write letter and proposal.

The Westport-Weston Foundation
c/o The Westport Bank & Trust Co.
P O Box 5177
Westport, CT 06881
(203) 222-6988

Qualifications: For residents of Weston and Westport.

Grant Amount: 29 grants awarded for $100 - $400.
Purpose: To help pay living and medical expenses.
Contact: Susanne M. Allen - Write letter.

Widow's Society
c/o Connecticut National Bank
777 Main St.
Hartford, CT 06115
Application address:
20 Bayberry Ln.
Avon, CT 06001
(203) 687-9660

Qualifications: For female residents of Connecticut.
Grant Amount: 117 grants awarded for $75 - $4,800.
Purpose: To help those in financial need.
Contact: Dorothy Johnson - Write letter or apply through social services.

DELAWARE
Borkee-Hagley Foundation, Inc.
P O Box 230
Wilmington, DE 19899
(302) 652-8616

Qualifications: For elderly residents of Delaware.
Grant Amount: 25 grants awarded for $100 - $15,000.
Purpose: To help with living and educational expenses.
Contact: Henry H. Sillman, Jr. - Write letter, formal application.

Delaware Department of Health and Social Services
Division of Economic Services
P O Box 906
CP Building
New Castle, DE 19720
(302) 421-6153

Qualifications: For residents of Delaware who are refugees.

Grant Amount: N/A

Purpose: To help with resettlement. Social services provided.

Contact: Thomas P. Eichler - Write letter.

Milton and Hattie Kutz Foundation
101 Garden of Eden Rd.
WIlmington, DE 19803
(302) 478-6200

Qualifications: Residents of Delaware.

Grant Amount: $44,500

Purpose: To help with living, education, and child welfare expenses.

Contact: Robert N. Kerbel - Write for guidelines. Deadline for scholarships - March 15.

DISTRICT OF COLUMBIA
Buchly Charity Fund of Federal Lodge No. !
1212 Wisconsin Ave, NW
Washington, DC 20007
Application Address:
7015 Leesville Rd.
Springfield, VA 22151

Qualifications: Widows and orphans of former members of Federal Masonic Lodge No. 1.

Grant Amount: 12 grants awarded for $500 - $6,700.

Purpose: To help those showing financial need after the death of husband / father.

Contact: Willard E. Griffing - write letter.

FLORIDA
Alfred I. duPont Foundation
P O Box 1380
Jacksonville, FL 32201
(904) 396-6600

Qualifications: Must be resident of Florida.

Grant Amount: 5 grants for $4,300

Purpose: To help those in financial need.
Contact: N/A - write letter.

Gore Family Memorial Foundation
501 East Las Olas
Fort Lauderdale, Fl 33302

Qualifications: For residents of Broward County.
Grant Amount: $526,187 for 504 grants.
Purpose: To help with medical and living expenses.
Contact: N/A - write letter. Formal application.

The Ryan Foundation
1511 West Broadway
Oviedo, FL 32765
(407) 365-8390

Qualifications: Residents of Florida
Grant Amount: 77 grants awarded for $13 -$7,479.
Purpose: To help those in financial need.
Contact: Jean Beede - call or write.

Roy M. Speer Foundation
1803 U.S. Highway 19
Holiday, FL. 34694-5536

Qualifications: Residents of Florida.
Grant Amount: $4,00 for one grant.
Purpose: To help with medical expenses or financial need.
Contact: Richard W. Baker - write letter.

Vero Beach Foundation for the Elderly
c/o First National Bank
255 South County Road
Palm Beach, FL 33480

Information: Relief aid to indigent residents of Vero Beach, Florida.

GEORGIA
Pine Mountain Benevolent Foundation Inc.
P.O. Box 2301
Columbus, GA 31902
Information: Welfare assistance to worthy & needy individuals in Georgia.

Savannah Widows' Society
P O Box 30156
Savannah GA 31410
Qualifications: For single female residents over 55 living in Chatham County.
Grant Amount: 108 grants for $10 - $8,400.
Purpose: To help those in financial need.
Contact: Becky Traxler - application required.

HAWAII
The Hawaii Community Foundation
222 Merchant St.
Honolulu, HI 96813
(808) 537-6333
Qualifications: Residents of Hawaii.
Grant Amount: 115 grants for $100 - $1,000.
Purpose: To help those in financial need.
Contact: Suzanne Toguchi - Call.

The May Templeton Hopper Foundation
1412 Whitney St.
Honolulu, HI 96822
(808) 944-2807
Qualifications: Elderly residents of Hawaii who have lived there for at least five years.
Grant Amount: 287 grants for $360 - $9,600.
Purpose: To help with living, medical, and general expenses.
Contact: Diana H Lord - Call or write. Deadline is the fifth of every month.

IDAHO
Rouch Boys Foundation
c/o Twin Falls Bank & Trust Department
P.O. Box 7
Twin Falls, ID 83303
Information: Relief aid to children in the Magic Valley area of Idaho.

ILLINOIS
The Clara Abbott Foundation
One Abbott Park Rd.
Abbott Park, IL 60064
(708) 937-1091
Qualifications: Current and former employees of
Abbott Laboratories and their families.
Grant Amount: 2,470 grants for $100 - $50,000 .
Purpose: To help those in financial need.
Contact: David C. Jeffries - Application required.

Crane Fund for Widows and Children
222 West Adams St. Room 849
Chicago, IL 60606
Qualifications: Residents of Illinois.
Grant Amount: 3 grants for $1,500 - $11,760
Purpose: To help those in financial need.
Contact: Trustees - Write letter.

The Cultural Society, Inc.
P O Box 1374
Bridgeview, IL 60455
(312) 434-6665
Qualifications: Muslims
Grant Amount: $125,050 for grants.
Purpose: To help those in financial need.
Contact: Mohammad Nasr - Write letter.

Reade Industrial Fund
c/o Harris Trust & Savings Bank
P.O. Box 755
111 West Monroe Street
Chicago, IL 60690
(312) 461-2613

Information: Grants to Illinois residents who have experienced a sudden financial or health catastrophe.

The Shifting Foundation
8000 Sears Tower
Chicago, IL 60606

Qualifications: Homeless, women, disadvantaged, and minorities.

Grant Amount: 6 grants for $4,000 - $10,000

Purpose: To help those in financial need.

Contact: Pat Culver - Application.

Swiss Benevolent Society of Chicago
P O Box 2137
Chicago, IL 60690

Qualifications: Elderly and people of Swiss ancestry residing in Chicago area.

Grant Amount: $53,450 for 53 grants.

Purpose: To help those with financial hardship.

Contact: Alan Weber - write letter, formal application required.

Tallman Boys Fund Trust
c/o First of America Trust Co.
189 East Court St.
Kankakee, IL 60901
(815) 937-3687

Qualifications: Protestant boys under 21 living in Kankakee County.

Grant Amount: $4,020 for grants.

Purpose: To help those who are homeless or provide general financial assistance.

Contact: Glen F. Rewerts, II - formal application, must be applied for by non-profit organization.

INDIANA

Mary Jane Luick Trust

c/o American National Bank & Trust Co.

110 East Main St.

Muncie, IN 47305

(317) 747-7510

Qualifications: Elderly female resident of Delaware County.

Grant Amount: 5 grants for $300 -$2,100

Purpose: To help those with medical expenses or financial need.

Contact: July Polson - Write letter.

Allen and Rose Mills Trust

c/o Irwin Union Bank & Trust Co.

500 Washington St.

Columbus, IN 47201

Qualifications: Residents of Bartholomew County.

Grant Amount: 5 grants for $100 - $1,639.

Purpose: To help with medical and living expenses.

Contact: Stephen Kirts - Write letter.

Smock Foundation

c/o Lincoln National Bank & Trust Company

P.O. Box 960

Fort Wayne, IN 46801

Information: Medical & nursing care to needy individuals of Presbyterian faith.

IOWA

Human Aid Society of Iowa

400 First Interstate Bank Building

Des Moines, IA 50309

Application Address:

550 39th St.
Des Moines, IA 50312
(515) 274-1450

Qualifications: For those in financial need.
Grant Amount: $7,294 for 200 grants.
Purpose: To provide money for necessities.
Contact: Joseph S. Brick - Write letter.

KANSAS
Brown Memorial Foundation
300 North Cedar
P O Box 187
Abilene, KS 67410
(913) 263-2351

Qualifications: For those and their families in need.
Grant Amount: 20 grants of $500 each.
Contact: N/A - Write letter.

Charlotte Hill Charitable Trust
P O Box 754
Winfield, KS 67156
(316) 221-4600

Qualifications: For single female residents over 60 living in Winfield or Arkansas City.
Grant Amount: 62 grants for $40 - $5,915.
Purpose: To help those in financial need.
Contact: Kay Roberts - formal application.

Victor Murdock Foundation
c/o Bank IV Wichita, N.A.
P O Box 1122
Wichita, KS 67201
(316) 261-4361

Qualifications: For primarily Wichita residents.

Grant Amount: 1 grant for $500.

Purpose: For general assistance.

Contact: Ted W. Schupp - write letter.

Topeka Community Foundation

5100 SW 10th

P O Box 4525

Topeka, KS 66604

(913) 272-4804

Qualifications: Fore residents of Topeka and Shawnee Counties.

Grant Amount: 40 grants for $415 - $5,000.

Purpose: For child welfare and general living expenses.

Contact: Karen Welch - application and proposal required. Deadline February 15.

LOUISIANA

Joe W. and Dorothy Dorsett Brown Foundation

1801 Pere Marquette Building

New Orleans, LA 70112

(504) 522-4233

Qualifications: Residents and hospitals in Louisiana.

Grant Amount: $43,953 for grants.

Purpose: For those in financial need.

Contact: D. P. Spencer - write proposal.

MAINE

Camden Home for Senior Citizens

66 Washington St.

Camden, ME 04843

(207) 236-2087

Application Address:

Belfast RD.

Camden, ME 04843

(207) 623-5527

Qualifications: For residents of Camden, Rockport, Hope, and Lincolnville.

Grant Amount: 201 grants for $50 - $300.

Purpose: For general living and medical expenses.

Contact: Charles Lowe - write letter.

Lena P. Frederick Trust Fund

c/o Key Trust Co. of Maine

P O Box 1054

Augusta, ME

04332-1054

(207) 623-5527

Qualifications: For residents of Belfast.

Grant Amount: $7,361 in grants awarded.

Purpose: For help with medical and living expenses.

Contact: Christina L. Cook - write or call.

Anita Card Montgomery Foundation

20 Mechanic St.

Camden, ME 04843-1707

Qualifications: For residents of Rockport, Camden, Lincolnville, and Hope

Grant Amount: 16 grants for $40 - $4,058

Purpose: To help with medical and living expenses.

Contact: Robert C. Perkins - Write letter.

Portland Female Charitable Society

c/o Janet Matty

P.O. Box 5202

Portland, ME 04101

Information: Dental care, prescriptions and hearing aids for needy residents of Portland, Maine

Portland Seamen's Friend Society
14 Lewis St.
Westbrook, ME 04092
Qualifications: For seamen in Maine.
Grant Amount: $36,000 for 50 grants.
Purpose: To help those in financial need.
Contact: Lewis G. Emery - write letter.

MARYLAND
The Baltimore Community Foundation
The Latrobe Building
Two East Read Street
Ninth Floor
Baltimore, MD 21202
(301) 332-4171
Qualifications: Widows and children of B & O Railroad employees.
Grant Amount: $153,900 for 50 grants.
Contact: Timothy D. Arbruster - write letter.

The Eaton Fund, Inc.
c/o Mercantile-Safe Deposit & Trust Co.
Two Hopkins Plaza
Baltimore, MD 21201
(301) 237-5521
Qualifications: Females over 60 who are residents of Baltimore.
Grant Amount: 9 grants for $900 - $2,400.
Purpose: To help those in financial need.
Contact: Patricia Bentz - write letter.

NFL Alumni Foundation Fund
c/o Sigmund M. Hyman
P.O. Box 248
Stevenson, MD 21153
(301) 486-5454

Information: Relief aid to physically or mentally disabled former National Football League alumni (prior to 1959).

Steeplechase Fund
400 Fair Hill Drive
Elkton, MD 21921

Qualifications: Injured jockeys or their widows.

Grant Amount: $38,995 for grants.

Purpose: To help those in financial need.

Contact: Charles Colgan - write letter.

Anna Emory Warfield Memorial Fund, Inc.
103 West Monument St.
Baltimore, MD 21201
(301) 547-0612

Qualifications: Elderly female residents of Baltimore.

Grant Amount: 42 grants for $900 -$3,925.

Contact: Thelma K. O'Neal - write letter.

MASSACHUSETTS
Association for the Relief of Aged Women of New Bedford
27 South Sixth Street
New Bedford, MA 02740

Information: Financial aid for elderly & needy women of New Bedford.

Boston Fatherless and Widows Society
c/o Goodwin, Proctor & Hoar
Exchange Place Room 2200
Boston, MA 02109-2881
(617) 570-1130

Qualifications: Residents of Boston who are widowed or orphans.

Grant Amount: 52 grants for $325 - $1,950.

Purpose: For medical and general living expenses.

Contact: George W. Butterworth, III - write letter.

Edwin S. Farmer Trust
133 Portland St.
Boston, MA 02114-9614

Qualifications: Residents of Arlington who are women or married.

Grant Amount: 7 grants for $100 - $2,840.

Purpose: To help those in financial need.

Contact: Harold E. Magnuson - Write letter.

German Ladies Aid Society of Boston, Inc.
2222 Centre St.
West Roxbury, MA 02132

Qualifications: Residents of West Roxbury.

Grant Amount: $2,498 in grants given.

Purpose: To help those with financial hardship.

Contact: N/A - write letter.

Howard Benevolent Society
14 Beacon St. Room 507
Boston, MA 02108
(617) 742-2952

Qualifications: Residents of Boston.

Grant Amount: 225 grants for $550.

Purpose: To help those who are ill or with financial hardship.

Contact: Marcia T. Burley - call or write.

Howland Fund for Aged Women
c/o Child and Family Service
1061 Pleasant St.
New Bedford, MA 02740
(508) 993-4232

Qualifications: Elderly female residents of New Bedford.

Grant Amount: 10 grants for $1,000 - $1,200.

Purpose: To help those in financial need.

Contact: Sally Ainsworth - formal application and interview.

Lend A Hand Society
34 1/2 Beacon St.
Boston, MA 02108
Qualifications: Residents of Boston.
Grant Amount: $130,029 for grants.
Purpose: To help those in financial need.
Contact: N/A - write letter.

Lotta Theatrical Fund
294 Washington St. Room 636
Boston, MA 022108
(617) 451-0698
Qualifications: For theatrical students and professionals.
Grant Amount: 12 grants for $500 - $3,000.
Purpose: For those in financial need.
Contact: Claire M. McCarthy - write letter.

Newburyport Howard Benevolent Society
P O Box 9
Newburyport, MA 01950
Qualifications: Families in Newburyport.
Grant Amount: $14,573 for grants.
Purpose: To help those with limited income.
Contact: N/A - write letter.

The Perpetual Benevolent Fund
c/o BayBank Middlesex
300 Washington St.
Newton, MA 02158
(617) 894-6500
Qualifications: Mainly for residents of Newton and Waltham.
Grant Amount: 280 grants for $400 - $600.
Purpose: To help with living expenses and necessities.
Contact: Majorie M. Kelley - call or write. Non-profit organization must apply on recipients behalf.

Katherine C. Pierce Trust
c/o State Street Bank & Trust Co.
P O Box 351
Boston, MA 02101
(617) 654-3357

Qualifications: Women.

Grant Amount: $250 - $5,000.

Purpose: For those with financial need.

Contact: Robert W. Seymour - write letter.

The Pilgrim Foundation
478 Torrey St.
Brockton, MA 02401-4654
(617) 586-6100

Qualifications: For families residing in Brockton.

Grant Amount: $54,831 in grants awarded.

Purpose: To help those in financial need.

Contact: N/A - formal application.

Charlotte M. Robbins Trust
c/o State Street Bank
P O Box 351
Boston, MA 02101
Application Address:
c/o State Street Bank
225 Franklin St.
Boston, MA 02110

Qualifications: Residents of Groton, Ayer, Harvard Littleton, and Shirley who are elderly couples or women.

Grant Amount: $6,000 for grants.

Purpose: To help with financial need.

Contact: Cheryl D. Curtin - write letter.

Salem Female Charitable Society
175 Federal St.
Boston, MA 02110
Application Address:
30 Chestnut St.
Salem, MA 01970

Qualifications: Female residents of Salem.

Grant Amount: 18 grants for $200 - $1,700.

Purpose: To help with financial need.

Contact: Jane A. Phillips - write letter.

Shaw Fund for Mariner's Children
c/o russell Brier & Co.
50 Congress St. Room 800
Boston, MA 02109

Qualifications: For mariners and their families residing in Massachusetts.

Grant Amount: $114,138 in grants awarded.

Purpose: For those in financial need.

Contact: Clare M. Tolias - write letter.

The Swasey Fund for Relief of Public School Teachers of Newbuyport, Inc.
31 Milk St.
Boston, MA 02109
(508) 462-2784
Application Address:
83 Summit Pl.
Newburyport, MA 01950

Qualifications: For teachers who have taught at least 10 years or retired teachers in Newburyport.

Grant Amount: 21 grants for $100 - $10,000.

Purpose: To help those in financial need and for educational expenses.

Contact: Jean MacDonald - formal application.

MINNESOTA
Duluth-Superior Area Community Foundation
316 MIssabe Building
227 West First Street
Duluth, MN 55802-1913
(218)726-0232

Qualifications: For residents of Douglas, Wisconsin, Koochiching, Bayfield, St. Ouis, Lake Cook, Aitkin, and Carlton counties.

Grant Amount: 15 grants for $362 - $3,000.

Purpose: To help with emergency and living expenses, also help with employment.

Contact: Holly C. Sampson - application required. Deadline - February 1, May 1, and October 1.

Gilfillin Memorial Inc.
W-555 First National Bank Building
St. Paul, MN 55101
(507) 282-2511

Information: Financial aid for dental, medical and surgical needs of people living within the state of Minnesota.

Hanna R. Kristianson Trust
P O Box 1011
Albert Lea, MN 56007
Application Address:
Clarks Grove, MN 56016
(507) 256-4415

Qualifications: Residents of Freeborn County over 50.

Grant Amount: 18 grants for $21 - $1,660.

Purpose: To help those in financial need.

Contact: Richard S. Haug - write letter.

The Saint Paul Foundation
1120 Norwest Center
St. Paul, MN 55101
(612) 224-5463

Qualifications: For employees of the 3M company and residents of St. Paul and Minneapolis.

Grant Amount: $130,121 for 105 grants.
Contact: Paul Verret - write letter.

MISSOURI
Ina Calkins Board
c/o Boatmen's First National Bank of Kansas City
14 West 10th St.
Kansas City, MO 64105
(816) 221-2800
Qualifications: Elderly residents of Kansas City.
Grant Amount: $33,000 for grants awarded.
Purpose: To help those in financial need.
Contact: David P. Ross - Write letter. Deadline - January 1, April 1,
July 1, and October 31.

Sarah Cora Gladish Endowment Fund
Forest Hills Estate, Apt c-11
Lexington, MO 64105
(816) 221-2800
Qualifications: Residents of Johnson, Jackson, or Lafayette Counties
who are accomplished or elderly musicians or artists.
Grant Amount: 6 grants for $200 -$350
Purpose: To help those with financial hardship.
Contact: Margaret Lomax - formal application. Deadline - July 1.

Herschend Family Foundation
c/o Jack R. Herschend
Silver Dollar City, Inc.
Marvel Cave Park, MO 65616
(417) 338-2611
Qualifications: Christian residents of Missouri.
Grant Amount: $250,435 for grants awarded.
Purpose: To help those in financial need.
Contact: Jack R. Herschend - write or call.

NEW YORK
Adams Memorial Fund Inc.
c/o Lebeouf, Lamb, Lelby and Macrae

520 Madison Avenue
New York, NY 10022
(212) 715-8000
Information: Welfare funds for elderly & indigent persons in the NY area.

The American Society of Journalist
and Authors Charitable Trust
The Llewellyn Miller Fund
1501 Broadway Suite 1907
New York, NY 10036
Qualifications: For professional writers who are disable or over 60.
Grant Amount: 4 grants for $1,250 - $2,500.
Contact: Murray Teigh Bloom - write letter.

The Bagby Foundation for the Musical Arts, Inc.
501 Fifth Ave.
New York, NY 10017
(212) 986-6094
Qualifications: For the elderly who have made contributions to music.
Grant Amount: 9 grants for $600 - $2,850.
Purpose: To help those in financial need.
Contact: Eleanor C. Mark - write letter.

Benedict Family Charitable Foundation, Inc.
82 Wall St.
New York, NY 10005
Qualifications: Residents of New York.
Grant Amount: $3,579 in grants.
Purpose: To help those in financial need.
Contact: Alfred Benedict - write letter.

The James Gordon Bennett Memorial Corporation
c/o New York Daily News
220 East 42nd St.
New York, Ny 10017
Qualifications: Journalist who have been employed for at least 10 years for a New York City daily newspaper.

Grant Amount: N/A
Purpose: To help those in financial need.
Contact: Denise Houseman

Beulah Cliff Rest
c/o Paul S. Longo
199 Main St
White Plains, NY 10601
(914) 919-2193

Qualifications: Females and female invalids.
Grant Amount: 51 grants for $200 -$400.
Purpose: Vacation grants.
Contact: Hastings Ross - write letter.

Broadcasters Foundation, Inc.
320 West 57th St.
New York, NY 10019

Qualifications: Members of the broadcast field and their families.
Grant Amount: 7 grants for $1,800 - $2,400.
Purpose: To help those in financial need.
Contact: N/A - formal application.

Brockway Foundation for the Needy of the Village and
Township of Homer, New York
c/o Key Bank
25 South Main St.
Homer, NY 13077 -1314

Qualifications: For residents of Homer.
Grant Amount: 23 grants for $180 - $690.
Purpose: To help those in financial need.
Contact: M. Lee Swartwout - write letter.

Carnegie Fund for Authors
1 Old Country Rd. Suite 113
Carle Place, NY 11514
(516) 877-2141

Qualifications: Authors who have published a "non-vanity" book.
Grant Amount: N/A

Purpose: To help those with illness or injury.
Contact: William L. Rothenberg - write letter.

Change, Inc.
P O Box 705
Cooper Station
New York, NY 10276
(212) 473-3742
Qualifications: For professional artists.
Grant Amount: $1,000 - $70,000.
Purpose: To help with medical and living expenses.
Contact: Denise LeBeau - write letter, include bills, need, letters of recommendation.

The Clark Foundation
30 Wall St.
New York, NY 10005
(212) 269-1833
Qualifications: For residents of New York City and upstate New York.
Grant Amount: 19 grants for $565 - $15,600.
Purpose: To help with medical expenses.
Contact: Edward W. Stack - write letter.
The Correspondents Fund
c/o Rosenman & Cohen
575 Madison Ave
New York, NY 10022-2511
Application Address:
c/o The New York Times
229 West 43rd St.
New York, NY 10036
Qualifications: For men and women who have worked in press or broadcasting in the United States.
Grant Amount: 3 grants for $2,500 - $3,000.
Purpose: To help those in financial need.
Contact: James L. Greenfield - write letter.

Josiah H. Danforth Memorial Fund
8 Fremont St.
Gloversville, NY 12078
Qualifications: For residents of Fulton County.
Grant Amount: 95 grants for $65 - $500
Purpose: To help with medical expenses.
Contact: N/A - write letter.

District Lodge No. 3, Sons of Norway Charitable Trust
c/o Frank C. Monnick
53 Ganevoort Blvd.
Staten Island, NY 10314
Qualifications: For those of Norweigian origin.
Grant Amount: 12 grants for $300 - $2,500.
Purpose: To help those in financial need.
Contact: Frank C. Monnick - write letter.

Adolph and Esther Gottlieb Foundation, Inc.
380 West Broadway
New York, NY 10012
Qualifications: Painters and sculptors who have at least 10 years
experience.
Grant Amount: Up to $10,000.
Purpose: To help with financial need.
Contact: Ellen Bryson - write letter.

The Havens Relief Fund Society
105 East 22nd St. Suite 805
New York, NY 10010
(212) 475-1990
Qualifications: Residents of New York City.
Grant Amount: $406,429 in grants.
Purpose: To help those in financial need.
Contact: Marilyn Lamarr - foundation members award funds to people
of their own choosing.

Robert F. Hildenbrand Foundation, Inc.
111 West Sunrise Hwy.
Freeport, NY 11520
(516) 379-3575
Qualifications: Residents of Freeport.
Grant Amount: 228 grants for $2 - $200.
Purpose: To help with living and medical expenses.
Contact: N/A - write letter.

Mary J. Hutchins Foundation, Inc.
110 William St.
New York, NY 10038
(212) 602-8529
Qualifications: Residents of New York City.
Grant Amount: 14 grants for $250 - $4,980.
Purpose: For those in financial need.
Contact: John F. Hirsch - write letter.

Ittleson-Beaumont Fund
c/o The C.I.T. Group Holdings, Inc.
135 West 50th St.
New York, NY 10020
(212) 408-6000
Application Address:
650 CIT Drive
Livingston, NJ 07039
Qualifications: Current or former CIT Financial Corporation employees.
Grant Amount: 20 grants for $285 - $18,000.
Purpose: To help those in financial need.
Contact: Clare Carmichael - write letter.

Jockey Club Foundation
40 East 52nd St.
New York, NY 10022
(212) 371-5970
Qualifications: For those involved with thoroughbred racing and

breeding.

Grant Amount: $394, 278 for grants.

Purpose: To help those in financial need.

Contact: Nancy Colletti - write letter, describe needs.

Mary W. MacKinnon Fund
c/o Wilber National Bank
Trust Department
245 Main St.
Oneonta, NY 13820
(607) 432-1700

Qualifications: Elderly residents of Sidney.

Grant Amount: $48,453 for grants.

Purpose: To help with medical expenses.

Contact: N/A - apply through doctor or hospital.

Max Mainzer Memorial Foundation, Inc.
570 Seventh Ave. Third Floor.
New York, NY 10018
(212) 921-3865

Qualifications: Members of the American Jewish K.C. Fraternity or their widows.

Grant Amount: 15 grants for $250 - $4,200.

Purpose: To help those in financial need.

Contact: N/A - write letter.

Israel Matz Foundation
14 East Fourth St. Room 403
New York, NY 10012
(212) 673-8142

Qualifications: Jewish writers, scholars, public workers or children.

Grant Amount: 28 grants for $600 - $3,900.

Purpose: To help those in financial need.

Contact: Milton Arfa - write letter.

Musicians Foundation, Inc.
200 West 55th St.

New York, NY 10019

(212) 247-5332

Qualifications: Professional musicians and their families.

Grant Amount: 39 grants for $500 - $2,000.

Contact: Brent Williams - write letter.

New York Society for the Relief of Widows and Orphans of Medical Men

c/o Davies & Davies

50 East 42nd St.

New York, NY 10017

Qualifications: For widows and orphans of physicians.

Grant Amount: $96,727 for grants.

Purpose: To help those in financial need.

Contact: Walter Wichern - write letter. Deadline November 15.

Nurses House, Inc.

350 Hudson St.

New York, NY 10014

(212) 989-9393

Qualifications: For current or former registered nurses.

Grant Amount: $45,648 in grants.

Purpose: To help with financial needs excluding medical or educational.

Contact: Patricia B. Barry - write letter, formal application.

Pen American Center

568 Broadway

New York, NY 10012

(212)334-1660

Qualifications: Writers.

Grant Amount: $50 - $1,000.

Purpose: To help those with AIDS or financial need.

Contact: Joan Dalin - write letter.

The Pollock-Krasner Foundation, Inc.

725 Park Ave

New York, NY 10021

(212) 517-5400

Application Address:

P O Box 4957

New York, NY 10185

Qualifications: For visual artists working overseas or in the United States.

Grant Amount: 143 grants for $2,000 - $20,000.

Purpose: To help with careers or emergency.

Contact: Charles C. Bergman - formal application. Include 10 slides of work and letter including need and biographical information.

Saranac Lake Voluntary Health Association, Inc.

70 Main St.

Saranac Lake, NY 12983-1706

Qualifications: Students and elderly residents of Saranac Lake.

Grant Amount: 3 grants for $4,498 - $31,613.

Purpose: To help with dental expenses.

Contact: N/A - write letter.

J.F. Schoellkopf Silver Wedding Fund

340 Elk St.

Buffalo, NY 14240

(716) 842-5535

Qualifications: Members and families of Mutual Aid Society.

Grant Amount: 11 grants for $1,550 - $1,750.

Purpose: To help those in financial need.

Contact: Arthur Maciejewski - write letter.

J. D. Shatford Memorial Trust

c/o Chemical Bank

30 Rockefeller Plaza

New York, NY 10112

Qualifications: Residents of Hubbards, Nova Scotia, and Canada.

Grant Amount: 70 grants for $331 - $24,172.

Purpose: To help those in financial need.

Contact: Barbara Strohmeier - formal application.

Society for the Relief of Women and Children
c/o Turk, Marsh, Kelly, and Hoare
575 Lexington Ave. 20th Floor
New York, NY 10022-6102

Qualifications: For residents of New York.

Grant Amount: 12 grants for $1,550.

Purpose: To help those who can no longer take care of themselves due to inevitable circumstances.

Contact: N/A - write for information.

St. George's Society of New York
71 West 23rd St.
New York, NY 10010
(212) 924-1434

Qualifications: British citizens reside in in New York.

Grant Amount: $101,003 for 85 grants.

Purpose: To help with living and medical expenses.

Contact: David Loovis - write for information.

St. Luke's Nurses Benefit Fund
c/o Alumnae Association of St. Luke's School of Nursing
411 West 114th St. Apt 6D
New York, NY 10025
Application Address:
47 Phillips Ln.
Darien, CT 06820

Qualifications: Graduates of St. Luke's School of Nursing.

Grant Amount: 1 grant for $2,000.

Purpose: To help with individual in financial need.

Contact: Martha Kirk - formal application.

Suffolk County Happy Landing Fund, Inc.
c/o Peter Opromolla
P O Box 383
St. James, NY 11780
(516) 366-4843

Qualifications: Police officers and their families living in Suffolk County.

Grant Amount: 3 grants for $1,000.
Purpose: To help those in financial need.
Contact: Peter Opromolla - formal application.

Otto Sussman Trust
P O Box 1374
Trainsmeadow Station
Flushing, NY 11370-9998
Qualifications: Residents of New Jersey, New York, Oklahoma, or Pennsylvania.
Grant Amount: 36 grants for $329 - $4,397.
Purpose: Help with medical and living expenses.
Contact: Edward S. Miller - write for information.

United Merchants and Manufacturers Employees Welfare Foundation
1407 Broadway Sixth Fl.
New York, NY 10018-5103
(212) 930-3999
Qualifications: Current or former employees (or families) of United Merchants and Manufacturers, Inc.
Grant Amount: 14 grants for $375 - $825.
Purpose: To help those in financial need.
Contact: Lawrence Marx, Jr - write letter.

Vonderlinden Charitable Trust
c/o Leonard Rachmilowitz
26 Mill St.
Rhinebeck, NY 12572
(914) 876-3021
Qualifications: Residents of upstate New York.
Grant Amount: 100 grants for $375 - $825.
Purpose: To help with medical and living expenses.
Contact: N/A - write letter.

Emma Reed Webster Aid Association, Inc.
c/o Frances E. Peglow

R.D. No. 2

Albion, NY 14411

Qualifications: Residents of upstate New York.

Grant Amount: 130 grants for $600.

Purpose: To help those in financial need.

Contact: Frances E. Peglow - write letter.

NORTH CAROLINA

Garrison Community Foundation of Gaston County Inc.

P.O. Box 123

Gastonia, NC 28053

(704) 864-0927

Information: Grants for medical purposes for children in North Carolina.

NEVADA

Stearns-Blodgett Trust

c/o First Interstate Bank of Nevada

P.O. Box 30100

Reno, NV 89520

(702) 784-3316

Information: Aid to indigent people who need ophthalmological care.

NEW JERSEY

Carroll Foundation

70 Enterprise Avenue

Secaucus, NJ 07094

Information: Assistance for needy individuals.

OHIO

Christian BusinessCares Foundation

P O Box 360691

Cleveland, OH 44136

(216) 621-0096

Qualifications: Residents of northeast Ohio.

Grant Amount: $100 - $250.

Purpose: To help with emergency situations.

Contact: N/A - write for information.

Columbus Female Benevolent Society
228 South Drexel Ave.
Columbus, OH 43209
Qualifications: For pensioned widows or needy infants.
Grant Amount: $32,806 for grants.
Purpose: To help with financial needs.
Contact: N/A - residents should recommend applicant.

Gay Fund
c/o Marjorie L. Ater
751 Grandon Avenue
Columbus, OH 43209
Information: Financial Aid for elderly, retired school teachers from Ohio.

Grace A. Gossens Testamentary Trust
c/o Ralph C. Boggs
240 Huron St. Suite 800
Toledo, OH 43604
Application Address:
416 West Wayne
Maumee, OH 43537
(419) 893-8603
Qualifications: Elderly women in rest homes in Maumee.
Grant Amount: 2 grants for $2,500 each.
Purpose: For those in financial need.
Contact: Alice J. Servais - write letter.

Meshech Frost Tesamentary Trust
c/o BancOhio National Bank Trust Division
155 East Broad St. Fifth Fl.
Columbus, OH 43251
Application Address:
109 South Washington St.
Tifflin, OH 44883
(419) 447-5211
Qualifications: For residents of Tiffin.
Grant Amount: 5 grants for $169 - $690

Purpose: To help those in financial need.
Contact: Kenneth H. Myers - write letter.

National Machinery Foundation, Inc.
Greenfield St.
P O Box 747
Tiffin, OH 44883
(419) 447-5211

Qualifications: Former employees or residents of Tiffin residing in Seneca county.
Grant Amount: 205 grants for $150 - $4,000.
Purpose: To help those in financial need.
Contact: D. B. Bero - write letter.

Virginia Wright Mothers Guild, Inc.
426 Clinton St.
Columbus, OH 43202-2741

Qualifications: For elderly females living in Columbus.
Grant Amount: $9,925 for grants.
Purpose: For those in financial need.
Contact: M. Courtwright - write letter.

OKLAHOMA
Johnson Educational and Benevolent Trust
900 First City Place
Oklahoma City, OK 73102
(405) 232-0003

Information: Financial aid for handicapped persons living in Oklahoma.

The R. H WIlkin Charitable Trust
P O Box 76561
Oklahoma City, OK 73147
(405) 235-7700

Qualifications: For cripped children residing in Oklahoma County.
Grant Amount: $14,855 for 28 grants.
Purpose: For help with medical expenses.
Contact: Peggy Pittman - write letter.

OREGON
Blanche Fischer Foundation
1001 SW Fifth Ave Suite 1550
Portland, OR 97204
(503) 323-9111
Qualifications: Physically disabled residents of Oregon.
Grant Amount: 148 grants for $100 - $1,000.
Purpose: To help those in financial need.
Contact: William K. Shepherd - formal appliction.

Clarke Testamentary Trust/Fund Foundation
U.S. National Bank of Oregon
P.O. Box 3168
Portland, OR 97208
(503) 228-9405
Information: Financial aid to cover medical costs for needy persons.

Sophia Byers McComas Foundation
c/o U.S. National Bank of Oregon
P O Box 3168
Portland, OR 97208
(503) 275-6564
Qualifications: For elderly residents of Oregon.
Grant Amount: $72,223 for grants.
Purpose: To help those not receiving welfare benefits who are in financial need.
Contact: Bank Trustee - write letter.

Scottish Rite Oregon Consistory Almoner Fund, Inc.
709 SW 15th Ave
Portland, OR 97205
Qualifications: Masons and their families living in Oregon.
Grant Amount: $19,437 for grants.
Purpose: To help those in financial need.
Contact: Walter Peters - write letter.

PENNSYLVANIA
Margaret Baker Memorial Fund Trust
Mellon Bank (East), N.A.
P O Box 7236
Philadelphia, PA 19101

Qualifications: Widows or single women over 30, or children under 14 living in Phoenixville.
Grant Amount: 17 grants for $108 - $750.
Purpose: To help those in financial need.
Contact: L. Darlington - write letter.

Female Association of Philadelphia
c/o Providents National Bank
1632 Chestnust St.
Philadelphia, PA 19103

Qualifications: For female residents of Philadelphia.
Grant Amount: $90,310 for grants.
Purpose: To help those in financial need.
Contact: Elizabeth Harbison - write letter.

Gibson Foundation
Two PPG Place, Suite 310
Pittsburgh, PA 15222
(412) 261-1611

Information: Hospital & medical coverage for those with <u>correctable</u> physical problems.

James T. Hambay Foundation
Dauphin Deposit Bank & Trust
P O Box 2961
Harrisburg, PA 17105-2961
(717) 255-2174

Qualifications: For blind or cripple children under 18 living in Harrisburg.
Grant Amount: $113,986 for 34 grants.
Purpose: For medical and camp expenses.
Contact: Joseph A. Marcri - write letter.

Edward W. Helfrick Senior Citizens Trust
400 Market St.
Sunbury, PA 17801
Qualifications: For elderly residents of the 107th Legislative District of Pennsylvania.
Grant Amount: 4 grants of $500 each.
Purpose: To help those with fire damage expenses or those who are ill.
Contact: N/A - write letter.

William B. Lake Foundation
Fidelity Bank, N.A.
Broad and Walnut Streets
Philadelphia, PA 19109
(215) 985-7320
Qualifications: For residents of Philadelphia.
Grant Amount: $30,000 for grants.
Purpose: To ehlp those with respiratory diseases.
Contact: Maureen B. Evans - write letter.

Merchants Fund
c/o Hemmenway and Reinhardt, Inc.
Four Park Ave.
Swarthmore, PA 19081-1723
Application Address:
P O Box 5920
Philadelphia, PA 19137
(215) 288-7131
Qualifications: Merchants and their families residing in Philadelphia.
Grant Amount: $207,057 for 48 grants.
Purpose: To help those in financia need.
Contact: Henry W. Kaufman - formal application.

Robert D. and Margaret W. Quin Foundation
Hazelton National Bank
101 West Broad St.
Hazelton, PA 18201

Qualifications: For students under 19 who live within 10 miles of Hazleton City Hall.

Grant Amount: 66 grants for $35 - $900.

Purpose: To help with educational and living expenses.

Contact: N/A - write letter.

St. Benedict's Charitable Society
1663 Bristol Pike
Bensalem, PA 19020
(215) 244-9900

Qualifications: For elderly or ill individuals.

Grant Amount: 4 grants for $100 - $1,800.

Purpose: To help with living and medical expenses.

Contact: Margaret Kuehmstedt - write letter.

The John Edgar Thomson Foundation
The Rittenhouse Claridge
201 South 18th St. Suite 318
Philadelphia, PA 19103
(215) 545-6083

Qualifications: Daughters of deceased railroad employees.

Grant Amount: 141 grants for $2,416.

Purpose: To help with expenses until the age of 22.

Contact: Gilda Verstein - formal application.

Western Association of Ladies for the Relief and Employment of the Poor.
c/o Fidelity Bank, N.S.
Broad and Walnut Streets
Philadelphia, PA 19109
(215) 431-4679

Qualifications: Residents of Philadelphia County.

Grant Amount: $43 - $1,500.

Purpose: To help those in financial need.

Contact: Marlane Bohon - social worker must apply on recipients behalf.

RHODE ISLAND
Bristol Home for Aged Women
c/o National Bank - Rhode Island Hospital Trust
One Hospital Trust Plaza
Providence, RI 02903
(401) 278-8752

Qualifications: For elderly female residents of Bristol.
Grant Amount: 8 grants for $100 - $4,900.
Purpose: To help those in financial need.
Contact: Shawn P. Buckless - write letter. Deadline June 1.

Robert B. Cranston - Theophilus T. Pitman Fund
18 Market Square
Newport, RI 02840
(401) 278-8700

Qualifications: Elderly residents of Newport County.
Grant Amount: $6,856 for grants.
Purpose: To help those in financial need.
Contact: D. C. Hambly, Jr - formal application.

Inez Sprague Trust
c/o Rhode Island Hospital Trust
One Hospital Trust Plaza
Providence, RI 02903
(401) 278-8700

Qualifications: Residents of Rhode Island.
Grant Amount: 23 grants for $79 - $1,500.
Purpose: To help with medical expenses.
Contact: Hospital Trust Trustee - write letter.

Townsend Aid for the Aged
c/o Fleet Nationa Bank
100 Westminister St.
Providence, RI 02903

Qualifications: For elderly residents of Newport.

Grant Amount: $74,700 for grants.

Purpose: To help those with financial need.

Contact: Samuel C. Wheeler - write for guidelines.

SOUTH CAROLINA

Graham Memoria Fund

P O Box 533

Bennettsville, SC 29512

(803) 479-6804

Application Address:

308 West Main St.

Bennettsville, SC 29512

Qualifications: Residents of Bennettsville.

Grant Amount: 37 grants for $200 - $500.

Contact: Chairperson - formal application.

Society for the Relief of Families of Deceased and Disable Indigent Members of the Medical Profession of the State of South Carolina

19 Guerard Rd.

Charleston, SC 29407

Qualifications: For families of deceased or disable doctors in South Carolina.

Grant Amount: 5 grants for $1,100 - $2,350.

Purpose: To help those in financial ned.

Contact: The Benevolent Committee.

TENNESSEE

The Ruby McCown Foundation

1625 Rushing Wind Ln

Knoxville, TN 37922

(615) 966 -9807

Qualifications: For residents of Knoxville.

Grant Amount: 3 grants for $6,250.

Contact: Glen McCown - write letter.

The Quarter Century Fund
c/o International Paper Company
6400 Poplar Ave.
Memphis, TN 38197-4031
Application Address:
c/o International Paper Company
1290 Ave of the Americas Ninth fl.
New York, NY 10104

Qualifications: For children or Widows of deceased members of Quarter Century Society, Inc.

Grant Amount: 6 grants for $200 - $1,500

Purpose: To help those in financial need.

Contact: John J. Dillon - write letter for guidelines.

State Industries Foundation
P O Box 307
Old Ferry Rd.
Ashland City, TN 37015
(615) 244-7040

Qualifications: For residents of Tennessee

Grant Amount: 310 grants for $150.

Purpose: To help those in financial need.

Contact: Joseph P. Lanier - write letter.

Hurlbut Memorial Fund
c/o First Tennessee Bank, N.A.
701 Market Street
Chattanooga, TN 37401
(615) 266-3029

Information: Aid for indigent cancer patients needing medical treatment in TN.

TEXAS
Dallas Cotton Exchange Trust

c/o MTrust Corporation, N.A.

P O Box 2320

Dallas, Tx 75221-2320

Application Address:

Dallas Cotton Exchange

c/o Joe Ferguson

Dixon Trust Co.

3141 Hood St. Suite 600

Dallas Tx. 75219

Qualifications: Former and current employees of the cotton merchandisin business.

Grant Amount: 6 granst for $1,750 - $3,300.

Purpose: To help those in financial need.

Contact: Joe Ferguson - formal application.

H. C. Davis Fund

P O Box 2239

San Antonio, TX 78298

Qualifications: Masons who are residents of the 39th Masonic District of Texas.

Grant Amount: $200 - $3,075.

Purpose: To help those who are ill.

Contact: N/A - write letter.

F. V. Hall, Jr. and Marylou Hall Children's Crisis Foundation

c/o NCNB Texas National Bank

P O Box 830241

Dallas TX 75283-0241

Qualifications: Children under 12 who reside in Tom Green County.

Grant Amount: $80,407 for grants.

Purpose: To help those whose families are having financial hardship.

Contact: Alice J. Gayle - formal application and interview.

Hugh A. Hawthorne Foundation
5634 Briar Dr.
Houston, TX 77056
(713) 840-8453

Qualifications: Residents of Ireland.
Grant Amount: 20 grants for $68 - $8,310.
Purpose: To help those in financial need.
Contact: Claudia Hawthorne - write letter.

Walter Hightower Foundation
c/o Texas Commerce Bank - El Paso
P O Drawer 140
El Paso, TX 79980
(915) 546-6515

Qualifications: Handicapped children under 21 who reside in west Texas or southern New Mexico.
Grant Amount: 657 grants for $50 - $1,000.
Purpose: For health care equipment.
Contact: Terry Crenshaw - formal appliction. Deadline July 1.

The Kings Foundation
P O Box 27333
Austin, TX 78755

Qualifications: Residents of Texas.
Grant Amount: 9 grants for $50 - $250.
Purpose: To help those in financial need.
Contact: N/A - write letter.

The Mary L. Peyton Foundation
Bassett Tower Suite 908
303 Texas Ave
El Paso, TX 79901

Qualifications: Residents of El Paso who are children of employees for the Peyton Packing Company or those who cannot work because of disabilities.

Grant Amount: 790 grants for $8 - $1,600.
Purpose: To help those in financial need.
Contact: James Day - write letter.

Lulu Bryan Rambaud Charitable Trust
c/o NCNB Texas
P O box 2518
Houston, TX 77252-2518
Qualifications: For elderly female residents of Houston and Harris County.
Grant Amount: 5 grants for $270 - $1,200.
Purpose: Medical expenses.
Contact: N/A - write letter.

Sunnyside Foundation, Inc.
8609 Northwest Plaza Dr. Suite 201
Dallas, TX 75225
(214) 692-5686
Qualifications: Children residing in Texas.
Grant Amount: 33 grants for $39 - $4,350.
Purpose: To help with needs including camps.
Contact: Mary Rothenflue - formal application.

VERMONT
Copley Fund
P O Box 696
Morrisville, VT 05661
Qualifications: Elderly residents of Lamoille County.
Grant Amount: $80,781 for 133 grants.
Purpose: To help with housing expenses.
Contact: Richard Sargent - write letter.

VIRGINIA
Harrison and Conrad Memorial Trust
c/o Sovran Bank

P O Box 26903
Richmond, VA 22204
Application Address:
Loudoun Memorial Hospital
Office of the Administrator
224 Cornwall St NW
Leesburg, VA 22075
(703) 777-3300

Qualifications: Children with diseases who live in Leesburg or Loudoun.

Grant Amount: $86,884 in grants.

Purpose: For families who cannot afford to pay medical bills.

Contact: Hospital Administrator - write letter. Deadline April 1.

William A. Roberts Trust F/B/O Orphan Children of Chase City, c/o Central Fidelity Bank
Trust Department
828 Main St.
Lynchburg, VA 24504

Qualifications: Orphan children of Chase City.

Grant Amount: 13 grants for $750 - $3,600.

Purpose: To help those in financial need.

Contact: Trust Department of Central Fidelity Bank - write letter.

WASHINGTON
Welch Trust
P.O. Box 244
Walla Walla, WA 99362

Information: Medical & welfare aid to needy persons in the state of Washington

George T. Welch Testamentary Trust
c/o Baker-Boyer National Bank
P O Box 1796
Walla Walla, WA 99362
(509) 525-2000

Qualifications: Residents of Walla Walla County.

Grant Amount: 29 grants for $53 - $1,500.

Purpose: Financial and medical aid.

Contact: Bettie Loiacono - formal application. Deadline February 20, May 20, August 20, and November 20.

WEST VIRGINIA
Jamey Harless Foundation, Inc.
Drawer D
Gilbert, WV 25621
(304) 664-3227

Qualifications: Residents of Gilbert.

Grant Amount: $4,722 for grants.

Purpose: To help during financial emergency.

Contact: Sharon Murphy - write letter for guidelines.

WISCONSIN
Oshkosh Foundation
c/o First Wisconsin National Bank of Oshkosh
P O Box 2448
Oshkosh, WI 54903
(414) 424-4283

Qualifications: Residents of Oshkosh.

Grant Amount: 22 grants for $137 - $30,560.

Purpose: To give financial and medical aid.

Contact: Sandra A. Noe - write letter.

Edward Rutledge Charity
P O Box 758
404 North Bridge St.
Chippewa Falls, WI 54729
(715) 723-6618

Qualifications: Residents of Chippewa County

Grant Amount: 269 grants for $5 - $600.

Purpose: To help those in financial need.

Contact: John Frampton - formal appliction and interview. Deadline July 1.

Theodore and Catherine Schulte Foundation
c/o Bank One
Wisconsin Trust, N.S.
P O Box 1308
Milwaukee, Wi 53201
Application Address:
P O Box 221
Racine, WI 53408

Qualifications: Retired Catholic priest who reside in Racine.
Grant Amount: 10 grants for $600 - $2,800/
Purpose: To help with housing expenses.
Contact: Trust Administrator - write letter.

Margaret Wiegand Trust
c/o Bank One Wisconsin Trust Co. N.A.
P O Box 1308
Milwaukee, WI 53201

Qualifications: Blind residents of Waukshia County.
Grant Amount: 5 grants for $135 - $4,031.
Purpose: To help with general living expenses and care.
Contact: Judith Holland - write letter.

Chapter 5
PRI GRANTS

P rogram-related investments (PRIs), which foundations use to further charitable objectives like low-income housing or expanded capital for manufacturing firms, are made in nonprofit organizations, profit-making businesses or individuals. These investments typically are outright grants, equity investments, letters of credit, donated services or direct loans.

PRIs can be especially beneficial to growing businesses. Unlike commercial enterprises, foundations can invest in charitable deals that don't immediately generate an acceptable rate of return. Foundations thus provide part of a business's capital through a PRI, allowing the investor to obtain the remaining financing from commercial lenders or investors. Individuals or profitable businesses sometimes use nonprofit corporations as a "flow through" to get around creating a separate organization.

PROGRAM GRANTS

CALIFORNIA
America Honda Foundation
P.O. Box 2205
Torrance, California 90509-2205
(213) 781-4090

Grant Opportunities: Grants for scholarship funds, fellowships, special projects, operating budgets, continuing support, research, building funds, equipment, seed money, annual campaigns, professorships, internships, matching funds, capital campaigns, conferences and seminars, exchange programs and program-related investments.

Amounts: $613,418 for 16 grants: high $71,854; low $2,500; average $25,000-$50,000.

Applications: letter or telephone

Deadlines: November 1, February 1, May 1 and August 1

The Corcoran Community Foundation
P.O. Box 655
Corcoran, California 93212
(209) 992-5551

Grant Opportunities: Awarded for operating budgets, continuing support, seed money, emergency funds, building funds, equipment, land acquisition, matching funds, consulting services, technical assistance, program-related investments, loans, special projects, publications, conferences and seminars.

Amounts: $104,000 for 26 grants: high $32,500; low $233. Also $12,000 for two loans.

Application: letter

Deadlines: submit proposal preferably in the month preceding board meetings.

The Wallace Gerbode Foundation
470 Columbus Avenue, Suite 209
San Francisco, California 94133
(415) 391-0911

Grant Opportunities: Support for innovative programs and projects with a direct impact on residents of the five San Francisco Bay Area counties or Hawaii.

Amounts: $994,529 for 96 grants; high $60,000; low $300.

Application: letter

Deadlines: none

The Luke B. Hancock Foundation
360 Bryant Street
Palo Alto, California 94301
(414) 321-5536

Grant Opportunities: Broad purposes -- local giving primarily for youth job training and employment.

Amount: $828,728 for grants.
Application: letter
Deadlines: none

The Parker Foundation
1200 Prospect Street, Suite 575
La Jolla, California 92037
(619) 456-3038

Grant Opportunities: Giving largely in the form of partial seed money and matching or challenge grants
Amount: $421,834 for 43 grants; high $55,000; low $100; average $2,000-$20,000
Application: letter
Deadlines: none

The San Francisco Foundation
685 Market Street, Suite 910
San Francisco, California 94105
(415) 543-0223

Grant Opportunities: Grants awarded for operating budgets, seed money, building funds, equipment, land acquisition, program-related investments, special projects and technical assistance. Grants are only issued to groups living within the San Francisco area.
Amounts: $37,753,057 for 683 grants; high $1,000,000; low $100; average $5,000-$75,000. Also $4,307,903 for five loans.
Application: application form required
Deadlines: none

Rosenberg Foundation
47 Kearny Street, Suite 804
San Francisco, CA 94108-5528
(415) 421-6105

Grant Opportunities: Given for programs benefiting children and youth, rural development projects and immigration issues.

Levi Strauss Foundation
1155 Battery Street
P.O. Box 7215

San Francisco, CA 94106

(415) 544-6579

Grant Opportunities: Matching funds, continuing support, seed money, emergency funds, building funds and equipment.

Weingart Foundation

1200 Wilshire Boulevard, Suite 305

Los Angeles, CA 90017-1984

(213) 482-4343

Grant Opportunities: Seed money, building funds, equipment, matching funds, special projects and research.

COLORADO

Coors (Adolph) Foundation

350-C Clayton Street

Denver, Colorado 80206

(303) 388-1636

Grants Opportunities: Grants given for building funds, general purposes, seed money and program-related investments.

Amount: $4,425,146, including $3,265,690 for grants.

Application: letter

Deadlines: 6 weeks prior to meetings

ONLY FOR RESIDENTS OF **COLORADO**

Gates Foundation

3200 Cherry Creek South Drive, Suite 630

Denver, Colorado 80209-3247

Grant Opportunities: Grants for continuing support, building funds, capital campaigns, endowment funds, matching funds, program-related investments, renovation projects, seed money, special projects, equipment, fellowships, general purposes, land acquisition, publications and technical assistance.

Amounts: $3,367,020 for 106 grants; high $850,000; average $5,000-$100,000

Application: telephone

Deadlines: February 1, April 15, August 1, and October 15

The Piton Foundation

511 16th Street, Suite 700

Denver, Colorado 80202

(303) 825-6246

Grant Opportunities: Grants awarded for operating budgets, seed money, emergency funds, consulting services, technical assistance and program-related investments.

Amounts: $5,660,983 for grants; high $350,000. Also $79,992 for 54 grants to individuals.

Application: letter

Lowe Foundation

Colorado Judicial Center

Two East 14th Avenue

Denver, Colorado 80203

(303) 837-3750

Grant Opportunities: Grants for building funds, equipment, general purposes, operating budgets, program-related investments and seed money.

Amounts: $115,000 for 21 grants; high $15,000; low $1,500; average $6,000.

Application: letter

Deadlines: submit proposal preferably in January; deadline February 28.

Fishback (Harmes C.) Foundation Trust

Eight Village Road

Englewood, Colorado 80110

(303) 789-1753

Grant Opportunities: Grants for capital campaigns, continuing support, endowment funds, program-related investments and scholarship funds.

Amounts: $76,300 for 34 grants; high $20,000; low $250.

Application: letter

Deadlines: none

CONNECTICUT

Connecticut Mutual Life Foundation

140 Garden Street

Hartford, Connecticut 06154

(203) 727-6500

Grant Opportunities: Grants given for operating budgets, continuing support, seed money, building funds, matching funds, consulting services, technical assistance, program-related investments, special projects, conferences and seminars.

Amounts: $769,691 for 102 grants: average $3,000-$6,000
Application: letter, full proposal, or telephone
Deadlines: none

The New Haven Foundation
One State Street
New Haven, CT 06510
(203) 777-2386

Grant Opportunities: Operating budgets, seed money, emergency funds, building funds, equipment, matching funds, consulting services, technical assistance, program-related investments and loans. Grants are only issued to groups living within the state of Connecticut.

DELAWARE

Crystal Trust
1088 DuPont Building
Wilmington, Delaware 19898

Grant Opportunities: Grants awarded for seed money, building funds, equipment, land acquisition, and program-related investments.
Amounts: $843,260 for 46 grants; high $100,000; low $2,000; average $10,000-$20,000.
Application: letter
Deadlines: October 1

Raskob Foundation for Catholic Activities Inc.
P.O. Box 4019
Wilmington, Delaware 19807
(302) 655-4440

Grant Opportunities: Grants for operating budgets, seed money, emergency funds, equipment, land acquisition, matching funds, conferences and seminars, program-related investments, renovation projects and special projects.
Amounts: $2,879,026 for grants.
Application: letter
Deadlines: applications accepted for spring meeting from December 15 to February 15; applications accepted for fall meeting from June 15 to August 15.

DISTRICT OF COLUMBIA

The Hitachi Foundation
1509 22nd Street, N.W.
Washington, D.C. 20037
(202) 457-0588

Grant Opportunities: Grants for general purposes, operating budgets, program-related investments, seed money, special projects and technical assistance.

Amounts: $525,323 for 24 grants; high $118,400; low $1,000; average $35,000. Also $15,000 for loans.

Application: letter of no more than three pages; if project is of interest, a more detailed proposal will be invited.

Deadlines: February 1, June 1, October 1

The Community Foundation of Greater Washington Inc.
1002 Wisconsin Avenue N.W.
Washington, D.C. 20007
(202) 338-8993

Grant Opportunities: Grants for seed money, emergency funds, technical assistance, program-related investments, loans, special projects, research, publications, conferences and seminars.

Amounts: $1,915,918 for 200 grants; high $140,850; low $100; average $1,000-$$10,000. Also $1,173,457 for six foundation-administered programs and $62,000 for loans.

Application: letter

Deadlines: May and October

FLORIDA

Edyth Bush Charitable Foundation Inc.
199 East Welbourne Avenue
P.O.Box 1967
Winter Park, Florida 32790-1967
(407) 647-4322

Grant Opportunities: Provides a limited number of program-related investment loans for construction, land purchase, emergency, or similar purposes to organizations otherwise qualified to receive grants.

Amounts: $2,254,585 for 68 grants; high $200,000; low $1,000; average $15,000-$50,000. Also $106,921 for four foundation-administered programs.

Application: telephone or full proposal
Deadlines: September 1 or January 1; May 30 if funds are available

The Wilder Foundation
P.O.Box 99
Key Biscayne, Florida 33149

Grant Opportunities: Support for general purposes, building funds, endowment funds, research scholarship funds and matching funds.
Amounts: $126,956 for 18 grants: high $55,000; low $80.
Application: proposal
Deadlines: submit proposal before September

The Dr. P. Phillips Foundation Inc.
60 West Robinson Street
P.O. Box 3753
Orlando, FL 32801
(305) 422-6105

Grant Opportunities: Building funds, operating budgets, and special projects

GEORGIA

Metropolitan Atlanta Community Foundation Inc.
The Hurt Building, Suite 449
Atlanta, Georgia 30303
(404) 688-5525

Grant Opportunities: Grants for seed money, emergency funds, building funds, equipment, land acquisition, technical assistance, program-related investments, special projects, publications, capital campaigns, matching funds and renovation projects.
Amounts: $10,223,081 for grants: high $1,000,000; low $50; average $3,000-$5,000.
Application: letter or telephone
Deadlines: June 1, September 1, December 1 and March 1

The Coca-Cola Foundation
One Coca-Cola Plaza
Atlanta, Georgia 30313
(404) 676-3740

Grant Opportunities: Grants for annual campaigns, scholarship funds, continuing support, operating budgets, program-related investments and special projects.

Amounts: $3,666,464 for 149 grants: high $371,031; low $200; and $500,000 for loans.

Application: proposal

HAWAII

Wallace Alexander Gerbode Foundation
470 Columbus Avenue, Suite 209
San Francisco, California 94133
(415) 391-0911

Grant Opportunities: Support for innovative positive programs and projects with a direct impact on residents of the five San Francisco Bay area counties and Hawaii.

Amounts: $994,529 for 96 grants; high $60,000; low $300.

Application: letter

Deadlines: none

IDAHO

Northwest Area Foundation
West 975 First National Bank Building
St. Paul, Minnesota 55101
(612) 224-9635

Grant Opportunities: Grants generally for experimental and demonstration projects that promise significant impact on the community.

Amounts: $6,967,105 for 196 grants; high $250,000; low $150; average $20,000-$60,000.

Application: telephone, letter or proposal

Deadline: varies

ILLINOIS

The Field Foundation of Illinois Inc.
135 South LaSalle Street
Chicago, Illinois 60603
(312) 263-3211

Grant Opportunities: Support for building funds, emergency funds, equipment, special projects and land acquisition.

Amounts: $1,475,357 for 69 grants: high $60,000; low $1,000; average

$10,000-$20,000.

Application: full proposal

The Meyer-Ceco Foundation
c/o The Ceco Corporation
One Tower Lane, Suite 2300
Oak Brook Terrace, Illinois 60181
(312) 242-2000

Grant Opportunities: Continuing support and program-related investments.

Amounts: $252,915 for 140 grants: high $32,000; low $100. Average $500-$1,500.

INDIANA

Cummins Engine Foundation
Box Number 3005
Columbus, Indiana 47202-3005
(812)377-3569

Grant Opportunities: Primarily for local community needs, youth and civil rights; grants also for national needs that combine equal opportunity and excellence.

Amounts: $1,711,063 for 120 grants: high $272,296; low $500; average $2,500-$15,000.

Application: full proposal or letter

Deadlines: none

Heritage Fund of Bartholomew County Inc.
P.O. Box 1547
Columbus, Indiana 47202
(812) 376-7772

Grant Opportunities: Grants given for operating budgets, continuing support, seed money, emergency funds, deficit financing, building funds, equipment, land acquisition, matching funds, consulting services, technical assistance, program-related investments, special projects, conferences and seminars.

Amounts: $9,938 for four grants.

Olive B. Cole Foundation Inc.
Cole Capital Corporation

3242 Mallard Cove Lane
Fort Wayne, Indiana 46804
(219) 436-2182

Grant Opportunities: Grants for seed money, building funds, equipment, land acquisition, matching funds, program-related investments, general purposes and continuing support.

Amounts: $337,462 for 28 grants: high $70,000; low $1,000; average $12,052. Also $118,018 for grants to individuals.

Application: form required; letter

The Indianapolis Foundation
615 N. Alabama Street, Room 119
Indianapolis, IN 46204
(317) 634-7497

Grant Opportunities: Given for research and community education programs.

IOWA
Northwest Area Foundation
West 975 First National Bank Building
St. Paul, Minnesota 55101
(612)224-9635

Grant Opportunities: Grants generally for experimental and demonstration projects that promise significant impact on the community.

Amounts: $6,967,105 for 196 grants; high $250,000; low $150; average $20,000-$60,000.

Application: telephone, letter or proposal
Deadline: varies

KANSAS
The Powell Family Foundation
10990 Roe Avenue
P.O. Box 7270
Shawnee Mission, Kansas 66207
(913) 345-3000

Grant Opportunities: Grants given for operating budgets, seed money, emergency funds, equipment, program-related investments, conferences and seminars, matching funds and general purposes. Grants are limited to groups, not private individuals.

Amounts: $1,191,538 for 119 grants; high $147,000; low $200.
Application: letter
Deadlines: 30 days preceding board meetings

LOUISIANA
The Lupin Foundation
3715 Prytania Street, Suite 403
New Orleans, Louisiana 70115
(504) 897-6125

Grant Opportunities: Grants for equipment, research, scholarship funds, special projects, matching funds, continuing support, general purposes, program-related investments, renovation projects and seed money. Grants are limited to groups, not private individuals.
Amounts: $1,222,469, including $774,650 for 52 grants: high $75,000; low $800; average $15,000.
Applications: application form required; brief proposal
Deadlines: none

MASSACHUSETTS
Godfrey M. Hyams Trust
One Boston Place, 33rd Floor
Boston, Massachusetts 02108
(617) 720-2238

Grant Opportunities: Grants given for operating budgets, continuing support, annual campaigns, seed money, building funds, equipment, land acquisition and matching funds.
Amounts: $2,793,499, including $2,481,387 for 170 grants: high $87,000; low $2,500; average $5,000-$20,000.
Application: full proposal
Deadlines: submit proposal preferably in fall or winter.

The Nathaniel and Elizabeth P. Stevens Foundation
P.O. Box 111
North Andover, Massachusetts 01845
(508) 688-7211

Grant Opportunities: Grants given for general purposes, seed money, emergency funds, building funds, equipment, land acquisition, special projects, matching funds and program-related investments.
Amounts: $343,620 for 47 grants: high $50,000; low $750; average

$2,000-$5,000.
Application: full proposal
Deadlines: none

MICHIGAN

Ann Arbor Area Foundation
121 West Washington, Suite 400
Ann Arbor, Michigan 48104
(313) 663-0401

Grant Opportunities: Grants for seed money, emergency funds, building funds, equipment, matching funds, program-related investments, research, special projects, publications, conferences, and seminars.
Amounts: $71,022 for 21 grants.
Application: telephone
Deadlines: middle of month prior to meetings

Hudson-Webber Foundation
333 West Fort Street
Detroit, Michigan 48226
(313) 963-8991

Grant Opportunities: Concentrates efforts and resources in support of physical revitalization of downtown Detroit.
Amounts: $2,176, 592 for 62 grants: high $213,000; low $2,400; average $10,000-$30,000. Also $188,871 for 236 grants to individuals and $43,946 for 11 employee matching gifts.
Deadlines: April 15, August 15 and December 15

Albert L. and Louise B. Miller Foundation Inc.
155 West Van Buren Street
Battle Creek, Michigan 49016
(616) 964-7161

Grant Opportunities: Local municipal improvement, grants for seed money, building funds, equipment, land acquisition, endowment funds and loans. Grants are only for groups living within the state of Michigan.
Amounts: $100,600 for 32 grants, high $18,000; low $400; average $3,000.
Application: application form required; letter
Deadlines: none

Greater Battle Creek Foundation
512 Michigan National Bank Building
Battle Creek, MI 49017
(616) 962-2181
Grant Opportunities: Given for charitable, scientific, literary and educational programs.

MINNESOTA
Charles K. Blandin Foundation
100 Pokegama Avenue North
Grand Rapids, Minnesota 55744
(218) 326-0523
Grant Opportunities: Support for seed money, emergency funds, loans, program-related investments, special projects, consulting services and technical assistance.Grants are only for groups living within the state of Minnesota.
Amount: $4,192,734 for 152 grants: high $450,000; low $500. Also $215,071 for 378 grants to individuals and $110,000 for two loans.
Application: letter
Deadlines: submit proposal preferably 2 months prior to board meetings: March 1, June 1, September 1 and December 1.

Mary Andersen Hulings Foundation
c/o Baywood Corporation
287 Central Avenue
Bayport, Minnesota 55003
(612) 439-1557
Grant Opportunities: Support for general purposes, operating budgets, seed money, building funds, program-related investments and research.
Amount: $191,665 for 62 grants: high $35,000; low $100.
Application: form required; letter or proposal
Deadlines: submit proposal preferably in March, June, September or December; no set deadlines.

The McNeely Foundation
444 Pine Street
St. Paul, Minnesota 55101
(612) 228-4444

Grant Opportunities: Grants for community funds including operating budgets, continuing support, annual campaigns, seed money, emergency funds, building funds, endowment funds and program-related investments.

Amount: $120,000 for 20 grants: high $40,000; low $500; average $3,000-$5,000.

Application: letter

Deadlines: submit proposal preferably in September or December

Northwest Area Foundation
West 975 First National Bank Building
St. Paul, Minnesota 55101
(612) 224-9635

Grant Opportunities: Grants generally for experimental and demonstration projects that promise significant impact on the community.

Amount: $6,967, 105 for 196 grants: high $250,000; low $150; average $20,000-$60,000.

Application: telephone, letter or proposal

Deadline: varies

The Saint Paul Foundation
1120 Norwest Center
St. Paul, Minnesota 55101
(612) 224-5463

Grant Opportunities: Grants for seed money, emergency funds, building funds, equipment, matching funds, special projects and program-related investments.

Amount: $13,033,824 for 381 grants: high $9,967,964; low $60. Also $324,168 for seven loans.

Application: telephone, letter or full proposal

Deadlines: three months before next board meeting

Ordean Foundation
501 Ordean Building
Duluth, MN 55802
(218) 726-4785

Grant Opportunities: Building funds, loans, operating budgets, matching funds and program-related investments. Grants are only for groups living within the state of Minnesota.

MISSOURI

The H & R Block Foundation
4410 Main Street
Kansas City, Missouri 64111
(816) 932-8424

Grant Opportunities: Support for general purposes, building funds, equipment, land acquisition, matching funds, program-related investments, operating budgets, seed money, emergency funds and deficit financing. Grants are limited to groups only, not private individuals.

Amount: $233,955 for 131 grants: high $$26,000; low $50; average $500-$25,000. Also $60,000 for 30 grants to individuals and $5,100 for 22 employee matching gifts.

Application: full proposal

Deadlines: 45 days prior to meetings

Hall Family Foundations
Charitable & Crown Investment - 323
P.O. Box 419580
Kansas City, Missouri 64141-6580
(816) 274-5615

Grant Opportunities: Broad purposes, within four main areas of interest: (1) youth, especially education and programs that include social welfare, health and charater building of youth people; (2) economic development; (3) the performing and visual arts; and (4) the elderly.

Amount: $155,550 for 110 grants to individuals and $3,768,407 for 52 grants: high $1,966,921; low $1,000; average $35,000. Also $130,600 for 89 loans.

Application: letter

Deadlines: 4 weeks before board meetings

MONTANA

Northwest Area Foundation
West 975 First National Bank Building
St. Paul, Minnesota 55101
(612) 224-9635

Grant Opportunities: Grants generally for experimental and demonstration projects that promise significant impact on the community.

Amount: $6,967,105 for 196 grants: high $250,000; low $150; average $20,000-$60,000

Application: telephone, letter or proposal
Deadline: varies

NEW JERSEY

Geraldine R. Dodge Foundation Inc.
95 Madison Avenue
P.O. Box 1239
Morristown, New Jersey 07960-1239
(201) 540-8442

Grant Opportunities: Grants for seed money, conferences and seminars, matching funds, general purposes, special projects, publications and continuing support.

Amount: $4,015,288 for 199 grants: high $285,500; average $5,000-$100,000.

Application: letter or full proposal

Deadlines: submit proposal preferably in March, June, September or December

NEW HAMPSHIRE

Norwin S. and Elizabeth N. Bean Foundation
c/o New Hampshire Charitable Fund
1 South Street
P.O. Box 1335 Concord, New Hampshire 03302-1335
(603) 225-6641

Grant Opportunities: Grants for general purposes, seed money, emergency funds, building funds, equipment, land acquisition, special projects, conferences and seminars, matching funds, loans, program-related investments and consulting services.

Amount: $274,691 for 31 grants: high $75,000; low $350; average $500-$5,000. Also $12,000 for one loan.

Application: letter or telephone

Deadlines: February 15, May 15, August 15 and Nov. 15

NEW MEXICO

Carlsbad Foundation Inc.
116 South Canyon
Carlsbad, New Mexico 88220
(505) 887-1131

Grant Opportunities: Support given in the form of loans, operating budgets, seed money, emergency funds, building funds, equipment, matching funds, consulting services, technical assistance, program-related investments, special projects, publications, conferences and seminars.

Amount: Expenditures: $249,513, including $62,853 for grants, $92,781 for grants to individuals, and $400,000 for one loan.

Walter Hightower Foundation
c/o El Paso National Bank
P.O. Drawer 140
El Paso, Texas 79980
(915) 546-6515

Grant Opportunities: Grants for general purposes, operating budgets, continuing support, annual campaigns, seed money, building funds, equipment, and program-related investments; grants also to individuals.

Amounts: $233,574 for grants: high $40,000

Application: form required; letter

Deadlines: July 1

NEW YORK

A. Lindsay and Olive B. O'Conner Foundation
P.O. Box D
Hobart, New York 13788
(607) 538-9248

Grant Opportunities: Grants are awarded for general purposes, continuing support, seed money, emergency funds, building funds, equipment, land acquisition, special projects, publications, conferences and seminars, matching funds, loans, technical assistance, and program-related investments.

Amounts: $1,262,964 for 45 grants: high $500,000; low $500; average $1,000-$20,000.

Application: letter

Deadlines: April 1

The Sherman Foundation Inc.
315 West 57th Street, Suite 2D
New York, New York 10019
(212) 489-7143

Grant Opportunities: Grants given for operating budgets, continuing support, seed money, emergency funds, matching funds, program-related investments, special projects, loans and general purposes. Does not make grants to private individuals, only groups.

Amount: $2,119,000 for 153 grants: high $10,000; low $3,000; average $5,000-$25,000.

Application: full proposal

Deadlines: none

The John Ben Snow Foundation Inc.
P.O. Box 376
Pulaski, New York 13142
(315) 298-6401

Grant Opportunities: Community betterment projects.

Amount: $257,600 for 13 grants: high $45,000; low $1,000; average $3,500.

Application: form required; letter

Deadlines: submit proposal between September and April; deadline is April 15.

The Statler Foundation
Statler Tower, Suite 508
Buffalo, New York 14202
(716) 852-1104

Grant Opportunities: Building funds, program-related investments and equipment.

Taconic Foundation Inc.
745 Fifth Avenue, Suite 1111
New York, NY 10151
(212) 758-8673

Grant Opportunities: Seed money, program-related investments, general purposes and continuing support.

NORTH CAROLINA

Broyhill Foundation Inc.
P.O. Box 700
Lenoir, North Carolina 28633

Grant Opportunities: Local giving for civic and community service

Amount: $573,059 for 244 grants: high $100,000; low $50; average $500-$5,000. Also $54,520 for 51 loans.
Application: form required; letter

James G. Hanes Memorial Fund/Foundation
c/o Wachovia Bank and Trust Company
P.O. Box 3099
Winston-Salem, North Carolina 27150
(919) 748-5269

Grant Opportunities: Support for community programs.
Amount: $1,300,053 for 39 grants: high $125,000; low $1,000; average $1,000-$50,000.
Application: form required; proposal
Deadlines: first day of month in which board meets

The Kathleen Price and Joseph M. Bryan Family
Foundation, Inc.
P.O. Box 1349
Greensboro, North Carolina 27402
(919) 379-7512

Grant Opportunities: Grants for community projects, seed money, building funds and program-related investments.
Amount: $4,105,500 for 29 grants: high $10,000; low $1,000; average $1,000-$10,000.
Application: letter
Deadlines: March 15 and September 15

NORTH DAKOTA
Northwest Area Foundation
West 975 First Bank Building
St. Paul, Minnesota 55101
(612) 224-9635

Grant Opportunities: Grants generally for experimental and demonstration projects that promise a significant impact on the community.
Amount: $6,967,105 for 196 grants: high $250,000; low $150; average $20,000-$60,000.
Application: telephone, letter or proposal
Deadline: varies

NORTHEASTERN STATES
Ellis L. Phillips Foundation
13 Dartmouth College Highway
Lyme, New York 03768
(603) 795-2790

Grant Opportunities: Grants for operating budgets, continuing support, annual campaigns, seed money, emergency funds, endowment funds, conferences and seminars.

Amount: $268,658 for 45 grants: high $30,158; low $1,000; average $1,000-$10,000.

Application: one- to three-page letter

OHIO
The William Bingham Foundation
1250 Leader Building
Cleveland, Ohio 44114
(216) 781-3275

Grant Opportunities: Grants for several purposes, special projects, seed money, building funds, equipment, publications, conferences and seminars, matching funds and program-related investments.

Amount: $640,244 for 27 grants: high $115,294; low $2,000; average $5,000-$30,000. Also $100,000 for one loan.

Application: letter of two pages or less

Deadlines: submit proposal preferably in February or July; deadline 2 months prior to board meeting dates.

The Cleveland Foundation
1400 Hanna Building
Cleveland, Ohio 44115
(216) 861-3810

Grant Opportunities: Grants serve mainly as seed money for innovative projects or for developing institutions or services addressing unmet needs in the community.

Amount: $17,100,149 for 675 grants: high $500,000; low $250; average $5,000-$50,000.

Deadlines: March 31, June 15, August 31 and Dec. 15

The Lorain Foundation
457 Broadway

Lorain, Ohio 44502

Grant Opportunities: Grants for general purposes.

Amount: $32,223 for grants.

Marathon Oil Foundation Inc.

539 South Main Street

Findlay, Ohio 45840

(419) 422-2121 Ext. 3708

Grant Opportunities: support for seed money, building funds, conferences and seminars, and program-related investments.

Amount: $1,789,407 for 368 grants: high $1,000,000; low $300. Also $197,778 for 50 grants to individuals.

Application: full proposal

Deadlines: none

Toledo Trust Corporation Inc. Foundation

c/o Trust Corporation Bank, Ohio

Three Seagate

Toledo, Ohio 43603

(419) 259-8217

Grant Opportunities: Grants given for operating budgets, continuing support, emergency funds, building funds, equipment, land acquisition, consulting services, technical assistance, and program-related investments.

Amount: $212,350 for 19 grants: high $148,000; low $100; average $1,000-$10,000.

Application: letter

Deadlines: none

OKLAHOMA

Phillips Petroleum Foundation Inc.

Phillips Building, 16th Floor

Bartlesville, Oklahoma 74004

(918) 661-6248

Grant Opportunities: Grants given for operating budgets, seed money, emergency funds, building funds, equipment, land acquisition, program-related investments, conferences and seminars, matching funds and continuing support.

Given: $3,595,030 for 712 grants; high $520,801; low $60
Application: proposal, letter or telephone
Deadlines: none

OREGON
The Jackson Foundation
c/o U.S. National Bank of Oregon
P.O. Box 3168
Portland, Oregon 97208
(503) 225-4461; (800) 547-1031 ext. 6558

Grant Opportunities: Grants for local giving, including funds for scientific research and technology.
Amount: $791,646 for 132 grants: high $64,200; low $300; aveage $2,000-$10,000. Also $764,330 for 18 loans.
Deadlines: none

Fredy Meyer Charitable Trust
1515 Southwest Fifth Avenue, Suite 500
Portland, Oregon 97201
(503) 228-5512

Grant Opportunities: Support for seed money, building funds, equipment, matching funds, technical assistance, program-related investments, special projects and research.
Amount: $6,365,583 for 94 grants: high $555,000; low $964; average $20,000-$75,000.
Application: form required; full proposal or letter
Deadlines: no set deadlines

Northwest Area Foundation
West 975 First National Bank Building
St. Paul, Minnesota 55101
(612) 224-9635

Grant Opportunities: Grants generally for experimental and demonstration projects that promise significant impact on the community.
Amount: $6,967,105 for 196 grants: high $250,000; low $150; average $20,000-$60,000.
Application: telephone, letter or proposal.
Deadline: varies

PENNSYLVANIA

Claude Worthington Benedum Foundation
223 Fourth Avenue
Pittsburgh, Pennsylvania 15222
(412) 288-0360

Grant Opportunities: Grants awarded for matching funds, consulting services, building funds, operating budgets, technical assistance, special projects, program-related investments and seed money. Grants are only for groups living within the state of Pennsylvania.

Amount: $5,646,092 for 73 grants; high $1,000,000; low $2,500; average $75,000.

Application: letter

Howard Heinz Endowment
DNG Tower, 30th Floor
625 Liberty Avenue
Pittsburgh, Pennsylvania 15222
(412)391-5122

Grant Opportunities: Local giving, usually with one-time, non-renewable grants for new programs, seed money and capital projects.

Amount: $4,637,323 for 108 grants: high $500,000; low $500; average $5,000-$150,000.

Application: letter, full proposal or telephone

Deadlines: none

Kennametal Foundation
P.O. Box 231
Latrobe, Pennsylvania 15650
(412)539-5203

Grant Opportunities: Giving for general purposes, including community funds. Support for building funds, equipment, endowment funds, program-related investments, research and matching funds.

Amount: $129,283 for 100 grants: high $33,198; low $25.

Application: letter

Deadlines: submit proposal preferably in January

Richard King Mellon Foundation
525 William Penn Place

Pittsburgh, Pennsylvania 15219

(412) 392-2800

Grant Opportunities: Grants awarded for seed money, building funds, equipment, land acquisition, endowment funds, research, matching funds, general purposes and continuing support.

Amount: $24,520,772 for 107 grants: high $9,000,000; low $2,500; average $10,000-$500,000.

Application: full proposal

Deadlines: submit proposal between January and April or July and September; deadlines April 15 and October 15.

The Pittsburgh Foundation

CNG Tower, 30th Floor

265 Liberty Avenue

Pittsburgh, Pennsylvania 15222

(412) 391-5122

Grant Opportunities: Funds used for programs to support special projects of regularly established agencies, capital and equipment needs, research of a non-technical nature and demonstration projects.

Amount: $4,289,491 for 664 grants: high $150,000; low $37; average $5,000-$50,000.

Application: letter, full proposal or telephone

Deadlines: 60 days prior to board meeting

Williamsport Foundation

102 West Fourth Street

Williamsport, Pennsylvania 17701

(717) 326-2611

Grant Opportunities: Grants given for building funds, emergency funds, equipment, general purposes, matching funds, program-related investments, seed money, special projects and loans.

Amount: $899,945 for 84 grants: high $115,000; low $24; average $1,000-$30,000.

Application: letter

Deadlines: none

RHODE ISLAND

Old Stone Bank Charitable Foundation

180 South Main Street

Providence, Rhode Island 02903

(401) 278-2213

Grant Opportunities: Grants awarded for seed money, building funds, land acquisition, program-related investments and special projects.

Amount: $238,798 for 24 grants: high $140,000; low $150.

Application: letter or telephone

Deadlines: first day of each month when board meets.

SOUTH DAKOTA

Northwest Area Foundation

West 975 First National Bank Building

St. Paul, Minnesota 55101

(612) 224-9635

Grant Opportunities: Grants generally for experimental and demonstration projects that promise significant impact on the community.

Amount: $6,967,105 for 196 grants: high $250,000; low 4150; average $20,000-$60,000.

Application: Telephone, letter, or proposal

Deadline: varies

SOUTHEASTERN STATES

Mary Reynolds Babcock Foundation Inc.

102 Reynolds Village

Winston-Salem, North Carolina 27106-5123

(919) 748-9222

Grant Opportunities: Grants for operating budgets, seed money, emergency funds, special projects and program-related investments.

Amount: $3,127,491 for 156 grants: high $175,000; low $1,000; average $10,000-$50,000. Also $200,000 for two loans.

Application: form required

Deadlines: submit proposal between December and February or June and August; deadlines March 1 and September 1.

TENNESSEE

Lyndhurst Foundation

701 Tallan Building

Chattanooga, Tennessee 37402

(615) 756-0767

Grant Opportunities: Support for general purposes, seed money, matching funds, operating budgets, program-related investments and special projects.

Amount: $2,827,077 for 50 grants: high $350,000; low $2,000; average $30,000-$150,000. Also $305,000 for 13 grants to individuals.

Application: application form required for grants to individuals; awards made only at the initiative of the foundation.

Deadlines: 4 weeks before board meetings

TEXAS

Communities Foundation of Texas Inc.
4605 Live Oak Street
Dallas, Texas 75204
(204) 826-5231

Grant Opportunities: Support for operating budgets, annual campaigns, seed money, emergency funds, building funds, equipment, land acquisition, matching funds, consulting services, technical assistance, special projects, program-related investments, research, publications, conferences and seminars.

Amount: $11,310,838 for 925 grants: high $1,050,923; average $10,000-$25,000.

Application: letter

Deadlines: 30 days before distribution committee meetings

Walter Hightower Foundation
c/o El Paso National Bank
P.O. Box Drawer 140
El Paso, Texas 79980
(915) 546-6515

Grant Opportunities: Grants for general purposes, operating budgets, continuing support, annual campaigns, seed money, building funds, equipment and program-related investments. Grants also to individuals.

Amount: $233,574 for grants: high $40,000

Application: application form required; letter

Deadlines: July 1

Meadows Foundation Inc.
Wilson Historic Block
2922 Swiss Avenue

Dallas, Texas 75204

(214) 826-9431

Grant Opportunities: Support for operating budgets, continuing support, seed money, emergency funds, deficit financing, building funds, equipment, land acquisition, matching funds, special projects, publications, conferences and seminars, program-related investments, technical assistance and consulting services.

Amount: $7,500,859 for 164 grants: high $1,000,000; low $607; average $25,000-$50,000.

Application: full proposal

Deadlines: none

Crystelle Waggoner Charitable Trust

c/o NCNB Texas

P.O. Box 1317

Fort Worth, Texas 76101

(817) 390-6925

Grant Opportunities: Support for general purposes, annual campaigns, building funds, conferences and seminars, emergency funds, endowment funds, equipment, land acquisition, operating budgets, program-related investment, publications, research, seed money, special projects and technical assistance.

Amount: $339,922 for 33 grants: high $50,000; low $2,000; average $10,000.

Application: letter

Deadlines: end of each quarter

WASHINGTON
Northwest Area Foundation

West 975 First National Bank Building

St. Paul, Minnesota 55101

(612) 224-9635

Grant Opportunities: Grants generally for experimental and demonstration projects that promise significant impact on the community.

Amount: $6,967,105 for 196 grants: high $250,000; low $150; average $20,000-$60,000.

Application: telephone, letter or proposal

Deadline: varies

WEST VIRGINIA
Claude Worthington Benedum Foundation

223 Fourth Avenue
Pittsburgh, Pennsylvania 15222
(412) 288-0360

Grant Opportunities: Grants awarded for matching funds, consulting services, building funds, operating budgets, technical assistance, special projects, program-related investments and seed money.

Amount: $5,646,092 for 73 grants: high $1,000,000; low $2,500; average $75,000.

Application: letter

WISCONSIN

Judd S. Alexander Foundation Inc.
500 Third Street, Suite 509
P.O. Box 2137
Wausau, Wisconsin 54402-2137
(715) 845-4556

Grant Opportunities: Grants for seed money, emergency funds, building funds, equipment, land acquisition, matching funds, technical assistance and program-related investments.

Amount: $270,472 for 56 grants: high $29,000; low $175. Also $157,723 for three loans.

Application: letter, full proposal or telephone

Deadlines: none

Alvin R. Amundson Charitable Remainer Trust
c/o Marshall and Ilsley Bank, Madison Trust Office
P.O. Box 830
Madison, Wisconsin 53701

Grant Opportunities: Local giving for community development.

Amount: $68,225 for 12 grants: high $38,225; low $1,000

La Crosse Foundation
P.O. Box 489
La Crosse, Wisconsin 54602-0489
(608) 782-1148

Grant Opportunities: Local giving for charitable purposes to benefit the citizens of La Crosse County, Wisconsin.

Amount: $142,059 for 45 grants: high $30,000; low $100; average $2,300. Also $9,816 for 20 grants to individuals.

Deadlines: submit proposal preferably 1 month before committee meetings.

Chapter 6

HOW TO OBTAIN
VENTURE CAPITAL

Becuase federal and state money is getting difficult to come by, and anyone interested in starting or expanding a business may find it difficult to do so, venture capital may be the answer. Venture capitalists are those willing to invest in a business or other venture for a percentage of the equity. Below is a listing of the various organizations that can provide you with information on venture capital.

Venture Capital Associations

The National Venture Capital Association (NVCA)
1655 North Fort Meyer Drive, Suite 700
Arlington, VA 22209
703-528-4370

The association answers questions regarding federal legislation and regulations regarding the venture capital process.

The Western Association of Venture Capitalists
3000 San Hill Road, Building 2, Suite 215
Menlo Park, CA 94025
415-854-1322
Includes 130 members.

National Association of Investment Companies
1111 14th Street NW, Suite 700
Washington, DC 20002
202-289-4336

Includes 150 members all of which are Specialized Small Business Investment Companies (SSBICs). A directory is provided for $5 that describes the companies individual requirements.

National Association of Small Business Investment Companies (NASBIS)

1191 North Fairfax Street, Room 200

Alexandria, VA 22314.

703-683-1601

The association has an abundant source of venture capital experts and literature. They also publish a directory of 300 small business investment companies with information on procedures, investment policies, and information on dollar limits on loans and investments. The directory is available for $10 by sending a check or money order to NASBIS Directory, P.O. Box 2039, Merrifield, VA 22116.

Venture Capital Network

201 Vassar Street

Cambridge, MA 02139

617-253-7163

Registration for this association costs $250. for 12 months and works to match entrepreneurs in need of capital with venture capital sources. It is a non-profit organization.

Government Agencies

U.S. Small Business Administration

Investment Division

Washington, DC 20416

The responsibility of this office is to license, regulate, and fund some 350 Small Business Investment Companies (SBICs) nationwide. By writing to the above address, you can receive a free directory of a listing of the names and addresses of SBICs. It is called the Directory of Operating Small Business Investment Companies. Other sources available include videotapes and publications on how to start a small business. For more information, call the SBA Small Business Answer Desk at 1-800-827-5722.

Venture Capital Clubs

The International Venture Capital Institute (IVCI)
P.O. Box 1333
Stamford, CT 06904
203-323-3143

The IVCI publishes the IVCI Directory of Domestic and International Venture Groups which includes a listing of contact information for all of the venture capital clubs, for a cost of $9.95.

Association of Venture Capital Clubs
265 East 100 South, Suite 300
P.O. Box 3358
Salt Lake City, UT 84110-3358
801-364-1100

Not only does this association assist in the creation of growth-oriented businesses, but they also encourage the starting of venture clubs. The association publishes an instruction manual for $50.

Below is a partial listing of other venture capital clubs in the United States.

Alabama

Birmingham Venture Club
P.O. Box 10127
Birmingham, AL 35202
205-323-5461
Attention: Patricia Tucker Fox

Mobile Venture Club
c/o Mobile Area Chamber of Commerce
451 Government Street
Mobile, AL 36652
205-433-6951

California
Sacramento Valley Venture Capital Forum
University of California Graduate School of Management
Davis, CA 95616
916-752-7395
Attention: Professor Richard Dorf

Orange Coast Venture Group
P.O. Box 7282
Newport Beach, CA 92658
714-754-1191
Attention: Mike Reagan

San Diego Venture Group
Girard Capital
4320 La Jolla Village Drive, Suite 210
San Diego, CA 92122
Attention: Gregory Beck

Northern California Venture Capital Association
1470 Wild Rose Way
Mountain View, CA 94043
415-965-4651
Attention: Tom Schwartz

Channel Islands Venture Association
500 Esplanada Drive, #810
Oxnard, CA 93030
805-644-5335
Attention: Mark Shappee

Connecticut
Connecticut Venture Group
30 Tower Lane
Avon, CT 06001
203-677-0183
Attention: Sam McKay

District of Columbia
Baltimore-Washington Venture Group
1545 18th Street NW, #319
Washington, DC 20036
202-438-0297
Attention: John Versteeg

Florida
Gold Coast Venture Capital Club
110 E. Atlantic Avenue, #208E
Delray Beach, FL 33444
305-272-1040 or 800-624-6009
Attention: Oscar Ziemba or Sy Lubner

Gulf Coast Venture Club
P.O. Box 5042
South Station
Fort Myers, FL 33901
813-939-5714

Georgia
Atlanta Venture Forum
2859 Paces Ferry Road, Suite 1400
Atlanta, GA 30339
404-584-1364
Attention: Mary King

Idaho
Treasure Valley Venture Capital Forum
Idaho Small Business Development Center
Boise State University College of Business
1910 University Drive
Boise, ID 83725
208-385-1640

Iowa
Venture Club of Iowa City
ICAD Group
Iowa City, IA 52240
319-354-3939

Minnesota
The Entrepreneur's Network
512 Nicollet Mall, Suite 500
Minneapolis, MN 55402
612-542-0682

Michigan
New Enterprise Forum
912 North Main Street
Ann Arbor, MI 48104
313-662-0550

New York
Rochester Venture Capital Group
100 Corporate Woods, Suite 300
Rochester, NY 14623
716-232-4160

Washington
Puget Sound Venture Club
14606 NE 51st Street, #C-1
Bellevue, WA 98007-3025
206-882-0605
Attention: Gary R. Ritner

Wisconsin
Wisconsin Venture Network
823 N. Second Street, Suite 605
Milwaukee, WI 53203
414-278-7070

There are also several other groups in the United States that publish their own materials to assist you with you venture. Among them are;

The CPA Firm Coopers & Lybrand
1251 Avenue of the Americas
New York, NY 10020
212-536-2000

There are several publications on venture capital provided by this firm including Three Keys to Obtaining Venture Capital, The Economic Impact of Venture Capital, Venture Capital: The Price of Growth, and Charting a Course for Corporate Venture Capital.

Venture Economics, Inc.
1180 Raymond Blvd.
Newark, NJ 07102
201-622-4500

This company provides research and consulting to various organizations on venture capital trends. Among its publications are:

Venture Capital Journal, a monthly journal that cites issues and trends in venture capital investment. The subscription rate is $695.

Pratt's Guide to Venture Capital Sources, an annual directory of 800 venture capital firms in the U.S. and Canada, with articles on how to raise venture capital. The cost is $175.

Venture Capital Journal Yearbook, an annual journal that summarizes venture activities from the previous year, including statistics and information about specific industries. The cost is $175.

Additional Reading Material

A Venture Capital Primer for Small Business, published by the U.S. Small Business Administration. Explains the various resources available for venture capitalists and how to develop proposals to obtain these resources. Send $.50 to SBA Publications, P.O. Box 30, Denver, CO 80201-0030. Ask for item number FM5.

Venture Capital Handbook, written by David Gladstone, Prentice Hall, Englewood Cliffs, NJ 07632, 1988, is a quick guide to obtaining capital for the purpose of starting, buying, or expanding a business. It also includes a state by state listing of venture capital companies.

The MacMillan Small Business Handbook, provides information about how to find venture capital and develop effective proposals to obtain that capital. The handbook also includes a list of Small Business Investment Companies and types of venture capital firms. The author is Mark Stevens, MacMillan Publishing Co., 866 Third Avenue, New York, NY 10022, 1988. The cost is $35.

Mancuso's Small Business Resource Guide, lists Small Business Administration regional offices, Small Business Development Centers, and Small Business Investment Companies. The author is Joseph R. Mancuso, Prentice Hall Press, Gulf & Western Bldg., New York, NY 10023, 1988. The cost is $19.95.

The Best of INC. *Guide to Finding Capita*l, by the editors of Inc. Magazine, Prentice Hall Press, New York, NY, 1988.

Help In Writing Proposals

You may also want to check out the following book from your local public library. Hall, Mary: *Developing Skills In Proposal Writing*, Continuing Education Publications, Portland, Oregon.

....

SAMPLE LETTER

John Doe
3456 Maple Road
Yourtown, OR

April 19, 1992

The ACE Grants
4560 Whittier Boulevard
Chicago, Il 30010

Dear Sirs:

I am researching the grant foundations and I would appreciate your sending me grant proposal guidelines, a list of your past recipients and your annual report.

Sincerely,

John Doe

SAMPLE LETTER

John Doe
3456 Maple Road
Yourtown, OR

April 19, 1992

The ACE Grants
4560 Whittier Boulevard
Chicago, Il 30010

Dear Sirs:

    I am researching the grant foundations and I would appreciate your sending me grant proposal guidelines, a list of your past recipients and your annual report.

Sincerely,

John Doe

Chapter 7
HELP FOR
THE DISABLED

VOCATIONAL REHABILITATION

All states have coordinated programs of vocational rehabilitation and independent living to help individuals with disabilities become employable, independent, and integrated into the community by providing a wide range of services, financial assistance, and training. An individualized written plan for rehabilitation and independent living is worked out for every eligible handicapped individual, through meetings of that individual and the counselors, to determine the individual's potential skills, and other resources.

During this process and throughout the rehabilitation, the program may provide a variety of services, including the following:

• A medical examination, to determine the extent of disability, one's suitability for employment, and specific rehabilitation assistance needed.

• Counseling and guidance to determine the individual's rehabilitation, independent living, and employment potential, and the type(s) of employment and independent living setting most suitable for him/her.

• Medical help to reduce or remove disability and improve or restore job performance. This help includes medical, surgical, psychiatric, and hospital services; artificial limbs, braces, hearing devices, and eyeglasses needed on the job.

• Job training at trade schools, rehabilitation centers, or at home.

• Educational opportunities, including payment of college tuition and fees and other education expenses as necessary, if college is required for the individual to be able to earn a livelihood.

• Financial assistance during the rehabilitation period for room and board, transportation, and other necessary assistance.

• Referral and job placement.

• On the job help, if needed, including expenses related to getting to your job or keeping your job.

FOR DEAF PERSONS

Special emphasis on rehabilitation services to hearing impaired persons has its origin at the Federal level within the Rehabilitation Services Administration at:

Deafness and Communicative Disorders Branch
Switzer Building, MS 2312
Washington, D.C. 20202
(202) 732-1401 (voice) or 732-1298 (TDD)

This office provides leadership and consultation to state agencies in developing rehabilitation programs and services for persons with from deafness and communicative disorders.

The Rehabilitation Services Administration maintains a liaison staff person in deafness rehabilitation in each of the ten RSA regional offices, and sponsors numerous rehabilitation counselors for special training in working with deaf clients. The agency also funds sever several projects around the country to assist underachieving deaf person whose maximum potential not been reached.

FOR DEAF/BLIND PERSONS

The Federal Government provides funds that help support the Helen Keller National Center for Deaf-Blind Youth and Adults. To explore your eligibility for the Center's rehabilitation programs, write:

Helen Keller National Center
111 Middle Neck Road
Sands Point, N.Y. 11050
(516) 944-8900 (voice or TTY)

EDUCATION

The Federal Government provides assistance at many lev levels to enable children, youth, and adults to receive education and training. Disabled persons share the same right to educational opportunities and services as everyone else.

National Information Center for
Children and Youth with Handicaps
1555 Wilson Blvd. Suite 508
Rosslyn, VA 22209
(703) 522-3332

SCHOOLS FOR THE BLIND

There are approximately 55 special schools for blind children throughout the country which provide specific educational and training curricula for grade levels K through 12. Examples of courses include: Braille, skills of daily living, orientation and mobility, plus the full range of regular academic curricula offered in other schools. Many of these schools will also accept blind students with multiple handicaps. For further information on schools in your area, contact your local school district.

FOR DEAF PERSONS

The Department of Education office supports post-secondary education of deaf individuals through six major programs across the country and 23 single and multi-state projects serving deaf-blind children and youth. For information, write:

Office of Special Education Programs
U.S. Department of Education
Washington, D.C. 20202

SCHOOLS FOR DEAF

Gallaudet University is funded by the Federal Government and was established to provide a liberal higher education for deaf persons. In addition to its undergraduate program, Gallaudet operates graduate programs at the master's and doctoral levels and a program of research. On agreement with the U.S. Department of Education (ED), Gallaudet operates a model Secondary School for the Deaf for students from the District of Columbia, Maryland, Virginia, West Virginia, Pennsylvania, and Delaware. The college also operates the Kendall Elementary Demonstration School which experiments in techniques and materials and disseminates information to educational facilities for deaf children. For more information write:

> Gallaudet University
> 800 Florida Avenue N.E.
> Washington, D.C. 20002

The national Technical Institute for the Deaf (NTID) in Rochester, NY., was created by public law as a special technical college for deaf students from all states. many receive financial assistance to study at NTID from their state vocational rehabilitation agencies. For more information, write to:

> Office of Career Opportunities
> National Technical Institute for the Deaf
> One Lomb Memorial Drive
> Rochester, NY 14623

Get Free Help ...
New Law Requiring Businesses
To Accomodate The Disabled

Recently, a new law was enacted that makes it illegal for any business to discriminate against individuals with mental or physical disabilities including terminally ill patients with AIDS for example. This means that employers and public places such as restaurants and hotels, must make adjustments to accomodate the disabled. New construction to existing facilities must be undertaken to accomodate the disabled, unless it poses a threat of undue hardship.

The law is called the American with Disabilities Act, and requires businesses with 25 or more employees to have made their adjustments by July of 1992, whether or not they have any disabled employees working for them. Companies with only 15 to 24 employees must make their changes by July of 1994. Furthermore, if the business serves the public such as a restaurant or retail store, the changes should have been made by January 26, 1992.

Uncle Sam Helps You Beat Fear Consultants

When new laws are enacted, usually an entirely new industry will appear with it containing high-priced lawyers and other specialists that will take advantage of a business's fear of the consequences of the new law. But, a business does not have to pay the exorbitant fees of these consultants because the same information can be extracted, free, from the government. Any assistance you need, whether it be with finances, arichitectural advice, choosing the plans, or contractors to implement those plans, can be obtained from Uncle Sam.

Why Was This Law Passed?

This law came about after a study was taken in 1988 by the Bureau of the Census. It states that there are 13 million Americans between the ages of 16 and 64 that do not suffer from a disability that confines them to an institution or hospital. Of these 13 million, 5 million are currently employed and 6 million more have the capability to work, if the law were to be enacted. And so it was. Putting the disabled to work, will reduce the government's outlay of $60 billion in benefits to the disabled, and it is expected to cost businesses between $1 to $1 billion dollars. The General Accounting Office and the U.S. Department of Labor estimate that changes can be made for as little as $50. for to accomodate half of the disabled workers, while 20% of the disabled could be employed with changes that cost $50 to $100, and another 20% can be employed with costs between $500 to $1000 each to employ. The amounts can be staggering, but there is help.

What Your Business Must Do And How To Do It

Because of the consequences of this law, 10 Regional Disability and Business Accomodation Centers were created to assist businesses with their problems. Many times, consultants will actually come out to your business to help, free, to determine the types of changes you need. The objectives of these centers are to help the entire community by disseminating information, providing direct technical assistance, providing referrals for specialized information and technical assistance, and training interested and affected individuals. The following regions are listed below.

Region I (CT, ME, MA, NH, RI, VT)

Jennifer Eckel, Director

ADA Regional Disability
and Business Accomodation Center

University of Southern Maine

Muskie Institute of Public Affairs

96 Falmouth Street

Portland, ME 04103

207-780-4430

207-780-4417 FAX

Region II (NJ, NY, PR)

Richard Dodds, Director

ADA Regional Disability
and Business Accomodation Center

United Cerebral Palsy Association

365 S. Broad Street

Trenton, NJ 08608

609-392-4004

609-392-3505 FAX

Region III (DE, DC, MD, PA, VA, WV)

Sharon Mistler, Director

ADA Regional Disability
and Business Accomodation Center

Independence Center of Northern VA

2111 Wilson Blvd.

Arlington, VA 22201

703-525-3268

703-525-6835 FAX

Region IV (AL, FL, GA, KY, MS, NC, SC, TN)

Shelly Kaplan, Director

ADA Regional Disability
and Business Accomodation Center

United Cerebral Palsy Association / U.S.-National Alliance of Business

1776 Peachtree Road

Atlanta, GA 30309

404-888-0022

404-888-9091 FAX

404-888-9006 TDD

Region V (IL, IN, MI, MN, OH, WI)

David Braddock, Director

ADA Regional Disability
and Business Accomodation Center

University of Illinois at Chicago

University Affiliated Program in Developmental Disabilities

1640 W. Roosevelt Road

Chicago, IL 60608

312-413-1647 VOICE/TDD

Region VI (AR, LA, NM, OK, TX)

Lex Frieden, Director

ADA Regional Disability
and Business Accomodation Center

Independent Living Research Utilization

The Institute for Rehabilitation and Research

2323 W. Shepard Blvd., Suite 1000

Houston, TX 77019

713-520-0232, 713-520-5785 FAX

713-520-5136 TDD

Region VII (IA, KS, NE, MO)

Jim DeJong, Director

ADA Regional Disability
and Business Accomodation Center

University of Missouri at Columbia

401 E. Locust Street

Columbia, MO 65201

314-882-3807

314-882-1727 FAX

Region VIII (CO, MT, ND, SD, UT, WY)

Randy W. Dipner, Director

ADA Regional Disability
and Business Accomodation Center

Meeting the Challenge, Inc.

3630 Sinton Road, Suite 103

Colorado Springs, CO 80907

719-444-0252

719-444-0269 FAX

Region IX (AZ, CA, HI, NV)

Erica Jones, Director

ADA Regional Disability
and Business Accomodation Center

Berkeley Planning Associates

440 Grand Avenue, Suite 500

Oakland, CA 94610

415-465-7884

415-465-7885 FAX

Region X (AK, ID, OR, WA)

Toby Olson, Director

Washington State Governor's Committee

ADA Regional Disability
and Business Accomodation Center

212 Maple Park, KG-11
Olympia, WA 98504
206-438-3168
206-438-4014 FAX
206-438-3167 TDD

The Requirements Of The Law

Although the above regional centers offer a vast amount of information, you may find that you still need more. The following sources can provide you with that additional information about the law and its implications.

President's Committee
on Employment of People with Disabilities
1331 F Street, NW, 3rd Floor
Washington, DC 20004
202-376-6200

Civil Rights Division
U.S. Department of Justice
Coordination and Review Section
P.O. Box 66118
Washington, DC 20035
202-514-0301
202-514-0381 TDD
202-514-0383 TDD

FEDERAL HANDICAPPED STUDENT FINANCIAL AID

There is no specific federal financial aid program to enable handicapped individuals to attend college except where the vocational rehabilitation agency has determined that the best preparation for a job for a particular individual is a college education. In these cases financial assistance may be provided. There are, however, five kinds of Federal financial aid programs available to all students in need:

Grants given on the basis of financial need. Money received does not have to be repaid.

Loans which must be repaid; (Perkins or guaranteed student loans);

Work-study programs in which students are given part-time jobs to help them through school;

Benefits, such as GI Bill, Social Security and Junior GI which do not have to be repaid.

To learn more about the various Federal student aid programs, write to:

Office of Student Financial Assistance
P.O Box 84
Washington, D.C. 20044

FEDERAL JOBS

All Federal jobs for regular appointment must be announced to the public and are filled on a competitive basis. There are a small number of special "A" appointment positions for handicapped individuals, however, which are not competitive under the following conditions:

Mentally retarded individuals referred by their vocational rehabilitation counselors;

Severely physically handicapped individuals referred through their vocational rehabilitation counselor or taking a 700 hour trial appointment.

SMALL BUSINESS ADMINISTRATION

Handicapped persons interested in going into business for themselves may qualify for Federal assistance and low cost loans from the Small Business Administration (SBA). If SAB office in your area write to:

Small Business Administration
Director, Office of business Loans
1441 L Street, N.W.
Washington, D.C. 20416

FINANCIAL ASSISTANCE

There are two basic Federal programs providing direct and continuing financial assistance to disabled persons.

SOCIAL SECURITY DISABILITY INSURANCE BENEFITS

Social Security disability insurance benefits may be paid to a disabled worker under 65 and his or her family when earnings are lost of reduced due to the worker's disability.

You may be considered "disabled" if you have a physical or mental impairment which (1) prevents you from working and (2) is expected to last for at least 12 months or to result in death. A person is considered "blind" with central visual acuity of 20/200 or less in the better eye with the use of corrective lenses or visual field reduction of 20 degrees or less.

Before a disabled worker and his or her family can get benefits, the worker must have credit for a certain amount of work under social security. The exact amount of work credit needed depends on the worker's age.

Monthly disability benefits can be paid to a disabled worker's

(1) Unmarried children under 18 (or under 19 if full-time high school or elementary school students);

(2) Unmarried children 18 or older who were severely disabled before 22 and continue to be disabled;

(3) Wife or husband 62 or older;

(4) Wife under 62 if she's caring for worker's child who is under 16 or disabled and getting a benefit based on the disabled worker's earnings.

NOTE: Children 18 or older who were disabled before 22 also can receive monthly benefits when either parent becomes entitled to retirement payments or dies after having worked long enough under social security. A disabled widow or widower or disabled surviving divorced wife 50 or older may be eligible for monthly survivors payments when a worker dies.

The people in any social security office will be glad to answer any questions you may have. They also have a wide variety of publications. Single copies are free. Local social security offices are listed in the telephone directory under "Social Security Administration."

SUPPLEMENTARY SECURITY INCOME

Supplementary security income (SSI) makes monthly payments to aged, disabled, and blind people who have limited income and resources (assets). To receive SSI payments on the basis of disability or blindness, you must meet the social security definition of "disabled" or "blind" (see pg 13). but, you do not need any social security work credits to get SSI payments. People may be eligible for SSI even if they have never worked. And, people who get SSI checks can get social security checks, too, if they are eligible for both.

Disabled and blind children, as well as adults, may qualify for SSI payments. It makes no difference how young a person is.

To be eligible for SSI, you must have limited income and resources, be a resident of the U.S. or Northern Mariana Island, and be either a U.S. citizen or a lawfully admitted immigrant.

Not all of you income and resources are counted in determining if you are eligible for SSI. Generally, the first $20 a month of unearned income and the first $65 a month in earnings are not counted. Income above these levels usually reduces the amount of the basic SSI payment. A home and the land adjacent to it are not counted. Personal effects or household goods, a car, and life insurance policies may not count, depending on their value. Burial funds and burial plots also may not count. The Federal Government does not put liens on recipients' homes.

States may add to the Federal SSI payments. The States also provide medicaid, food stamps, and various social and rehabilitation services.

For more information about SSi, contact your local social security office.

MEDICAL ASSISTANCE

The primary sources of Federal medical assistance for disabled persons are Medicare and Medicaid; Crippled Children's Services; and the Early Periodic Screening, Diagnosis and Treatment Program.

MEDICARE

The health insurance program is designed to serve everyone over 65 years old of age and disabled persons under 65 years old of age who:

(1) have been entitled to receive Social Security disability benefits for a total of 24 months; or

(2) who need dialysis treatments or kidney transplant because of permanent kidney failure.

The program is not based on income, but is available regardless of financial need.

The Medicare program has two parts:

Part A: Hospital insurance at no premium that helps pay for care while in the hospital and for related health care services after leaving the hospital. Certain deductible and coinsurance amounts apply.

Part B: Voluntary medical insurance at a monthly premium that helps pay doctor bills and other approved medical services.

MEDICAID

Medicaid (Medical Assistance Program) is a joint Federal/state program to provide physical and related health care services to persons with low incomes. Disabled persons may be eligible for Medicaid on the basis of their income.

Because eligibility is determined by your state program of public assistance (welfare) on the basis of broad Federal guidelines, there are requirements and types of services covered. Generally, persons may be eligible for Medicaid if they are receiving welfare or Security Income or are blind or disabled. Medicaid services are available in all states.

Individuals with higher incomes may be eligible for Medicaid Supplemental Medical Care Assistance, or their children may be eligible if medical expenses exceed a given percentage of their annual income.

Each state establishes its own elgibility requirements for Medicaid.

Further information on Medicaid and assistance in applying is available for your local or state welfare or public assistance office.

CRIPPLED CHILDREN'S SERVICES

Crippled Children's Services (CCS) is a joint Federal/state program to provide medical and related services to handicapped children from birth to age 21.

All states must provide medical diagnosis and evaluation free for all children. (No state residence period is required before such services are provided). The range and cost of additional treatment or hospital care services vary from state to state. All programs accept third party payments such as Medicaid, Blue Cross and Blue Shield and other medical insurance.

For further information on what is available to your handicapped child, contact your local, county or state health department.

EARLY PERIODIC SCREENING, DIAGNOSIS AND TREATMENT PROGRAM (EPSDT)

The EPSDT program screens children from poor families to identify whether health care or related services may be necessary, and provides preventive and remedial care.

Children receiving state Aid to Families with Dependent Children benefits, and children whose parents or guardians are receiving Medicaid, and/or local or state public assistance benefits are eligible for EPSDT.

EPSDT programs vary from state and are administered by either state public assistance (welfare) or health departments.

For more information on EPSDT contact your physician, local or state health department or public assistance office.

OFFICE OF CIVIL RIGHTS

A disabled person has rights guaranteed by law to education, employment, health care, senior citizens activities, welfare, and any other public or private services in programs or activities that receive Federal assistance.

It is the responsibility of the Office for Civil rights in the Department of Education and the Office for Civil Rights in the Department of Health and Human Services to enforce Federal laws prohibiting discrimination against persons on the basis of race, color, national origin, sex, age, or handicap in federally assisted programs or activities, and to investigate discrimination complaints brought by individuals under these statutes. If you feel that your rights have been violated-because of you disability or your child's disability-by a hospital, school, or any other institution in any of their Federally assisted programs or activities, write, giving details, to the Office for Civil Rights of the Department of Education (ED) (about schools and post-secondary institutions), and of the Department of Health and Human Services (HHS) (about hospitals, social services) in your region.

Region I (Conn., Maine, Mass., N.H., R.I., VT.)
Office for Civil Rights, ED
McCormack P.O. & Courthouse, Rm 222
Boston, MA 02109
(617) 223-9662

Office for Civil Rights, HHS
John F. Kennedy Federal Bldg., Rm 2403
Boston, MA 02203
(617) 565-1304

Region II (N,J., N.Y., Puerto Rico, Virgin Islands.)
26 Federal Plaza, 33rd Floor
New York, NY 10278

ED: (212) 264-4633
HHS: (212) 264-3313

Region III (Del., D.C., Md., Pa., Va., W. Va)
3535 Market Street, Rm 6300
Philadelphia, PA 19101
ED: (215) 596-6772
HHS: (215) 596-1262

Region IV (Ala., Fla., Ga., Ky., Miss., N.C., S.C., Tenn.)
101 Marietta Street, Atlanta, GA 30323
ED: (404) 331-2954-27th Floor
HHS: (404) 331-2779-15th Floor

Region V (ILL., Ind., Mich., Minn., Ohio, Wis.)
300 South Wacker Drive
Chicago, IL 60606
ED: (312) 353-2520-8th Floor
HHS: (312) 886-2356-33rd Floor

Region VI (Ark., La., N.M., Okla., Texas)
1200 Main Tower Building,
Dallas, TX 75202
ED: (214) 767-3985-Suite 2200
HHS: (214) 767-4056-Suite 1360

Region VII (Iowa, Kan., Mo., Neb.)
Office for Civil Rights, ED
10220 N. Executive Hills Blvd.
Kansas City, MO 64153
(816) 374-2474-8th Floor

Office for Civil Rights, HHS
601 E. 12th Street, Rm. 248

Kansas City, MO 64106

(816) 374-6367

Region VIII (Colo., Mont., N.D., S.D., Utah, Wyo.)

1961 Stout Street

Denver, Co 80294

ED: (303) 844-5595-3rd Floor

HHs: (303) 844-2024-Suite 804

Region IX (Ariz., Calif., Hawaii, Nev., Guam Turst Terr. Pac. Islands, Amer. Samoa)

Office for Civil Rights, ED

221 Main Street

San Francisco, CA 94105

ED: (415) 227-8020- 10th Floor

Office for Civil Rights, HHs

50 United Nations Plaza, Rm 322

San Francisco, CA 94103

(415) 536-8586

Region X (Alaska, Idaho, Ore., Wash.)

2901 Third Avenue

Seattle, WA 98121

ED: (206) 442-1636-M/S 106

HHS: (206) 442-0473-M/S 510

OFFICE OF FEDERAL CONTRACT COMPLIANCE

Every employer doing business with the Federal Government under contract for more than $2,500 must take "affirmative action" to hire handicapped people. If you believe that you have been denied a job by such a contractor because of your diability, a complaint can be filed with the :

Office of Federal contract Compliance
Department of Labor
Washington, D.C. 20210

HOUSING LOANS

If you have a disability and need to adapt your home to your needs, you may be eligible for a Title i Home Improvement Loan insured by the U.S. Department of Housing and Urban Development (HUD). The HUD-insured loan can be used to remove architectural barriers, hazards, or inconvenient features in the home. Improvements can be handled on a do-it-yourself basis or through a contractor. The loans are applied for through bands or other lending institutions. HUD insures the lender against possible loss. For further information contact the nearest office of HUD.

Low income individuals may be eligible for loans from the Farmers Home Administration to purchase or repair a home which is on a farm or in a very rural area. For more information, write to:

Farmers Home Administration
Department of Agriculture
Washington, D.C. 20250

RENT ASSISTANCE

Low income families (including those with disabilities) may be eligible for housing assistance payments from HUD. Payments by HUD are made directly to the owners of rental units to make up the difference between the HUD-approved rental amount and the amount the tenant is required to pay. Tenants pay an average of 30% of their adjusted income (gross income less certain deductions and exceptions). Rental assistance payments under this arrangement are not considered additional income to the tenant who is also eligible for Supplemental Security Income payments from the Social Security Administration.

For further information on rent assistance or other housing programs benefiting disabled persons, write to:

Special Advisor on the Handicapped
U.S. Department of Housing & Urban Development
Room 10184
Washington, D.C. 20410

Chapter 8
HOW THE SMALL BUSINESS ADMINISTRATION CAN HELP YOU!

The U. S. Small Business Administration (SBA) helps the nation's small businesses through several programs and efforts. SBA assists new or growing businesses in meeting their financial needs; counsels small firms with problems; offers special assistance to minority and woman-owned businesses; helps small businesses secure government contracts; and acts as a special advocate for small businesses which deal with other federal agencies, states and the private sector. The SBA solidifies our nation's free-enterprise system, encourages competition and improves the national economy.

The proceeds from business loans can be used for working capital, purchase of inventory, equipment and supplies, or for building construction and expansion.

SBA offers two basic types of business loans

Bank Guaranteed Loans

1. SBA "bank guaranteed loans" made by private lenders are tied to funds appropriated by Congress. However, these SBA loans are of a larger amount than funds appropriated for direct loans. Most SBA loans are of the guaranteed type.

SBA can guarantee up to 90 percent of a loan made by a bank or other private lender.

2. Loans offered directly by the SBA are also taken from funds appropriated by Congress specifically for this purpose. Those direct loan monies are limited, however, and demand always exceeds supply. The SBA has recently reserved a growing share of its direct loans for small firms which have difficulty raising funds in the private sector.

Generally, SBA loans are available only to applicants unable to receive private financing or an SBA-guaranteed or participation loan. They usually carry interest rates lower than private market rates.

Economic Opportunity Loans

"Economic opportunity" loans are offered to socially and economically disadvantaged persons. Loans are also available to small firms which have been hindered by government regulation and are involved in manufacturing, selling, installing, servicing or developing specific energy projects. In addition, local development companies offer programs helping small businesses in urban or rural communities.

"Small Business Investment Companies" (SBICs) are licensed, regulated and controlled financially by the SBA. They provide regular loans and equity capital to growing firms.

A list of agency offices and special loan programs can be obtained from any SBA office.

Despite its diverse programs, SBA cannot help all the small businesses or persons interested in starting a small firm because agency funds and personnel are limited. Consequently, SBA--Small Business Advocate--has collaborated with the private sector to make funds available to millions of small-business entrepreneurs. The nation's banks have instituted their own loan programs to satisfy the needs and wants of a small business. SBA has cooperated with several certified banks to eliminate red tape and paperwork in agency-guaranteed loans. Other companies also have been used as SBA "non-bank lenders."

Such an approach will allow the private lender to increasingly become the "retailer" and the SBA the "wholesaler."

The agency may not legally offer or guarantee a loan if a business can obtain funds from a bank or other private source. Therefore, the borrower must attempt to receive private financing from at least one bank or lending institution before applying to SBA.

Loans cannot be made to newspapers or businesses involved in gambling and other questionable activities. To receive a loan, a company must satisfy specific standards of size and annual receipts. It must also remain independently owned, operated and not dominant in its field.

There will be no discrimination in employment or services to the public (including loan applicants) based on race, color, religion, national origin, sex or marital status.

The size requirements for business loan eligibility are as follows:

Manufacturing -- Number of employees may be as high as 1,500, depending on the industry.

Wholesaling -- Annual sales may range between $9.5 and $22 million, depending on the industry.

Services -- Annual receipts may fluctuate between $2 million and $8 million, depending on the industry.

Retailing - Annual sales and receipts may differ from $2 million to $7.5 million, depending on the industry.

Special and general trade construction -- Average annual receipts for the last three fiscal years may range from $1 to $2 million, depending on the industry.

Agriculture - Annual receipts must not exceed $1,000,000.

NOTE: The total number of employees per firm may become the single measurement of size for certain small businesses.

A loan applicant must:
- Demonstrate ability to operate a business successfully.

- Possess enough capital in an existing firm so the business can operate on a financially sound level.
- Indicate some assuring of payment on a proposed loan.
- Demonstrate an ability to repay the loan and other debts by providing a satisfactory earnings record.
- Possess sufficient personal resources to be able to with stand possible losses.
- Realize that loans contributed directly by SBA have a maximum allowance of $150,000.
- Understand that the bank-guaranteed loan program allows the agency to guarantee up to 90 % of a loan or a maximum of $500,000, whichever is less.

NOTE: SBA may offer loans up to $150,000 on an "immediate participation" basis with a bank when neither private financing nor a loan guarantee is available. The bank dispenses a portion of the loan at market interest rates, while the balance of the loan is dispensed by SBA at lower interest rates.

Economic opportunity loans are limited to $100,000 under each kind of lending program.

Handicapped assistance loans offer a limit of $350,000 under the guaranteed program and $100,000 when made directly by the SBA.

A limit of $500,000 for a guaranteed loan and $350,000 for a direct or immediate participation loan is made for energy loans.

Small companies are eligible for loans if they were displaced by the government. If they were adversely affected by occupational safety and health legislation, strategic arms limitation actions, air and water pollution control legislation, military base closings or emergency energy shortage situations, small companies may receive loans.

The Local Development Company carries a maximum loan of $500,000.

While business loans usually have a maximum maturity of 10 years, working capital loans are limited to seven years. A 20-year maximum is given for loans which include construction or acquisition of real estate.

Maximum allowable interest rates, which the SBA sets and banks charge on guaranteed loans, are tied to the money in the federal reserve and change periodically.

Economic opportunity and handicapped assistance loans carry a 15-year maturity, while displaced business loans and economic injury loans carry a 30-year maturity.

At least one of the following is permissible security for a loan:
- A land mortgage, building and/or equipment.
- Assignment of warehouse receipts for saleable products.
- A mortgage of chattels.
- Guarantees or personal endorsements and occasionally assignment of current receivables.

Those already in business should:
1. Draw a current financial statement or balance sheet listing all assets and liabilities of the business.
2. Keep a profit and loss statement for the current period.
3. List an up-to-date personal financial statement of the owner and each partner or stockholder holding at least 20 % of the corporate stock in the business.
4. Offer collateral as security for the loan.
5. State the precise purpose and amount of the loan requested.
6. Request a direct loan from the bank. If you are turned down, ask the bank to make the loan under SBA's Loan Guarantee plan or Immediate Participation plan.
7. Contact one of 110 SBA field offices if a guaranteed or participation loan is not available.

Those desiring to start a business should:
1. Describe the kind of business you intend to open.
2. Explain your business experience and management skills.
3. Draw out an estimate of the amount you need to invest in the business and how much you will have to borrow
4. Make a current financial statement listing all personal

assets and liabilities.

5. Detail an operational budget of the first business year.

6. Offer collateral as security for the loan.

7. Follow steps five and six above.

8. Is there specific aid for the small, disadvantaged businessman?

Small Business Investment Companies (SBICs) originated through the Small Business Investment Act in 1958 to provide equity capital and long-term loan funds for small businesses. The SBIC is privately owned and licensed, regulated and partially financed by the U.S. Small Business Administration to make equity investments and long-term loans available to small firms. The SBIC may also offer management assistance, financing, expansion and modernization.

Section 301(d) licensees are awarded equity funds, long-term loans and management assistance by SBIC's. They are governed by similar regulations and offer a program which is especially responsive to the disadvantaged business community.

SBA can usually provide a 301(d) licensee $2 of continuous government funds for every dollar of private capital.

Under certain conditions, section 301(d) licensees are eligible for SBA purchases of 3% preferred stock and a subsidized interest rate on their debentures for the first five years, subject to repayment of that subsidy before any distribution is made to stockholders other than SBA. To attain additional tax benefits, section 301(d) licensees may be organized on a non-profit basis.

SBA may guarantee up to 90% of bank loans, lease guarantees and management assistance made by a leading institution to a SBIC portfolio concern.

Chapter 9
SBA PROGRAMS

LOANS FOR HIGH UNEMPLOYMENT AREAS.

Direct and guaranteed loans from $1,000 to $315,000 are available for those who open businesses in high unemployment areas or possess low incomes. By starting a business in a low employment or poor area, you can hire workers cheaply. To receive a loan application, contact:

Director of the Office of Financing
Small Business Administration
1441 L St., NW,
Washington, DC 20416
(202)653-6570

MANAGEMENT HELP FOR DISADVANTAGED BUSINESSES

The SBA provides financial and management assistance to racial minorities and those with low incomes who are opening a business in a low-income area. To receive information regarding this government aid, contact:

Assistant Administrator for Management Assistance
Small Business Administration
1441 L Street, NW, Room 317
Washington, DC 20416
(202)653-6874

PHYSICAL DISASTER LOANS

To obtain information about the governmental assistance you can receive in the event of such natural disasters as fires, hurricanes, earthquakes, tidal waves, etc., contact:

Director, Office of Disaster Loans
Small Business Administration
1441 L St., NW
Washington, DC 20416
(202) 653-6878

SMALL BUSINESS LOANS FOR SPECIAL BUSINESSES

Up to $500,000 in guaranteed and direct loans can be obtained for building, expanding or converting your business buildings and purchasing equipment and materials. Contact:

Director, Office of Financing
Small Business Administration
1441 L St., NW
Washington, DC 20416
(202)653-6570

BOND GUARANTEES

Contractors or those in the construction business can receive information about surety bonds of up to $1 million by contacting:

Chief of the Surety Bond Guarantee Division
Small Business Administration
4040 N. Fairfax Dr.
Arlington, VA 22203
(703)235-2907

SMALL BUSINESS ENERGY LOANS

Information about loans to finance plant construction, expansion, conversion or any energy-related equipment or service for a business can be obtained by contacting:

Business Loans Dept.
Small Business Administration
1441 L St., NW
Washington, DC 20416
(202)653-6570

SMALL BUSINESS POLLUTION CONTROL GUARANTEES

Businesses requiring pollution-control elements can receive information about guaranteed loans of up to $5,000,000 by contacting:

Chief, Pollution Control Financing Division
Office of Special Guarantees
Small Business Administration
4040 N. Fairfax Dr., Suite 500
Arlington, VA 22203
(703) 235-2902

OTHER SBA SERVICES

The SBA offers additional services to individuals currently operating or intending to open their own small business. To find out what statistics and information are available from the SBA, contact:

Office of Economic Research
1100 Vermont Ave., NW, Room 1100
Washington, DC

Small business counseling may be available through a business school near you. To find out, write:

SBA's Office of Management Counseling Services
1441 L St., NW, Room 317
Washington, DC

In addition, you can call or write a local SBA field office to receive information on purchasing SBA films.

SMALL BUSINESS ADMINISTRATION DISTRICT OFFICES

For many services, it is often quicker and more convenient to contact your local SBA district office. The Washington DC address is:

Small Business Administration
1441 L St., NW
Washington, DC 20416

Region 1: Maine, Vermont, New Hampshire, Massachusetts, Connecticut, Rhode Island

Small Business Administration
60 Batterymarch St., Boston, MA 02110; (617)223-3204

Small Business Administration
150 Causeway St., Boston, MA 02114; (617)223-3224

Small Business Administration
1550 Main St., Springfield, MA 01103; (413)785-0268

Small Business Administration
40 Western Ave., Room 512, Augusta, ME 04330;
(207)622-8378

Small Business Administration
55 Pleasant St., Room 211, Concord, NH 03301;
(603)224-4041

Small Business Administration
One Hartford Square West, Hartford, CT 06106;
(203)722-3600

Small Business Administration
87 State St., Room 204, Montpelier, VT 05602;
(802)229-0538

Small Business Administration
380 Westminster Hall, Providence, RI 02903;
(401)351-7500

Region 2: New York, New Jersey, Puerto Rico, Virgin Islands

Small Business Administration
26 Federal Plaza, Room 29-118, New York, NY 10278;
(212)264-7772

Small Business Administration
26 Federal Plaza, Room 3100, New York, NY 10278;
(212)264-4355

Small Business Administration
35 Pinelawn Rd., Room 102E, Melville, NY 11747;
(516)454-0750

Small Business Administration
Carlos Chardon Ave., Room 691, Hato Rey, PR 00919;
(809)753-4002

Small Business Administration
Veterans Dr., Room 283, St. Thomas, VI 00801;
(809)774-8530

Small Business Administration
60 Park Place, Newark, NJ 07102; (201)645-2434

Small Business Administration
100 S. Clinton St., Room 1071, Syracuse, NY 13260;
(315)423-5383

Small Business Administration
111 W. Huron St., Room 1311, Buffalo, NY 14202;
(716)846-4301

Small Business Administration
333 E. Water St., Elmira, NY 14901; (607)733-4686

Region 3: Pennsylvania, Delaware, West Virginia, Maryland, Virginia
Small Business Administration
231 St. Asaphs Rd., Suite 400, Philadelphia, PA 19004;
(212)264-7772

Small Business Administration
100 Chestnut St., Suite 309, Harrisburg, PA 17101;
(717)782-3840

Small Business Administration
20 N. Pennsylvania Ave., Wilkes-Barre, PA 18701;
(717)826-6497

Small Business Administration
844 King St., Room 5207, Wilmington, DE 19801;
(302)573-6294

Small Business Administration
109 N. 3rd St., Room 302, Clarksburg, WV 26301;
(304)623-5631

Small Business Administration
628 Charleston National Plaza, Charleston, WV 25301;
(305)347-5220

Small Business Administration
960 Penn Ave., Pittsburgh, PA 15222; (412)644-2780;
(412)644-2780

Small Business Administration
400 N. 8th St., Room 3015, Richmond, VA 23240;
(804)771-2617

Small Business Administration
8600 LaSalle Rd., Room 630, Towson, MD 21204;
(301)962-4392

Small Business Administration
1111 18th St., NW, Washington, DC 20036; (202)634-4950

Region 4: North Carolina, South Carolina, Georgia, Tennessee, Kentucky, Florida, Alabama, Mississippi

Small Business Administration
1375 Peachtree St., NE, Atlanta, GA 30367; (404)881-4999

Small Business Administration
1720 Peachtree St., NW, Atlanta, GA 30309;
(404)881-4749

Small Business Administration
908 S. 20th St., Room 202, Birmingham, AL 35205;
(205)254-1344

Small Business Administration
230 S. Tryon St., Room 700, Charlotte, NC 28202;
(704)371-6563

Small Business Administration
1835 Assembly, Columbia, SC 29202; (803)765-5376

Small Business Administration
100 W. Capitol St., Suite 322, Jackson, MS 39269;
(601)960-4378

Small Business Administration
111 Fred Haise Blvd., Biloxi, MS 39530; (601)435-3676

Small Business Administration
600 Federal Place, Room 188, Louisville, KY 40201;
(502)582-5971

Small Business Administration
2222 Ponce De Leon Blvd., Miami, FL 33134;
(305)350-5521

Small Business Administration
404 James Robertson Prkwy., Nashville, TN 37219;
(615)251-5881

Region 5: Ohio, Indiana, Illinois, Michigan, Minnesota, Wisconsin
Small Business Administration
219 S. Dearborn St., Room 838, Chicago, IL 60604;
(312)353-0359

Small Business Administration
1240 E. 9th St., Room 317, Cleveland, OH 43215;
(216)552-4180

Small Business Administration
85 Marconi Blvd., Columbus, OH 43215; (614)469-6860

Small Business Administration
550 Main St., Room 5028, Cincinnati, OH 45202;
(513)684-2814

Small Business Administration
477 Michigan Ave., Room 515, Detroit, MI 48226;
(313)226-6075

Small Business Administration
220 W. Washington St., Room 310, Marquette, MI 49885;
(906) 225-1108

Small Business Administration
575 N. Pennsylvania St., Indianapolis, IN 46204;
(317) 269-7272

Small Business Administration
501 E. Monroe St., Room 160, South Bend, IN 46601;
(219)232-8361

Small Business Administration
212 E. Washington Ave., Room 213, Madison, WI 53703;
(608)232-8361

Small Business Administration
310 W. Wisconsin Ave., Milwaukee, WI 53203;
(414)291-3941

Small Business Administration
100 N. 6th St., Suite 610, Minneapolis, MN 55403;
(612)349-3550

Small Business Administration
4 N. Old Capitol Plaza, Springfield, IL 62701;
(217)492-4416

Region 6: Arkansas, Louisiana, Texas, New Mexico, Oklahoma

Small Business Administration
8625 King George Dr., Bldg. C, Dallas, TX 75235;
(214)767-7643

Small Business Administration
1100 Commerce St., Room 3036, Dallas, TX 74242;
(214)767-0605

Small Business Administration
4100 Rio Bravo, El Paso, TX 79902; (915) 543-7586

Small Business Administration
221 W. Lancaster Ave., Fort Worth, TX 76102;
(817)334-5463

Small Business Administration
5000 Marble Ave., NE, Albuquerque, NM 87100;
(505)766-3430

Small Business Administration
222 E. VanBuren St., Room 500, Harlingen, TX 78550;
(512)423-8934

Small Business Administration
400 Mann St., Suite 403, Corpus Christi, TX 78550;
(512)888-3331

Small Business Administration
2525 Murworth, Houston, TX 77054; (713)660-4401

Small Business Administration
320 W. Capitol, Room 601, Little Rock, AR 72201;
(501)378-5871

Small Business Administration
1611 10th St., Suite 200, Lubbock, TX 79401;
(806)762-7466

Small Business Administration
1661 Canal St., Suite 2000, New Orleans, LA 70112;
(504)589-6685

Small Business Administration
200 NW 5th St., Oklahoma City, OK 73102; (405)231-4301

Small Business Administration
727 E. Durango St., San Antonio, TX 78206;
(512)229-6250

Small Business Administration
300 E. 8th St., Room 780, Austin, TX 78501;
(512)482-5288

Region 7: Missouri, Iowa, Kansas, Nebraska

Small Business Administration
911 Walnut St., Kansas City, MO 64106; (816)374-5288

Small Business Administration
309 N. Jefferson, Room 150, Springfield, MO 65803;
(417)864-7670

Small Business Administration
373 Collins Rd., NE, Cedar Rapids, IA 52402;
(319)399-2571

Small Business Administration
210 Walnut St., Des Moines, IA 50309; (515)284-4422

Small Business Administration
300 S. 19th St., Omaha, NB 68102; (402)221-4691

Small Business Administration
815 Olive St., Room 242, St. Louis, MO 63101;
(314)425-6600

Small Business Administration
110 E. Waterman St., Witchita, KS 67202; (316)269-6571

Region 8: Colorado, North Dakota, South Dakota, Utah, Montana, Wyoming

Small Business Administration
1405 Curtis St., Denver, CO 80202; (303)844-5441

Small Business Administration
721 19th St., Room 407, Denver, CO 80202;
(303)844-2607

Small Business Administration
100 E. B St., Room 401, Casper, WY 82602;
(307)261-5761

Small Business Administration
657 2nd Ave., Room 218, Fargo, ND 58108; (701)237-5771

Small Business Administration
301 S. Park, Room 528, Helena, MT 59626; (406)449-5381

Small Business Administration
125 S. State St., Salt Lake City, UT 84138; (314)524-5800

Small Business Administration
101 S. Main Ave., Sioux Falls, SD 57102; (605)336-2980

Region 9: California, Hawaii, Nevada

Small Business Administration
450 Golden Gate Ave., Room 15307, San Francisco, CA
94102; (415)556-7487

Small Business Administration
221 Main St., San Francisco, CA 94102; (415)556-0642

Small Business Administration
2202 Monterey St., Room 108, Fresno, CA 93721;
(209)487-5189

Small Business Administration
660 J St., Room 215, Sacramento, CA 95814;
(916)440-4461

Small Business Administration
301 E. Steward St., Las Vegas, NV 89125; (702)385-6611

Small Business Administration
300 Ala Moana, Room 2213, Honolulu, HI 96850;
(671)472-7277

Small Business Administration
350 S. Figueroa St., Los Angeles, CA 90071;
(213)688-2956

Small Business Administration
2700 N. Main St., Room 400, Santa Ana, CA 92701;
(714)836-2494

Small Business Administration
3030 N. Central Ave., Suite 1201, Phoenix, AZ 85012;
(602)241-2200

Small Business Administration
880 Front St., Suite 4-S-29, San Diego, CA 92188;
(619)293-5440

Region 10: Alaska, Idaho, Oregon, Washington

Small Business Administration
2615 4th Ave., Room 440, Seattle WA 98121;
(206)442-5676

Small Business Administration
915 Second Ave., Room 1792, Seattle, WA 98174;
(206)442-5534

Small Business Administration
701 C St., Room 1068, Anchorage, AK 99501:
(907)271-4022

Small Business Administration
101 12th Ave., Fairbanks, AK 99701; (907)452-0211

Small Business Administration
1005 Main St., Boise, ID 83701; (208)334-1696

Small Business Administration
1220 SW Third Ave., Room 676, Portland, OR 97204;
(503)221-5221

Small Business Administration
920 Riverside Ave., Room 651, Spokane, WA 99210;
(509)456-5310

Department of Agriculture
Office of Grants and Program Systems
Department of Agriculture, Room 323
Aerospace Center
901 D Street, SW
Washington, DC 20250
202-401-4002

Department of Defense
Small Business and Economic Utilization
Office of Secretary of Defense, Room 2A340
Pentagon
Washington, DC 20301
800-225-DTIC

Department of Education
Dr. Ed Esty
The Brown Building
1900 M Street, NW, Room 722
Washington, DC 20208
202-708-5366

Department of Energy
SBIR Program
U.S. Department of Energy
ER-16
Washington, DC 20585
301-353-5867

Department of Health and Human Services
Mr. Richard Clinkscales, Director
Office of Small and Disadvantaged Business Utilization
Department of Health and Human Services
200 Independence Avenue, SW, Room 513D
Washington, DC 20201
202-245-7300

Department of Transportation
SBIR Program
Transportation System Center
Department of Transportation
Kendall Square
Cambridge, MA 01242
617-494-2051

Environmental Protection Agency
EPA Small Business Ombudsman
401 M Street, SW, A149-C
Washington, DC 20460
800-368-5888

National Aeronautics and Space Administration
SBIR Program
National Aeronautics and Space Administration
1225 Jefferson Davis Hwy., Room 1304
Crystal City, VA 22202
703-271-5650

National Science Foundation
Mr. Ritchie Coryell
Mr. Roland Tibbetts
SBIR Program Managers
National Science Foundation
1800 G Street, NW
Washington, DC 20550
202-653-5002

Nuclear Regulatory Commission
Mr. Francis Gillespie, Director

Administration and Resource Staff
Office of Nuclear Regulatory Research
Nuclear Regulatory Commission
Washington, DC 20555
301-427-4301

Department of Agriculture

Office of Grants and Program Systems
Department of Agriculture, Room 323
Aerospace Center
901 D Street, SW
Washington, DC 20250
202-401-4002

Department of Defense

Small Business and Economic Utilization
Office of Secretary of Defense, Room 2A340
Pentagon
Washington, DC 20301
800-225-DTIC

Department of Education

Dr. Ed Esty
The Brown Building
1900 M Street, NW, Room 722
Washington, DC 20208
202-708-5366

Department of Energy

SBIR Program
U.S. Department of Energy
ER-16
Washington, DC 20585
301-353-5867

Department of Health and Human Services

Mr. Richard Clinkscales, Director
Office of Small and Disadvantaged Business Utilization
Department of Health and Human Services
200 Independence Avenue, SW, Room 513D

Washington, DC 20201
202-245-7300

Department of Transportation
SBIR Program
Transportation System Center
Department of Transportation
Kendall Square
Cambridge, MA 01242
617-494-2051

Environmental Protection Agency
EPA Small Business Ombudsman
401 M Street, SW, A149-C
Washington, DC 20460
800-368-5888

National Aeronautics and Space Administration
SBIR Program
National Aeronautics and Space Administration
1225 Jefferson Davis Hwy., Room 1304
Crystal City, VA 22202
703-271-5650

National Science Foundation
Mr. Ritchie Coryell
Mr. Roland Tibbetts
SBIR Program Managers
National Science Foundation
1800 G Street, NW
Washington, DC 20550
202-653-5002

Nuclear Regulatory Commission
Mr. Francis Gillespie, Director
Administration and Resource Staff
Office of Nuclear Regulatory Research
Nuclear Regulatory Commission
Washington, DC 20555
301-427-4301

Chapter 10
SELL IDEAS
TO THE GOVERNMENT

Technological innovation, small science and technology based firms are encouraged by the SBIR to participate in government-funded research. The SBIR was designed to stimulate technological innovation by providing challenging opportunities to meet the research and development needs of the Federal government. There are eleven federal agencies in all that utilize this program. They include; The Departments of Defense, Health and Human Services, Energy, Agriculture, Commerce, Transportation, and Education; the National Aeronautics and Space Administration; the Nuclear Regulatory Commission; the National Science Foundation; and the Environmental Protection Agency.

To qualify for SBIR funding, the business must have 500 or fewer employees, must not be a non-profit or foreign-owned organization, and the research must be conducted in the United States.

There are generally three phases to the program. Phase 1 has as its purpose to determine if the research idea is technically feasible, if the firm can do the high quality research necessary, and whether sufficient progress was made to continue to Phase II. Phase II has as its purpose, to begin research of the process of the idea and develop it, and usually the cost is limited to a maximum of $500,000 for up to two years. And finally, Phase III requires the pursuit of potential commercial applications, usually funded by venture capitalists. Because it is a very competitive program (approximately one proposal out of ten is accepted in Phase I and five out of ten in Phase II), the U.S. Small Business Administration publishes the Pre-Solicitation Announcement (PSA) in December, March, June, and September of each year. This publication provides information about SBIR details of solicitations that are about to be released, since solicitations by the government are only released once a year. Also available is the Commercialization Matching System that contains information about all businesses awarded with SBIR funding and their financing sources that have supported Phase III of the program. Both of these sources help the business concern to track the activities of the Federal agencies and define their potential needs. For more information about the SBIR program or receiving the PSA, contact the Office of Innovation, Research and Technology, Small Business Association, 1441 L Street, NW, Washington, DC 202-205-6450.If you would like more information on the SBIR program, representatives from the following agencies can assist you.

Department of Agriculture
Office of Grants and Program Systems
Department of Agriculture, Room 323
Aerospace Center
901 D Street, SW
Washington, DC 20250
202-401-4002

Department of Defense
Small Business and Economic Utilization
Office of Secretary of Defense, Room 2A340
Pentagon
Washington, DC 20301
800-225-DTIC

Department of Education
Dr. Ed Esty
The Brown Building
1900 M Street, NW, Room 722
Washington, DC 20208
202-708-5366

Department of Energy
SBIR Program
U.S. Department of Energy
ER-16
Washington, DC 20585
301-353-5867

Department of Health and Human Services
Mr. Richard Clinkscales, Director
Office of Small and Disadvantaged Business Utilization
Department of Health and Human Services
200 Independence Avenue, SW, Room 513D

Washington, DC 20201
202-245-7300

Department of Transportation
SBIR Program
Transportation System Center
Department of Transportation
Kendall Square
Cambridge, MA 01242
617-494-2051

Environmental Protection Agency
EPA Small Business Ombudsman
401 M Street, SW, A149-C
Washington, DC 20460
800-368-5888

National Aeronautics and Space Administration
SBIR Program
National Aeronautics and Space Administration
1225 Jefferson Davis Hwy., Room 1304
Crystal City, VA 22202
703-271-5650

National Science Foundation
Mr. Ritchie Coryell
Mr. Roland Tibbetts
SBIR Program Managers
National Science Foundation
1800 G Street, NW
Washington, DC 20550
202-653-5002

Nuclear Regulatory Commission
Mr. Francis Gillespie, Director
Administration and Resource Staff
Office of Nuclear Regulatory Research
Nuclear Regulatory Commission
Washington, DC 20555
301-427-4301

Chapter 11
FREE HELP FOR INVENTORS

I f anyone has ever tried to turn an idea into an actual product, they know how many thousands of dollars it can cost to get the help of a private invention company and a patent attorney. But, no more. Now, depending on the service, you can get the help free or at a fraction of the cost from university-sponsored programs, non-profit groups, state affiliated programs, and even profit-making companies.

A good place for an inventor to start is with the various inventor organizations that can help with licensing, financing and marketing. They are also a good place to meet people in the field such as other inventors, patent attorneys and manufacturers. These people are often experts on the process of invention-to-product and be of great assistance.

To get more information about various invention groups or programs, call the Small Business Development Center Office in Washington, DC at 202-205-6766. Or, contact any of the offices below for further assistance.

Alabama
Office for the Advancement of Developing Industries
University of Alabama - Birmingham
1075 13th South
Birmingham, AL 35205
205-934-2190
This office provides assistance in the commercialization and patent process, as well as provides critical reviews of the invention. Assessments are made on the idea's potential marketability. There is a service charge for assistance.

Alaska

Small Business Development Center
University of Alaska
430 W. 7th Avenue, Suite 110
Anchorage, AK 99501
907-274-7232

This office provides free counseling to inventors regarding commercialization and patent processors, and connects inventors with others, such as manufacturers, who can be of help.

Arizona

Arizona State Research Institute
Technology Transfer & Industry Liaison Office
Arizona State University
Temple, AZ 85287
602-965-4795

This office also serves as a counselor to inventors regarding commercialization and patent processes. The University is a depository for the U.S. Patent and Trademark Office and so provides PTO forms and publications.

Arkansas

Arkansas Inventors Congress
P.O. Box 411
Dardanell, AR 72334
Contact: Garland Bull
501-229-4515

This group provides counseling on all aspects of the invention process, as well as provides assessments on the marketability of the invention. PTO forms and publications are available, however, this group requires dues.

California

Inventors of California
215 Rheem Boulevard
Moraga, CA 94556
415-376-7541

The Inventors of California group holds information seminars with speakers, connects inventors to manufacturers, and for a fee, will provide assessments of inventions. Dues are mandatory.

Colorado
Affiliated Inventors Foundation, Inc.
2132 E. Bijou Street
Colorado Spring, CO 80909
719-635-1234

This office provides preliminary appraisals and evaluations for a fee, of inventions, as well as provides assistance in the commercialization process.

Connecticut
Inventors Association of Connecticut
P.O. Box 3325
Westport, CT 06880
Contact: Murray Schiffman
203-251-1174

Programs, seminars and speakers are offered, as well as a directory of members' inventions. Annual dues are $35.

Delaware
Small Business Development Center
University of Delaware
Purnell Hall
Newark, DE 19716
302-451-2747

Services include free management counseling and seminars, and advice on the commercialization process. Information is available by appointment only.

District of Columbia
U.S. Department of Commerce
U.S. Patent and Trademark Office
Washington, DC
202-377-2000

Florida
Tampa Bay Inventors Council
P.O. Box 2254
Largo, FL 34649
813-391-0315

Counseling is available on commercialization and the patent processes, connections are made between inventors, manufacturers, venture capitalists, and patent attorneys, and the Council provides critical reviews of inventions. Annual dues are $30.

Georgia
Inventors Association of Georgia
241 Freyer Dr., NE
Marietta, GA 30060
404-427-8024

Counseling is available to members, as are regular meeting where members share their progress on inventions. A newsletter is published by the Association and annual dues are $50 for corporate members and $25 for individuals.

Hawaii
Inventors Council of Hawaii
P.O. Box 27844
Honolulu, HI 96827
808-595-4296

Monthly meetings, workshops and newsletters are provided to members and the Council serves as a Patent Information Center for the state. Annual dues are $25.

Idaho
Idaho Research Foundation, Inc.
University of Idaho
P.O. Box 9645
Moscow, ID 83843
208-883-8366

Counseling is available, as well as reviews of inventions. Also available is a computer based data search and marketing service. The foundation takes a percentage of intellectual property royalties.

Illinois
Technology Commercialization Center
205 A South Main Street
Normal, IL 61761-6901
309-438-7127

Counseling, regular meetings with topical speakers, and critical reviews of inventions are provided by this center, however a service fee is required.

Indiana
The Inventors and Entrepreneurs Society of Indiana, Inc.
c/o Purdue University Calumet
Hammond, IN 46232
219-989-2354

The Society also serves residents of Illinois, Kentucky, and Michigan.

Counseling, monthly meetings, newsletters, and assessments of inventions' marketability. Annual dues are $30.

Iowa
Drake Business Center
Drake University
25th and University
Des Moines, IA 50311-4505
515-271-2655

Evaluations of inventions, counseling, and referrals are provided by the center. A fee of $100 is required for an invention's assessment.

Kansas
Kansas Association of Inventors, Inc.
2015 Lakin
Great Bend, KS 67530
316-792-1375

Monthly chapter meetings, inventions' potential marketability, newsletters, and referrals to persons in the field are all services provided by the association that primarily serves Kansas residents, but also has members in other states and Canada. Annual dues are $35.

Kentucky
Center for Entrepreneur and Technology
University of Louisville
Burhans Hall, Room 114
Shelby Campus
Louisville, KY 40292
502-588-7854

Counseling and invention reviews are available. No fees are required.

Louisiana
Technology Innovation Center
P.O. Box 44172
Lafayette, LA 70704-4172

Counseling, assistance in prototype development and selection of a patent attorney are services provided by the center. A registration fee of $100 is required and the center takes a percentage of future profits in exchange for certain services and requires reimburesements of its expenses.

Maine
Center for Innovation and Entrepreneurship
University of Maine

Maine Tech Center
16 Gadfrey Drive
Orono, ME 04473
207-581-1465

Center provides counseling, invention reviews, patent and financial assistance, and conducts inventors' forums. Newsletters and bulletins are also provided. There are fees for communicative and educational services and materials.

Maryland

Office of Energy-Related Inventions
National Institute of Standards and Technology
Gaithersburg, MD 20899
301-975-5500

Evaluations of promising non-nuclear energy-related inventions are conducted for independent inventors and small businesses aiming to obtain direct grants from the U.S. Department of Energy. Average awards have been $70,000.

Massachusetts

Inventors Association of New England
P.O. Box 335
Lexington, MA 02173
617-862-5008

Counseling, regular meetings with speakers, newsletters, and invention reviews are all provided by this association that covers eastern New England. Annual dues are $35.

Michigan

Inventors Council of Michigan
Metropolitan Center for High Technology
2727 Second Avenue
Detroit, MI 48201
313-963-0616

The council works with the statewide Small Business Development Centers to counsel inventors on commercialization of their inventions, patent processes, and provides referrals of other inventors, manufacturers, venture capitalists, and patent attorneys.

Minnesota

Minnesota Project Innovation, Inc.
1200 Washington Avenue South, Suite M-100
Minneapolis, MN 55415

612-338-3280
Affiliated with the Minnesota Department of Energy and Economic Development, U.S. Small Business Administration, and various private companies, this project provides referrals to inventors for technical assistance in refining their inventions.

Mississippi
Confederacy of Mississippi Inventors
4759 Nailor Road
Vicksburg, MS 39180
601-636-6561
Counseling, newsletters, quarterly meetings and public fairs are provided by this group. Annual dues are $12.

Missouri
Missouri Ingenuity, Inc.
T-16 Research Park
Columbia, MO 65211
314-882-2822
This group provides general consultations and referrals to other inventors, manufacturers, venture capitalists, and patent attorneys. There are fees for some services and the group is supported by the state of Missouri, the city of Columbia, and the University of Missouri.

Montana
Montana Science and Technology Alliance
46 North Last Chance Gulch, Suite 2B
Helena, MT 59620
406-449-2778
This group provides financial assistance to early stage, technology-based companies seeking commercialization of their inventions.

Nebraska
Nebraska Technical Assistance Center
University of Nebraska - Lincoln
W 191 Nebraska Hall
Lincoln, NE 68588-0535
402-472-5600
800-742-8800 (In NE)
This center offers counseling and referrals

Nevada
Nevada Inventors Association
P.O. Box 9905
Reno, NV 89507

Contact: Don Costar

Monthly meetings, newsletters, and workshops are provided by this association that maintains networking as its biggest success. Annual dues are $25.

New Hampshire
Service Corps of Retired Executives (SCORE)
Stewart Nelson Building
143 Main Street
Concord, NH 03302
603-226-7763

Counseling is available for marketing and commercialization of inventions.

New Jersey
Corporation for the Application of Rutgers Research
Rutgers, The State University of New Jersey
P.O. Box 1179
Piscataway, NJ 08854
908-932-4038

Counseling, reviews of inventions, and assessments of inventions' marketability are services provided by the corporation. Equity for services is required.

New Mexico
Thunderbird Technical Group
(aka Albuquerque Invention Club)
P.O. Box 30062
Albuquerque, NM 87190
Contact: Dr. Albert Goodman
505-266-3541

Monthly meetings and presentations are held. Annual dues are $10.

New York
Center for Technology Transfer
State University of New York College of Oswego
209 Park Hall
Oswego, NY 13126
315-341-3011

Counseling, reviews of inventions, and prototype fabrication and development are services provided by the center. Fees or royalties and laboratory and materials costs are required.

North Carolina
Innovation Research Fund
North Carolina Technology Development Authority
2 Davis Drive
Research Triangle Park, NC 27709
919-990-8558

Financial assistance is provided to support commercialization of inventors' ideas. Royalties from sales are taken.

North Dakota
Center for Innovation and Business Development
University of North Dakota
University Station, Box 8103
Grand Forks, ND 58202
701-777-3132

Counseling, referrals of other inventors, manufacturers, and venture capitalists, seminars and workshops are provided. There are fees for some services.

Ohio
Docie Marketing
9855 Sand Ridge Road
Millfield, OH 45761
614-797-4434

Counseling and reviews of inventions are services provided by this profit-making company.

Oklahoma
Invention Development Center
8230 SW 8th Street
Oklahoma City, OK 73128
405-376-2362

Regular meetings, counseling, and critical reviews of inventions are provided to the center's members. Annual dues are $25.

Oregon
Contact the Small Business Development Center for more i n f o r - mation at
Southern Oregon State 503-482-5838
Oregon Institute of Technology 503-885-1760
Eastern Oregon State 800-452-8639

Pennsylvania
American Society of Inventors
P.O. Box 58426

Philadelphia, PA 19102-8426
215-546-6601

Counseling, reviews of inventions, and assessments of inventions' marketability are services provided by the society.

Rhode Island
Service Corps of Retired Executives (SCORE)
c/o U.S. Small Business Administration
380 Westinghouse, Room #511
Providence, RI 02903
401-528-4571

Advice is offered by volunteer experts in the field of marketing and the commercialization process.

South Carolina
Center for Applied Technology (CAT)
Emerging Technology Center
Clemson University
511 Westinghouse Road
Pendleton, SC 29670
CAT Center 803-646-4000
Emerging Technology Center 803-646-4020

Counseling, reviews of inventions, and assessments of inventions' marketability are services provided by this center that works with the Small Business Development Center, South Carolina Research Authority, and Battelle Institute. There is a nominal fee for some services.

South Dakota
Dakota State University
SBIR PTAC Assistance Center
East Hall, Room 3
Madison, SD 57042
605-256-5555

Guidance is available on commercialization, the patent process, and marketability of inventions. Grants are available.

Tennessee
Venture Exchange Forum
P.O. Box 23184
Knoxville, TN 37933-1184
615-694-6772

Monthly meetings and referrals are provided. Annual dues are $25.

Texas
Texas Inventors Association

4000 Rock Creek Drive, #100
Dallas, TX 75204
Counseling is available, as well as information meetings.

Utah
Utah Small Business Development Center
University of Utah
College of Business
Salt Lake City, UT 84111
801-581-7915
Workshops, seminars, conferences, counseling, and publications are provided by the business center that only charges for workshops.

Vermont
Economic and Development Office
State of Vermont
109 State Street
Montpelier, VT 05609
Contact: Curt Carter
802-828-3221

Virginia
Technology Commercialization
Virginia's Center for Innovative Technology
2214 Rock Hill Road
Herndon, VA 22070
703-689-3043
Counseling is available, as well as financial assistance to colleges and universities setting up innovation centers.

Washington
Innovation Assessment Center
2001 6th Avenue, Suite 2608
Seattle, WA 98109
206-464-5450
As a part of the Small Business Development Center, counseling, evaluations, and assistance with the patent processes is available. There are fees for some services.

West Virginia
Small Business Development Center
West Virginia Institute of Technology
Montgomery, WV
304-442-3105

Counseling is available.

Wisconsin
Center for Innovation and Development
University of Wisconsin - Stout
206 Frylund Hall
Menomonie, WI 54751
715-232-5026

Counseling, reviews of inventions, assessments of inventions' marketability, and prototype development are services provided by the center, some for a fee.

Wyoming
Small Business Development Center
Casper College
350 West A, Suite 200
Casper, WY 82601
Contact: Barbara Stuckert
307-235-4827

Assistance is provided on patenting, commercialization, and intellectual property rights.

Canada
Inventors Association of Canada
P.O. Box 281
Swift Current, SA S9H3V6
306-773-7762

The association provides referrals to inventors in the U.S. and Canada and counseling on the inventions themselves.

┌─────────────────────────────┐

Chapter 12
HELP FOR HOME-BASED BUSINESSES

└─────────────────────────────┘

D id you know that Uncle Sam wants to give you money? The government has all the information you need to run a successful home-based business and offers it free. The Fortune 500 companies depend on government assistance, so why shouldn't you? Not only does the government provide financial assistance, but it also provides information regarding the start-up of a new business, low-cost insurance, marketing, assistance with bargain office furniture, computer equipment, and file cabinets, and much, much more.

The biggest advantage to running a home-based business is that you have minimal overhead. No wasted office space to rent, no unnecessary employees, no huge insurance bills. The safest way to start a business is to start one in your own home with the help of Uncle Sam.

Free Videos
On How To Start A Business In Your Home

Office of Business Development & Marketing
Small Business Administration (SBA)
409 3rd Street, SW
Washington, DC 20416
202-205-6665
        or
Oklahoma State University
Agricultural Communications
111 Public Information Building
Stillwater, OK 74078
405-744-3737

Home-Based Business: A Winning Blueprint is a special video developed by the SBA to guide the individual through the steps necessary for running a successful home-based business. You can review the video for free for 30 days, and if you decide to purchase it, send $39.00 to SBA, "Successes," Department A, P.O. Box 30, Denver, CO 80202-0030.

Home-Based Business Basics also is a video that helps individuals conduct market research, balance finances, handle legal problems, and establish a market base. The video is offered on a free loan basis or if you want to purchase it, the cost is $30.

How To Write Off Your Car And Home, And Summer Vacation As A Business Expense

Taxpayer Services
Internal Revenue Service (IRS)
U.S. Department of the Treasury
1111 Constitution Avenue, NW, Room 2422
Washington, DC 20224
800-424-3676

Get a free copy of *Business Use Of A Car* (#917), *Business Use Of Your Home* (#587), and *Travel, Entertainment, and Gift Expenses* (#463) that explain the deductions allowed for the various expenses.

Free Tax Consulting By The Experts

Internal Revenue Service (IRS)
1111 Constitution Avenue, NW
Washington, DC 20224
800-424-1040

The best information is free information. Your local IRS office, or the office above, will provide you with essential tax information regarding your home-based business.

Free Seminars
On Starting A Business At Home

Contact: Your County Cooperative Extension Service
(Under County Government in your telephone book)

Although services may vary, your local Cooperative Extension Service can provide you with lots of information on seminars, workshops, and meetings regarding your home-based business.

Cheap Crime Insurance
For Your Business Equipment

Federal Crime Insurance
P.O. Box 6301
Rockville, MD 20850
301-251-1660
800-638-8780

If your home is ever burglarized, your home-based business could suffer large losses if computer or office equipment is stolen. That's why the federal government subsidizes the cost of insurance with a federal crime insurance program if you live in one of the following states; AL, CA, CT, DE, DC, FL, GA, IL, KS, MD, NJ, NY, PA, RI, TN, Puerto Rico, or the Virgin Islands. Contact the office above for more information about this program.

Free Accounting Help

Contact: Your State Department of Economic Development Office for the Small Business Development Center nearest you.

Rather than going out and hiring an expensive accountant, the SBDC can provide you with your own expert who will sit down with you and help you develop your own bookkeeping and recordkeeping system, for free.

How To Pick A Work-At-Home Franchise

Bureau of Consumer Protection
Federal Trade Commission
6th and Pennsylvania Avenue, NW
Washington, DC 20580
202-326-2970
   or
International Franchising Association
1350 New York Avenue, NW
Washington, DC 20005
202-628-8000
   or
Your State Franchising Office

You can receive several publications from the FTC and the International Franchising Association that will assist you in how to evaluate and buy a franchise. The FTC may also be able to provide you with detailed backgrounds on the franchise you wish to purchase in certain states.

Work At Home
On A $100,000 Government Contract

Contact: Your State Department of Economic Development Office for the Small Business Development Center Nearest   You or Your U.S. Congressman or Senator

Just because you operate your business out of your home, does not mean you can't get your share of government contracts. And it doesn't matter what business you are in. Both federal and state governments utilize the services of artists, writers, and even janitors. Contact your congressman who can do a computer search of the current government contract opportunities available to see if you can take advantage of one of them.

Free Inspections Of Your Home
For Health And Safety Hazards

National Institute for Occupational Health and Safety
4676 Columbia Parkway
Cincinnati, OH 45226
800-356-4674

If you suspect that your work environment may be hazardous, then the NIOHS can provide a free inspection. If you meet any of the following criteria, the NIOHS can provide you with more information;

* Do you have trouble hearing at work?
* Does your job cause you mental stress?
* Do you conduct repetitive movements, such as typing or lifting?
* Do you ever feel a tingling in your hands?
* Are you exposed to hazardous chemicals?
* Do you use a computer for most of the day?

How To Get Free Health Care
If You Can't Afford Health Insurance

Public Health Service
Health Resource and Services Administration
Department of Health and Human Services
Rockville, MD 20857
800-638-0742
800-492-0359 (In MD)

With the costs of health care rising every year, it is no surprise that most people cannot afford it. However, some people may be eligible to receive free health care under the Hill-Burton Law that requires hospitals and clinics receiving assistance from the federal government, to also provide assistance to those who cannot afford to pay for health care. Call the number above to find out if you qualify and where the nearest program to you is located.

Free Home-Based Business Start-Up Guide

Office of Business Development & Marketing
Small Business Administration (SBA)
Washington, DC 20416
202-205-6665

How To Start A Home-Based Business is published by the SBA to assist individuals in getting a successful head start. This publication is part of the *Focus On The Facts* series of publications that also helps business owners in planning, marketing, finances, and pricing.

$50,000 To Work On Your Invention

Office of Innovation, Research and Technology
U.S. Small Business Administration
1441 L Street, NW
Washington, DC 20416
202-205-6450
    or
Energy-Related Inventions Program
National Institute of Standards and Technology
Building 411, Room A115
Gaithersburg, MD 20899
301-975-5500

Both offices have provided funds to individuals who work for specific projects under the government. Contact the offices above to find out if your business qualifies for any of the current opportunities available.

Get Legal Help At Little Or No Cost

Contact: Your State Department of Economic Development Office for the Small Business Development Center nearest you.
We all know that attorneys can come with a high price tag attached for their services. So why not get those same services for your home-based business at a fraction of the cost, and sometimes free? Contact the office above for more information.

The Government Will Sell
Your Service Or Product
In Other Countries

Contact: Your State Department of Economic Development
Office or Your State Office Of International Marketing
There is a whole world of business markets overseas perhaps waiting for
your product or service to arrive. But don't hire an expensive marketing
consultant, when you can get assistance for free. There are several programs offered by the government that will conduct market studies for your
product in another country, contact other businesses that may want to sell
your product or service, and provide you with financial assistance.

Find A Free Government Expert
On Any Topic

For the various Federal Government offices, contact your
local U.S. Government Federal Information Center or the
main Federal Information Center at 301-722-9000.
There is virtually a government expert on every topic, service, and product from underwear and toothpaste, to pasta and 900 number businesses. Contact the offices above for more information on your questions.

Free Marketing Help

Contact: Your State Office of Economic Development for
the Small Business Development Center nearest you.
Part of planning a successful business is to understand who exactly you
want to sell your product or service to. Marketing consultants can be
expensive, so it is best to contact the office above for free assistance.
They will refer you to experts through the Service Corps of Retired
Executives (SCORE) who can help you with analyzing your competition,
customers, and suppliers.

$10,000 To Start
A Craft Business In Your Home

Contact: Your State Office of Economic Development for the Small
Business Development Center nearest you.
Although there are no specific money programs for home-based busi-

nesses, the office above can assist you with finding a program tailored to your needs. For example, The USDA's Farmers Home Administration provides financial assistance (grants and loans) to businesses located in rural areas with poor economies and high unemployment.

80% Discount
On Office Equipment And Supplies

U.S. General Services Administration
18th & F Streets, NW
Washington, DC 20405
202-557-7785

Need any typewriters, computers, postage meters, paper clips, or any other office equipment and supplies? Don't go and spend thousands of dollars on this merchandise when you can get it at a fraction of the cost from the government. The General Services Administration (GSA) locates equipment that isn't needed by the government and auctions it off a rock-bottom prices. Contact the office above so that they can put you on a mailing list to notify you of up-coming auctions, or locate the office nearest you for more information.

Atlanta
GSA, Surplus Sales Branch,
75 Spring Street, Atlanta,
GA 30303; 404-331-0972

Boston
GSA, Surplus Sales Branch,
10 Causeway Street, 9th Floor,
Boston, MA; 617-565-7316

Chicago
GSA,
230 S. Dearborn Street,
Chicago, IL 60604; 312-353-6061

Denver
GSA, Surplus Sales Branch,
Denver Federal Center, Building 41,
Denver, CO 80225; 303-236-7705

Fort Worth
GSA, Surplus Sales Branch,

819 Taylor Street,
Fort Worth, TX 76102; 817-334-2351

Kansas
GSA, Surplus Sales Branch,
6F BPS 4400, College Blvd., Suite 175,
Overland, KS 66211

New York
GSA, Surplus Sales Branch,
26 Federal Plaza, Room 20-2016,
New York, NY 10278; 212-264-4824

Philadelphia
GSA, Surplus Sales Branch,
9th & Market Sts.,
Philadelphia, PA 19107; 215-597-SALE

San Francisco
GSA, Surplus Sales Branch,
525 Market Street, 32nd Floor,
San Francisco, CA 94105; 415-974-9189

Washington State
GSA, Surplus Sales Branch,
GSA Center,
Auburn, WA 98002; 206-931-7562

Washington, DC
GSA,
6808 Loisdale Road, Building A,
Springfield, VA 22150; 703-557-7785

Other offices that may be contacted that auction office equipment and
supplies include;

Internal Revenue Service
800-829-1040

U.S. Postal Service
202-268-2000

U.S. Customs Service
405-357-9194

Department of Defense
616-961-7331

Free Book On How To
Raise Money For Your Small Business

Office of Business Development & Marketing
Small Business Administration (SBA)
409 3rd Street, SW
Washington, DC 20416
202-205-6665

Raising money for your home-based business can be simple if you have the right information. The Small Business Administration has published another booklet as part of their *Focus On The Facts Series*, and it's called *How To Raise Money For A Small Business*. This publication contains lots of helpful information for everything from writing a loan proposal to SBA financial programs.

How To Set Up
A Self-Employed Retirement Plan

Taxpayer Services
Internal Revenue Service
U.S. Department of the Treasury
1111 Constitution Avenue, NW, Room 2422
Washington, DC 20224
800-424-3676

You can get a free copy of *Self-Employed Retirement Plans* (#560) from this IRS office that explains Keogh plans for self-employed individuals and certain partners in partnerships.

Free Consultants (SCORE)

Contact: Your Local U.S. Small Business Administration (SBA) Office or the SBA Hotline at 800-827-5722

Running a small business can require the help of several experts i.e. accounting, marketing. Your local SBA can refer you to several consultants who will help you work out your problems for free. SCORE members are there to assist small business owners with obstacles they may run across in the daily operations of the business.

Free Videos Show How To
Start Or Expand A Small Business

Office of Business Development & Marketing
Small Business Administration
409 3rd Street, SW
Washington, DC 20416
202-205-6665

If you are trying to market your business, the SBA has three videos that can be reviewed for 30 days with the option to purchase them, to assist you. The titles are; *Marketing: Winning Customers With A Workable Plan* ($30) that guides you in developing a marketing plan to identify your customers' needs; *The Business Plan: Your Roadmap To Success* ($30) helps you in developing a plan that will find you capital, growth, and profitability; and *Promotion: Solving The Puzzle* ($30) helps you develop a promotional strategy with a balance in advertising, public relations, direct mail, and trade shows to attract more customers.

Get A Tax Break For
Hiring And Training New Employees

Employment Training Administration
Office of Public Affairs
U.S. Department of Labor, Room S-2322
Washington, DC 20210
202-535-0236

Your business may qualify for a federal tax credit if your business employs dislocated workers, or workers who have lost their jobs because of competition. It is called the Targeted Jobs Tax Credit and is run by the state and local governments to give businesses a tax break for hiring these types of individuals. To find out if any of your employees may qualify, contact your state Department of Labor. They may also help you locate these workers and file the paperwork with the appropriate agency. When contacting the office, also ask about the Job Training Partnership Act that requires that the government pay a part of the salary of a disadvantaged employee, such as the handicapped or a minority, if your business meets certain requirements.

Tax Information For
Home-Based Businesses

Taxpayer Services

Internal Revenue Service
U.S. Department of the Treasury
1111 Constitution Avenue, NW, Room 2422
Washington, DC 20224
800-424-3676

The IRS provides business owners with free publications on the current tax laws affecting their certain type of business. Below is a list of the various publications offered and their order numbers.

Accounting Periods And Methods (#538) - explains accounting periods and how they relate to federal taxes.

Bankruptcy And Other Debt Cancellation (#908) - explains bankruptcy and discharge of debt from an income tax perspective.

Business Expenses (#535) - explains which expenses are tax deductible and which are not.

Business Use Of A Car (#917) - discusses how to deduct your car expenses when it is used for your home-based business.

Business Use Of Your Home (#587) - discusses how to deduct expenses when your home is used for business.

Circular E, Employer's Tax Guide (#15) - contains information on the tax aspects of employing others in your business.

Condemnations And Business Casualties And Thefts (#549) - explains how tot ake a tax deduction for casualties and thefts to your business property.

Depreciation (#534) - shows how to write off the depreciation of your business' assets over a period of time.

Earned Income Credit (#596) - discusses the advantages of the Earned Income Credit and who qualifies for it.

Educational Expenses (#508) - explains how you can deduct educational expenses if you take courses related to your business.

Examination Of Returns, Appeal Rights, And Claims For Refund (#556) - if your business is ever subject to an examination of your tax filings, this booklet provides useful information regarding the procedures.

Interest Expense (#545) - explains how to deduct interest payments on business-related loans.

Moving Expenses (#521) - explains how to deduct moving expenses when you relocate your home-based business.

Sales And Other Dispositions Of Assets (#544) - discusses how to calculate the gain and loss on the sale or disposition of assets used in your business.

Self-Employed Retirement Plans (#560) - explains Keogh plans for self-employed individuals and certain partners of partnerships.

Self-Employment Tax (#533) - explain the certain taxes that a self-employed individual must pay, such as social security tax.

Tax Guide For Small Business (#334) - explains the tax responsibilities for sole proprietorships, partnerships, corporations, and S corporations.

Tax Information For Direct Sellers (#911) - if your home-based business involves direct selling, this booklet provides helpful information on the tax aspects of door-to-door selling, sales parties, etc.

Tax Information On Corporations (#542) - explains the tax aspects of incorporating your home-based business.

Tax Information On Partnerships (#541) - explains the tax aspects of running your home-based business as a partnership.

Tax Information On S Corporation (#589) - explains the tax aspects of home-based businesses classified under subchapter S of the tax code.

Taxpayers Starting A Business (#583) - provides examples of records for individuals just starting a business on what information they need to keep record of and how to accurately file a tax return with these records.

Travel, Entertainment, And Gift Expenses (#463) - explains how to deduct business-related travel, including meals and entertainment, as well as how to record and report these expenses to the IRS.

Is Your Name Legal?
Trademark Search Library

Patent and Trademark Office
U.S. Department of Commerce
2011 Jefferson Davis Highway, Room 2C08
Arlington, VA 22202
703-557-5813

If you have decided on a name for your business, you must make sure that it doesn't already exist. The Trademark Search Library contains the registration of all trademarks, slogans, and logos and the information is available to the public. Contact the address above to find out more information about researching and applying for a trademark.

Do A Patent Search Yourself And Save Money

Office of Patent Depository Library Programs
Patent and Trademark Office
U.S. Department of Commerce
1921 Jefferson Davis Highway, Room 306
Arlington, VA 22202
703-577-9686

Hiring a lawyer or researcher to do your patent search can be very expensive. So, instead why not do it yourself. There are about 70 Patent Depository Libraries across the country that maintain files of all past and current patents issued. For a Patent Depository Library near you call 800-435-7735 or, in Virginia call 800-543-2313.

Protect Your Idea For $6.00

Commissioner of Patents and Trademarks
Patent and Trademark Office
U.S. Department of Commerce
2121 Crystal Drive
Arlington, VA 22202
703-557-3225

Rather than going through the time and money that it takes to do a patent search, you may want to apply for a Disclosure Statement. A Disclosure Statement allows you to protect your idea for $6.00 and serves as evidence of the dates of conception of your invention. It lasts for only two years, but gives you enough time to determine if your idea is marketable and sellable.

Videos On Starting A Child Care Business

Video Production
Texas A & M University
107 Reed McDonald Building
College Station, TX 77843
409-845-2840
    or
Contact: Your County Cooperative Extension Service under
County Government in your telephone book

If you are planning to open a day care, then don't miss out on the valuable information offered by the Texas Agricultural Extension Service. *Better Kid Care - Family Day Care Training* is a 4 part video program that covers child development, nutrition, health and safety, and business management. Contact one of the offices above to find out how you can get a copy of this video.

Chapter 13
FREE MONEY
FOR THE ARTIST

The National Endowment for the Arts and National Endowment for the Humanities are agencies which fund arts and humanities in the United States.

The humanities include the study of language, linguistics, literature, history, law, philosophy, archaeology, comparative religion, ethics, art history, art criticism and social studies.

Frequently, nonprofit organizations receive money from federal arts and humanities agencies. For information about these programs, contact:

Information Office
National Endowment for the Arts
1100 Pennsylvania Avenue, NW
Washington, DC 20506
(202)682-5400

Information Office
National Endowment for the Humanities
1100 Pennsylvania Avenue, NW, Room 409
Washington, DC 20506 (202)786-0438

The Arts Review, a magazine distributed by the National Endowment for the Arts, lists available grants and funding for the arts. To inquire about a $10 per year subscription, contact:

Superintendent of Documents
United States Government Printing Office
Washington, DC 20402
(202)783-3238

For general magazine information, contact:

> Publications Division
> National Foundation on the Arts and Humanities
> 1100 Pennsylvania Avenue, NW, Room 614
> Washington, DC 20506
> (202)682-5570

Those dedicated to a full-fledged career in the arts may consider forming their own non-profit organization or theater company. Artists, including actors and musicians who give recitals and concerts, are eligible for federal grants once they achieve "professional" status. For information, write:

> Grants Office
> National Endowment for the Arts
> 2401 E Street, NW
> Washington, DC 20506

Matching grants, in which the government matches the private or nonprofit donation for a project, are available for radio and television documentaries.

Radio, film and video documentaries can receive up to $50,000 in direct money and $15,000 in matching grants from the government.

For information, contact:

> National Endowment for the Arts, Grants Office
> 2401 E Street, NW
> Washington, DC 20506

For information regarding community-related arts programs, exhibits and workshops, contact:

> Division for the Support for Local Arts Agencies
> National Endowment for the Arts
> 1100 Pennsylvania Avenue, NW
> Washington, DC 20506
> (202)682-5431

Inquiries about federal grants up to $150,000 offered to professional dance companies should be made to the above address.

> # Chapter 14
> # HELP FOR WOMEN

T here is no doubt that women have become more common and more successful in the business world. For example, over the past 15 years, the number of businesses owned by women has nearly doubled. In addition, women-owned businesses were awarded more than $2 billion in federal prime contracts recently, as compared to only $180 million about ten years ago. This dramatic change has caused the government to take a second look at women as the most powerful group of emerging business owners.

Believe it or not, the government labels women-owned businesses as "disadvantaged," so instead of getting angry why not take advantage of the help the government is offering disadvantaged business owners. There are several state and federal programs that were created to help women compete and succeed in the business environment including low-interest loans and special government contracts. Below are some of the programs and information that women can obtain for success in the operations of their own business.

Federal Government Set-Asides For Women Entrepreneurs

Contact: Your state office of Economic Development
(Located in your state capitol)
    or
Government Printing Office
Superintendent of Documents
Washington, DC 20402
202-783-3238

A certain percentage of federal contracts are guaranteed to go to women entrepreneurs. For assistance in selling your product or service to the government, contact the office above to obtain a copy of *Women Business Owners: Selling To The Federal Government.* The cost is $3.75.

Creative Financing For Women Entrepreneurs
Office of Women's Business Ownership
U.S. Small Business Administration
409 3rd Street, SW
Washington, DC 20416
202-205-6673

The Office of Women's Business Ownership provides seminars for women who have been turned down for loans from regular banks. They provide creative ways of financing a business.

Free Mentors For New Women Entrepreneurs
Office of Women's Business Ownership
U.S. Small Business Administration
409 3rd Street, SW
Washington, DC 20416
202-205-6673

The Small Business Administration's Women's Network For Entrepreneurial Training (WNET) was created to provide women with role models who have been through the process of starting a business. The network will provide you with a mentor who will meet with you at least once a week for an entire year, for free. She will teach you from her own experiences and will guide you through the establishment of your business. To qualify for the program, you must have been in business for at least a year and have gross receipts of $50,000 or more. Contact the office above for more information.

Call Your Local Women's Business Ownership Representative
Because women entrepreneurs have special needs, the U.S. Small Business Administration has added staff members who specialize in the needs and problems of women-owned businesses such as networking, financial assistance, bidding on government contracts and programs, etc. For information sources and free counseling, contact the WBO representative nearest you.

Alabama
Judy York
U.S. Small Business Administration
2121 8th Avenue, North Suite 200

Birmingham, AL 35203-2398
205-731-1344

Alaska
Joyce Jansen
U.S. Small Business Administration
Federal Building, #67
222 West 8th Avenue
Anchorage, AK 99513-7559
907-271-4022

Arizona
Nina Rivera
U.S. Small Business Administration
2005 North Center, 5th Floor
Phoenix, AZ 85004-4599
602-379-3737

California
Sharon May
U.S. Small Business Administration
71 Stevenson Street, 20th Floor
San Francisco, CA 94105-2939

Lisa Zuffi
U.S. Small Business Administration
211 Main Street, 4th Floor
San Francisco, CA 94105-1988
415-744-6771

Peggy Gammie
U.S. Small Business Administration
660 J Street, Suite 215
Sacramento, CA 95814-2413
916-551-1431

Leslie Niswander
U.S. Small Business Administration
2719 N. Air Fresno Drive, 5th Floor
Fresno, CA 93727-1547
209-487-5189

Darlene McKinnon
U.S. Small Business Administration
800 Front Street, Room 4-S-29

San Diego, CA 92188-0270
619-557-7252 EXT. 46

Georgia Johnson
U.S. Small Business Administration
901 W. Civic Center Dr., Suite 160
Santa Ana, CA 92703-2352
714-836-2494

Marie Teeple
U.S. Small Business Administration
330 N. Brand Boulevard, Suite 1200
Glendale, CA 91203-2304
213-894-2956

Colorado
Dora D'Amico
U.S. Small Business Administration
999 18th Street, Suite 701
Denver, CO 80202
303-294-7033

Judy Hamrock
U.S. Small Business Administration
721 19th Street
Denver, CO 80202
303-844-3986

Connecticut
Kathleen Duncan
U.S. Small Business Administration
330 Main Street, 2nd Floor
Hartford, CT 06106
203-240-4642

District of Columbia
Jeanne Alexander
U.S. Small Business Administration
1111 18th Street, NW
Washignton, DC 20036
202-634-1500 EXT. 258

Florida
Kim Lucas

U.S. Small Business Administration
7825 Bay Meadows Way, Suite 100B
Jacksonville, FL 32256
904-443-1912

Carla Schworer
U.S. Small Business Administration
1320 S. Dixie Highway, Suite 501
Coral Gables, FL 33146
305-536-5521

Georgia
Paula Hill
U.S. Small Business Administration
1720 Peachtree Street, NW, 6th Floor
Atlanta, GA 30309
404-347-2356

Hawaii
Donna Hopkins
U.S. Small Business Administration
30 Ala Moana, Room 2213
P.O. Box 50207
Honolulu, HI 96850-4981
808-541-2973

Idaho
Sharon Barber
U.S. Small Business Administration
1020 Main Street, Suite 290
Boise, ID 83702
208-334-1780

Illinois
Nancy Smith
U.S. Small Business Administration
300 S. Riverdale, Room 1975S
Chicago, IL 60606
312-353-4252

Sam McGrier
U.S. Small Business Administration
500 W. Madison Street, Suite 1250
Chicago, IL 60606

312-353-4578

Valerie Ross
U.S. Small Business Administration
511 W. Capitol Street, Suite 302
Springfield, IL 62704
217-492-4416

Indiana
Don Owen
U.S. Small Business Administration
429 N. Pennsylvania Street, Suite 100
Indianapolis, IN 46204

Iowa
Dianne Reinerston
U.S. Small Business Administration
373 Collins Road, NE
Cedar Rapids, IA 52402
319-393-8630

Sandy Jerde
U.S. Small Business Administration
210 Walnut Street, Room 749
Des Moines, IA 50309
515-284-4762

Kansas
Linda McMaster
U.S. Small Business Administration
110 E. Waterman Street
Wichita, KS 67202
316-269-6191

Kentucky
Carol Hatfield
U.S. Small Business Administration
Dr. Luther King Jr. Pl., Room 18
Louisville, KY 40202-2254
305-536-5521

Maine
Bonnie Erickson
U.S. Small Business Administration

40 Western Avenue, Room 512
Augusta, ME 04330
207-622-8242

Maryland
Mindye Allentoff
U.S. Small Business Administration
10 North Calvert Street, 4th Floor
Baltimore, MD 21202
301-962-2235

Massachusetts
Barbara Manning
U.S. Small Business Administration
155 Federal Street, 9th Floor
Boston, MA 02110
617-451-2040

Mildred Cooper
U.S. Small Business Administration
10 Causeway Street, Room 265
Boston, MA 02222-1093
617-565-5636

Harry Webb
U.S. Small Business Administration
1550 Main Street, Room 212
Springfield, MA 01103
413-785-0268

Michigan
Cathy Gase
U.S. Small Business Administration
477 Michigan Avenue
Detroit, MI 48226
313-226-6075 EXT 23

Minnesota
Cynthia Collett
U.S. Small Business Administration
610 C Butler Square
Minneapolis, MN 55403
612-370-2312

Missouri
Patty Jenners

U.S. Small Business Administration
911 Walnut Street, 13th Floor
Kansas City, MO 64106
816-426-5311

Neida Heusinkvelt-Bopp
U.S. Small Business Administration
1103 Grand Avenue, 5th Floor
Kansas City, MO 64106
816-374-6701

LaVerne Johnson
U.S. Small Business Administration
815 Olive Street, Suite 242
St. Louis, MO 63101
314-539-6600

LuAnn Hancock
U.S. Small Business Administration
620 S. Glenstone, Suite 110
Springfield, MO 65802-3200
417-864-7670

Mississippi
Ada Turner & Penny Melton
U.S. Small Business Administration
One Hancock Plaza, Suite 1001
Gulfport, MS 39501
601-683-4449

Montana
Michelle Johnston
U.S. Small Business Administration
301 S. Park Avenue, Room 528
Helena, MT 59525-0054
406-449-5381

Nebraska
Betty Gutheil
U.S. Small Business Administration
11145 Mill Valley Road
Omaha, NB 68154
402-221-3626

Nevada
Marie Papile
U.S. Small Business Administration
301 E. Stewart, Box 7527, Downtown Station
Las Vegas, NV 89125-2527
702-388-6611

New Hampshire
Sandra Sullivan
U.S. Small Business Administration
55 Pleasant Street, Room 211
Concord, NH 03301
603-225-1400

New Jersey
Diana Parra
U.S. Small Business Administration
Military Park Building
60 Park Place, 4th Floor
Newark, NJ 07102
201-645-3683

New York
Sheila Thomas
U.S. Small Business Administration
26 Federal Plaza, Room 3108
New York, NY 10278
212-264-1046

Georgia Ellis
U.S. Small Business Administration
26 Federal Plaza, Room 3100
New York, NY 10278
212-264-1762

Stephanie Ubowski
U.S. Small Business Administration
100 S. Clinton Street, Room 1071
Syracuse, NY 13260
315-423-5375

Thomas Agon
U.S. Small Business Administration
333 E. Water Street
Elmira, NY 14901
607-734-8142

Carol Kruszona
U.S. Small Business Administration
111 W. Huron Street, Room 1311
Buffalo, NY 14202
716-846-4517

Josephine Bermudez
U.S. Small Business Administration
35 Pinelawn Road, Room 102E
Melville, NY 11747
516-454-0753

Sharon Kelleher
U.S. Small Business Administration
445 Broadway, Room 236-A
Albany, NY 12207
518-472-6300

Marcia Ketchum
U.S. Small Business Administration
Federal Building,
100 State Street
Rochester, NY 14614
716-263-6700

North Dakota
Marelene Koenig
U.S. Small Business Administration
657 2nd Avenue, North, Room 218
P.O. Box 3088
Fargo, ND 58102
701-239-5131

Ohio
Rosemary Darling
U.S. Small Business Administration
1240 E. 9th Street, Room 317
Cleveland, OH 44199
216-522-4194

Janice Sonnenburg
U.S. Small Business Administration
85 Marconi Boulevard
Columbus, OH 43215
614-469-6860 EXT. 274

Gene O'Connell
U.S. Small Business Administration
550 Main Street, Room 5028
Cincinnati, OH 45202
513-684-2814

Oregon
Inge McNeese
U.S. Small Business Administration
222 SW Columbia Avenue, Room 500
Portland, OR 97201-6605
503-326-5202

Pennsylvania
Daniel Sossaman
U.S. Small Business Administration
475 Allendale Square Road, Suite 201
King of Prussia, PA 19406
215-962-3729

Doris Young
U.S. Small Business Administration
475 Allendale Square Road, Suite 201
King of Prussia, PA 19406
215-962-3818

Mary Merman
U.S. Small Business Administration
960 Penn Avenue, 5th Floor
Pittsburgh, PA 15222
412-644-2785

Rhode Island
Linda Smith
U.S. Small Business Administration
380 Westminister Mall
Providence, RI 02903
502-528-4598

South Carolina
Kim Hite
U.S. Small Business Administration
1835 Assembly Street, Room 358
Columbia, SC 29202
803-253-3360

South Dakota
Darlene Michael
U.S. Small Business Administration
101 S. Main Avenue, Suite 101
Sioux Falls, SD 57102
605-330-4231

Tennessee
Saundra Jackson
U.S. Small Business Administration
50 Vantage Way, Suite 201
Nashville, TN 37228
615-736-7176

Texas
Gwen Syers
U.S. Small Business Administration
10737 Gateway West, Suite 320
El Paso, TX 79902
915-540-5564

David Royal
U.S. Small Business Administration
400 Mann Street, Suite 403
Corpus Christi, TX 78401
512-888-3333

Utah
Suzan Yoshimura
U.S. Small Business Administration
Federal Building
125 S. State Street
Salt Lake City, UT 84138-1195
801-524-3203

Vermont
Brenda Foster
U.S. Small Business Administration
87 State Street, Room 204
P.O. Box 605
Montpelier, VT 05602
802-828-4422

Virginia
Fannie Gergoudis
U.S. Small Business Administration
400 N. 8th Street, Room 3015
P.O. Box 10126
Richmond, VA 23240
804-771-2765

Washington
Gwen Elliott
U.S. Small Business Administration
2615 4th Street, Room 440
Seattle, WA 98121
206-553-2460

Connie Alvarado
U.S. Small Business Administration
915 2nd Avenue, Room 1792
Seattle, WA 98174
206-553-4436

Coralie Myers
U.S. Small Business Administration
West 601 First Avenue, 10th Floor East
Spokane, WA 99204
509-353-2815

West Virginia
Debra Flannigan
U.S. Small Business Administration
168 W. Main Street
P.O. Box 1608
Clarksburg, WV 26302
304-623-5631

Wisconsin
Valerie Ross
U.S. Small Business Administration
511 W. Capitol Street, Suite 302
Springfield, IL 62704
217-492-4416

Wyoming
Kay Stucker
U.S. Small Business Administration
100 E. B Street, Room 401
P.O. Box 2839
Casper, WY 82602
307-261-5761

Georgia
YMCA of Greater Atlanta
957 N. Highland Avenue, NE
Atlanta, GA 30306
404-872-4747

Illinois
Women's Business Development Center
230 N. Michigan Avenue, Suite 1800
Chicago, IL 60601
312-853-3477

Women's Business Development Center
SBDC/Joliet Junior College
214 N. Ottawa, 3rd Floor
Joliet, IL 60431
815-727-6544 EXT 1312

Women's Business Development Center
Kankakee Community College
4 Dearborn Square
Kankakee, IL 60901
815-933-0375

Women Business Owners Advocacy Program
SBDC/Rock Valley College
1220 Rock Street
Rockford, IL 61101
815-968-4087

Women's Economic Venture Enterprise
229 16th Street
Rock Island, IL 61201
309-788-9793

Indiana
Indiana Regional Minority Supplier Development Council, Inc.
300 E. Fall Creek Parkway, ND
P.O. Box 44801
Indianapolis, IN 46244-0801
317-923-2110

Michigan
EXCEL! Women Business Owners Development Team
200 Renaissance Center, Suite 1600
Detroit, MI 48243-1274
313-396-3576

Minnesota
BI-CAP, Inc., Women in New Development WIND-
P.O. Box 579
Bemidji, MN 56601
218-751-4631

Missouri
NAWBO of St. Louis
911 Washington Avenue, Suite 140
St. Louis, MO 63101
314-621-6162

New Mexico
Women's Economic Self-Sufficiency Team WESST Corp.
414 Silver Southwest
Albuquerque, NM 87102
505-848-4760

Women's Economic Self-Sufficiency Team WESST Corp.
Taos County Economic Development Corp.
P.O. Box 1389
Taos, NM 87571
505-758-1161

New York
American Woman's Economic Development Corp.
641 Lexington Avenue, 9th Floor
New York, NY 10022
212-688-1900

Texas
Center for Women's Business Enterprise
1200 Smith Street
2800 Citicorp Building
Houston, TX 77002
713-658-0300

Center for Women's Business Enterprise
301 Congress Avenue, Suite 1000
Austin, TX 78701
512-476-7501

Southwest Resource Development
8700 Crownhill, Suite 700
San Antonio, TX 78209
512-828-9034

Wisconsin
Women's Business Initiative Corp.
1020 N. Broadway
Milwaukee, WI 53202
414-277-7004

Woman-To-Woman
Entrepreneur Help Centers

For women who are interested in starting or expanding their existing business, the Small Business Administration has co-funded 19 demonstration centers to assist women with all aspects of business including accounting, marketing, legal matters, employee relations, and budgeting. These centers are non-profit and funded by public/private agencies, so they do charge nominal fees for some of their services.

California
American Woman's Economic Development Corp.
301 E. Ocean Boulevard, Suite 1010
Long Beach, CA 90802
213-983-3747

West Co.,
A Woman's Economic Self-Sufficiency Training Program
413 N. State Street
Ukiah, CA 95482
707-462-2348

West Co.,
A Woman's Economic Self-Sufficiency Training Program
333 C North Franklin Street
Fort Bragg, CA 95437
707-964-7571

Colorado
Mi Casa, Business Center for Women
571 Galapago Street
Denver, CO 80204
303-573-1302

District of Columbia
American Woman's Economic Development Corp.
2445 M Street, NW, Room 490
P.O. Box 65644
Washington, DC 20035
202-857-0091

State Women
Business Assistance Programs

Along with the federal government, state governments are now beginning to recognize the power of women in business, and so have developed special assistance programs and information sources for women. Only about half of the states have such programs, but remember that some states may have programs in the near future.

Alabama
Office of Minority Business Enterprise (OMBE)
Alabama Development Office
401 Adams Avenue
Montgomery, AL 36130
800-248-6889 (Out Of State) 800-248-0033 (In State)
This office assists women and minorities in all aspects of a business from preparing business plans to participating in state and federal procurement opportunities.

Arkansas
Arkansas Industrial Development Commission
One State Capitol Mall
Little Rock, AR 72201
501-682-1060
This office provides information on business loan packaging, bonding information, seminars, workshops, referrals to other agencies, and general business counseling.

California
Office of Small and Minority Business
Department of General services
1808 14th Street, Suite 100
Sacramento, CA 95814
916-322-5060
This office assists women who are interested in participating in state procurement opportunities, as well as general business counseling and assistance.

Colorado
Minority Business Office
Office of Business development
1625 Broadway Street, Suite 1710
Denver, CO 80202
303-892-3840
Act as a referral service and hold business planning seminars.

Illinois
Small Business Advocate
Illinois Department of Commerce and Community Affairs
State of Illinois Center
100 W. Randolph Street, Suite 3-400
Chicago, IL 60601
312-814-2829
This office provides information on how to deal with state, federal, and local agencies when a small business is experiencing a bureaucratic stand-still.

Indiana
Indiana Department of Commerce
Office of Minority and Women Business Development Division
One North Capitol, Suite 501
Indianapolis, IN 46204-2288
317-232-8820, 800-824-2476

Women and minorities receive assistance from this office in all phases of a business' development including management and technical assistance, procurement, contract bidding, seminars, and workshops.

Iowa
Targeted Small Business Program Manager
Department of Economic Development
200 E. Grand Avenue
Des Moines, IA 50309
515-242-4813

Under this program, women can receive direct loans, subsidies, or grants of up to $25,000, as well as loan guarantees of up to 75% of the project cost not to exceed $40,000 for start-up and expansion.

Kansas
Office of Minority Business
Existing Industry Development Division
Kansas Department of Commerce
400 SW 8th Avenue, 5th Floor
Topeka, KS 66603-3957
913-296-3805

This office provides assistance to women and minorities who are interested in participating in public and private procurement opportunities, as well as general business counseling and assistance.

Kentucky
Office of Minority Affairs
State Office Building, Room 904
501 High Street
Frankfort, KY 40622
502-564-3601

This office assists women-owned businesses interested in procurement programs for state highway-related contracts.

Louisiana
Louisiana Economic Development Corporation
Department of Economic Development
P.O. Box 94185
Baton Rouge, LA 70804-9185
504-342-5675

This program provides women- and minority-owned businesses with loans or loan guarantees for up to $250,000 for use in financing construction, conversion, or expansion of business facilities. The office also provides direct loans to businesses that have been turned down at least twice by a financial institution for a loan.

Maine
Maine Department of Transportation
Division of Equal Opportunity/Employee Relations
State Station House #16
Augusta, ME 04333
207-289-3576

Women-owned businesses can get certified under the Disadvantaged/Minority/Women Business Enterprise Program to obtain government contracts.

Massachusetts
State Office of Minority and Women Business Assistance
Department of Commerce
100 Cambridge Street
Boston, MA 02202
617-727-8692

This office provides assistance to women- and minority-owned businesses interested inparticipating in the state's procurement programs.

Michigan
Michigan Department of Commerce
525 W. Ottawa
P.O. Box 30225
Lansing, MI 48909
800-831-9090, 517-335-2166

Under the Women Business Owners Service program, women can receive assistance with problem solving, finances, and developing a business plan.

Minnesota
Department of Administration
Materials Management Division
112 Administrative Boulevard
St. Paul, MN 55155
612-296-2600

This office helps women-owned businesses receive certification to participate in state procurement opportunities. When a business has been certified, it receives a 6% preference on government contract bids over businesses that have not been certified.

Mississippi
Department of Economic and Community Development
P.O. Box 849
1200 Walter Sillers Building

Jackson, MS 32905
601-359-3449
This office provides low-interest loans for up to 50% of a project's cost, if a woman-owned business can prove that it is economically-disadvantaged.

Missouri
Council on Women's Economic Development & Training
1442 Aaron Court, Suite E
P.O. Box 1684
Jefferson City, MO 65102-1684
314-751-0810
Provides women-owned businesses with programs, seminars, and conferences.

Montana
DBE Program Specialist
Civil Rights Bureau
Montana Department of Highways
2701 Prospect Avenue
Helena, MT 59620
406-444-7906
The DBE Program Specialist is an individual specialized in disadvantaged- and women-owned businesses and is there to provide assistance to women-owned businesses in getting certified to bid on federal highway construction contracts.

New Jersey
Office of Women Business Enterprise
CN 835
Trenton, NJ 08625
609-292-3862
This office provides information to women interested in starting, expanding, or buying a company of their own.

New York
Division of Minority and Women's Business
Department of Economic Development
State Capitol, Room 235
Albany, NY 12224
518-474-1238
    or
1515 Broadway, 52nd Floor
New York, NY 10036

212-930-9000

This office provides consulting and technical assistance to minority- and women-owned businesses. Its main focus is on financial assistance, but also provides guidance in bidding for state and federal procurement contracts.

North Carolina
Minority Business Development Agency
430 N. Salisbury Street
Raleigh, NC 27611
919-571-4154

This office offers management workshops and seminars to women- and minority-owned businesses to inform, support, and assist in their problems.

Ohio
Minority Development Financing Commission
Ohio Department of Development
P.O. Box 1001
Columbus, OH 43266-0101
800-282-1085, 614-466-4945

Women can get all kinds of assistance with their business matters under the Women's Business Resource Program. All program services are free. This office publishes a directory of all women-owned businesses in Ohio called Ohio Women Business Leaders.

Oklahoma
Oklahoma Department of Commerce
Small Business Division
6601 Broadway Extension
Oklahoma City, OK 73116-8214
405-841-5227

Women can get a lot of different information under the Women-Owned Business Assistance Program such as information about business planning, marketing, technical issues, financing, and government procurement.

Oregon
Office of Minority, Women & Emerging Small Businesses
155 Cottage Street, NW
Salem, OR 97310
503-378-5651

Assists women-owned and small businesses that are disadvantaged in getting certified to participate in the state's procurement programs.

Pennsylvania
Bureau of Women's Business Development
Forum Building, Room 462
Harrisburg, PA 17120
717-787-3339

This office provides counseling, referrals, and other information to assist women in all of their business problems.

Rhode Island
Office of Minority Business Assistance
Department of Economic Development
7 Jackson Walkway
Providence, RI 02903
401-277-2601

This office assists women in becoming certified to participate in state and federal programs.

Tennessee
Office of Minority Business Enterprise
Department of Economic & Community Development
Rachel Jackson Building, 7th Floor
320 6th Avenue, North
Nashville, TN 37219-5308
800-342-8470, 615-741-2545

Information, referrals, procurement assistance, advocacy, and other services are offered to women and minority businesses.

Washington
Office of Minority and Women's Business Enterprises
406 S. Water St., MS FK-11
Olympia, WA 98504-4611
206-753-9653

This office assists women in becoming certified to participate in state programs that give certified individuals a 5% preference when bidding on procurement contracts.

Wisconsin
Women's Business Services
Department of Development
P.O. Box 7970
Madison, WI 53707
800-435-7287, 608-266-1018

This office helps women obtain information regarding the loan programs offered by the state and also keeps track of the top 10 women-owned businesses in the state.

Chapter 15
SELL YOUR
GOODS AND SERVICES
TO THE GOVERNMENT

The government purchases everything from toothbrushes to bombs from people, so why can't they buy things from you? All you need is to follow the 8 steps below and get yourself into the purchasing loop with a government contract.

Step I

When the federal government needs something, or rather when each department needs something, they place an order with the procurement office of that department. Many of these offices publish a guide called *Doing Business With The Department of* _____, that includes the office's procurement policies, procedures, and programs, a list of procurement offices, contact people, subcontracting opportunities, and a solicitation mailing list. There is also and office within each department called the Office Of Small and Disadvantaged Business Utilization, that its primary purpose is to encourage small businesses with government contracts. Another great source of information is the Small Business Administration Office in your state that can provide you with a listing of U.S. Government Procurement Offices.

Step II

After you have understood the process, you will next want to find out who is buying what and from whom is it being purchased, how much and when the transaction will occur. There are a few sources from where you can get this information listed below.

Daily Procurement News

Every weekday, a complete listing of products and services over $25,000 wanted by the government is published by *Commerce Business*

Daily (CBD). Each list includes the product or service wanted, a description, the name and address of the agency, deadlines for proposals, phone numbers for more specific information, and the solicitation number. The subscription rate is $208 per year and can be obtained by contacting the Superintendent of Documents, U.S. Government Printing Office, Washington, DC 20402, 202-783-3238.

Federal Procurement Data Center (FPDC)

Consolidated information about federal purchases is made available by this agency to assist you in determining how the government works, how much was spent last quarters on various goods and services, which departments made those purchases, and who the contractors were. The FPDC summarizes this information with two reports; The FPDC standard report is free and is basically a condensed form of over 60 federal agencies and their purchasing activities including charts and graphs that compare purchases by state, product, service codes, method of procurement, and contractors. It is a quarterly report and contains vital information of amounts spent on small, women-owned, and minority businesses. The FPDC special report is the second type of summary report and is prepared on request for a fee. These types of reports are designed to assist you in analyzing government procurement and data trends, locate competitors and federal markets for your goods and services. For more information, you can contact the Federal Procurement Data Center, General Services Administration, 7th and D Street, SW, Room 5652, Washington, DC 20407, 202-401-1529.

Other Contracts

If you are aiming for a contract of less than $25,000, you will be placed on a department's list for solicitation bids on the contracts. You can obtain a mailing list form from the Procurement Office, the Office of Small and Disadvantaged Business Utilization, or your local Small Business Association Office. Don't overlook this opportunity for such small purchases. Last year the government spent $18.7 billion dollars on them.

Step III - Subcontracting Opportunities

Sometimes a department's prime contract will require that the prime contractor utilize subcontracting opportunities, and all federal procurement offices or Offices of Small and Disadvantaged Business Utilization (SBDU) can provide you with a vast amount of information on subcontracting. Call your local Small Business Administration (SBA)

Office at 1-800-827-5722 for information about subcontracting and look for special publications provided by prime contractors that can assist you. The SBA has made agreements with thousands of prime contractors who in return cooperate with small firms. Many times it is a requirement by law that the SBA assure that prime contractors provide opportunities for subcontractors.

Step IV - Small Business Administration's 8 (a) Program

Black Americans, Hispanic Americans, Native Americans, and Asian Pacific Americans are sometimes socially or economically disadvantaged and at the same time own a business. The SBA 8 (a) program was designed to help these firms stay competitive in the marketplace. The program sometimes provides participating firms with procurement, marketing, financial, management, and technical assistance. If your firm participates, a Business Opportunity Specialist will be assigned to you to assist in locating assistance to help your firm reach its objectives. The SBA has a system called the Procurement Automated Source System (PASS) that puts your company online so that it is available to all government agencies and major corporations who may need your product or service. To apply for this program, you must attend an interview with an SBA field office representative in your area. Contact your local Small Business Administration for more information, or call 1-800-827-5722 for the SBA office nearest you.

Step V - Bond

If you plan on dealing with the government, sometimes a surety bond is required, especially if a construction contract is involved. The SBA can assist firms in obtaining surety bonds for contracts that do not exceed $1,250,000, and to qualify is dependent on the firm's capabilities and past performance. The SBA is authorized to guarantee as much as 90% of losses suffered by a surety resulting from a breach of the bond contract.

Step VI - Publications

To understand government contracts better, the Government Printing Office publishes several sources to assist you. To order any of the publications listed below, contact the Superintendent of Documents, Government Printing Office, Washington, DC 20402, 202-783-3238.

- U.S. Government Purchasing and Sales Directory - Cost $5.50. This directory is a listing of products and services purchased by the military civilian agencies with an explanation of the ways in which the SBA helps firms obtain government contracts.

- Guide to the Preparation of Offers for Selling to the Military - Cost $4.75.

- Small Business Specialists - Cost $3.75.

- Small Business Subcontracting Directory - Cost $ 7.00. Subcontracts available within the Department of Defense. The directory contains an alphabetical listing by state of the current Department of Defense prime contractors and their addresses.

- Women Business Owners;Selling to the Federal Government - Cost $3.75.

- Selling to the Military - Cost $8.00.

Step VII - What Is GSA?

The GSA is the General Services Administration and represents the government in directing and coordinating its purchases, sales, and services. The GSA gets its supply from private enterprise and provides the supply to all branches of the federal government. There are many activities that the GSA is responsible for including planning and managing lease contracts, purchases, or construction of buildings, buys and delivers goods and services, negotiates prices and terms of various contracts, and handles travel arrangements for its federal travelers. For a copy of Doing Business with the GSA, the GSA's Annual Report, or any other information regarding this agency, contact the Office of Publication, General Services Administration, 18th and F Streets, NW, Washington, DC 20405, 202-501-1235. Other information is available from the Office of Design and Construction, GSA, 18th and F Streets, NW, Washington, DC 20405, 202-501-1888. A booklet is also available, Guide to Specifications and Standards, by contacting the Specifications Sections, General Services Administration, 7th and D Streets, SW, Room 6654, Washington, DC 20407, 202-708-9205.

Step VIII - Bid And Contract Protests

Sometimes disputes may arise between agencies and bidders for government contracts, and so they are resolved by the General Accounting Office (GAO). A free publication titled, Bid Protests at GAO; A Descriptive Guide, explains the GAO's procedures on determining legal questions that may affect a bid for a government contract. For more information contact the Information Handling and Support Facilities, General

Accounting Office, Gaithersburg, MD 20877, 202-275-6241; For contract appeals, the GSA Board of Contract Appeals steps in to resolve these disputes between a contractor and the GSA, Department of Treasury, Education, Commerce, and other independent government agencies, as well as bid protests over automated data processing (ADP) contracts. Any contractor can appeal adverse decisions made by either Board to the U.S. Court of Appeals for the Federal Circuit. For more information, contact the Board of Contract Appeals, General Services Administration, 18th and F Streets, NW, Washington, DC 20405, 202-501-0720. Your government contract should specify which Board you should contact if a problem arises.

NOTES

_____

_____

_____

_____

_____

_____

_____

_____

_____

_____

_____

_____

_____

_____

> # Chapter 16
> # HELP FOR
> # SELLING GOODS
> # TO THE GOVERNMENT

o assist you in entering the federal procurement process, there are state offices that you can contact for information. One such office is the Small Business Administration (SBA), which can provide you with a list of Federal Procurement Offices in your own state. Your local Small Business Development Center (Economic Development) is also another good source of information because it is funded by both federal and state and is associated with the state university system. You may find that your state has an established program to help businesses learn about the bidding process, available resources, and all about how the procurement system operates. These offices are called Procurement Assistance Offices (PAOs) and can help you match your product or service to the appropriate agency. PAOs are partially funded by the Department of Defense in order to assist businesses with Defense Procurement. A current listing of PAOs is available by contacting:

Defense Logistics Agency
Office of Small and Disadvantaged Utilization
Building 3, Cameron Station
Alexandria, VA 22304
703-274-6471

Your Congressman Can Help You

If you encounter problems in the process of trying to get into the Federal Procurement process, your congressman can help. Because they want business to flourish in their own state, congressmen do their best to help companies obtain federal contracts. They can assist you often by sending a letter to accompany your bid or by requesting a review of your product if that is what you are trying to market, determining and resolving any problems, and can keep you informed on the status of your bid. Look in the phone book for your Senators' or Representatives' phone numbers or call them in Washington at 202-224-3121.

Small Business Set-Asides

If you own a small business, you are at an advantage because the Small Business Administration encourages government purchasing agencies to set-aside special opportunities for small business owners. These types of opportunities can be identified by a set-aside clause in the request for proposals or the invitation for bids. Getting on a bidders' list or checking the Commerce Business Daily can keep small businesses aware of their opportunities. For more information, contact your local Small Business Administration (To find the office nearest you, phone 1-800-827-5722), or your local Procurement Assistance Office.

Veterans Assistance

A Veterans Affairs Officer is available in each Small Business Administration District Office, and is there to assist veteran-owned businesses in obtaining government contracts. Keep in mind that although there are no set-aside clauses for veteran-owned businesses, the Veterans Administration does their best to fill its contracts with these businesses. For more information, contact your local SBA office.

Woman-Owned Business Assistance

A Women's Business Representative is available in each SBA District Office who can provide businesses owned by women with information regarding the government procurement process. Although current government policy requires government contracting officers to increase purchases from women-owned businesses, women must still be the lowest responsive and responsible bidders to win the contracts. A publication that is helpful to the woman who owns a business is Women Business Owners: Selling To The Federal Government. It provides information on the procurement opportunities available with the government. For more information contact your local SBA or PAO Office.

Minority And Labor Surplus Area Assistance

If you are a business owner who is socially or economically disadvantaged, the 8 (a) program was designed to assist your business to become independently competitive in the marketplace. Each business will be assigned a Business Opportunity Specialist to assist the firm in procurement, marketing, finances, and technical assistance. The SBA maintains the Procurement Automated Source System (PASS) that basically markets the firm's capabilities on-line so that all government agencies and major corporations may purchase products or services from these firms. To apply for this program, you must attend an interview with an SBA field office representative in your area. Contact your local Small Business Administration for more information, or call 1-800-827-5722 for the SBA office nearest you. There are set-aside clauses for labor-surplus areas and your local SBA Office can tell you if you live in such an area.

Alabama
University of Alabama at Birmingham
School of Business
Ms. Patricia E. Thompson
UAB Station
Birmingham, AL 35294
205-934-7260

Alaska
University of Alaska at Anchorage
Small Business Development Center
Ms. Jan Fredericks
430 West Seventh Avenue, Suite 110
Anchorage, AK 99501
907-274-7232

Arizona
Arizona Procurement Technical Assistance Network
Arizona Department of Commerce
Ms. Jenny L. James
3800 N. Central Avenue, Bldg. D
Phoenix, AZ 85012
602-280-1348

National Center for American Indian Enterprise Development
National Center Headquarters
Mr. Steve L.A. Stallings
953 E. Juanita Avenue
Mesa, AZ 85204
602-831-7524

Arkansas
Southern Arkansas University (SAU)
Mr. Robert E. Graham
P.O. Box 1239, Hwy 19 North

Magnolia, AR 71753
501-235-4375

California
Private Industry Council of Imperial County, Inc.
Ms. Martha Finnegan
1411 State Street
El Centro, CA 92243
619-353-5050

Tulare County Economic Development Corp.
Contract Procurement Center
Mr. Robert Jensen
2380 W. Whitendale Avenue
Visalia, CA 93278
209-627-0766

Colorado
Regents, University of Colorado BAC
Business Advancement Centers
Ms. Karen Eye
4700 Walnut, Suite 101
Boulder, CO 80301
303-444-5723

Connecticut
Small Business Development Center
University of Connecticut
West Hartford Campus
1800 Asylum Avenue
West Hartford, CT 06117
203-241-4986

Delaware
Development Office
99 Kings Highway
Dover, DE 19901
302-739-4271

Florida
University of West Florida
Florida Procurement Technical Assistance Program
Mr. Jerry Cartwright
11000 University Parkway, Bldg. 38

Pensacola, FL 32514
904-474-3016

Georgia
Columbus College
Division of Continuing Education
Dr. Edward Booth
Columbus, GA 31993-2399
404-568-2023

Georgia Tech Research Corporation
Georgia Institute of Technology
Mr. Charles P. Catlett
O'Keefe Building, Room 207
Atlanta, GA 30332
404-894-6121

Hawaii
State of Hawaii
Department of Business, Economic Development and Tourism
Mr. Larry Nelson
P.O. Box 2359
Honolulu, HI 96804
808-548-7736

Idaho
Business Network
Mr. Larry Demirelli
Department of Commerce
700 W. State Street
Boise, ID 83720
208-334-2470

Illinois
State of Illinois
Department of Commerce and Community Affairs
Mr. Mark Potrilli
620 East Adams, 6th Floor
Springfield, IL 62701
217-524-5696

Indiana
Indiana Institute for New Business Ventures
Government Marketing Assistance Group

Mr. A. David Schaff
One North Capitol, Suite 1275
Indianapolis, IN 46204-2026
317-232-8843

Iowa
State of Iowa
Iowa Department of Economic Development
Mr. Allen Williams
200 East Grand Avenue
Des Moines, IA 50309
515-242-4700

Iowa Procurement Outreach Center
c/o Kirkwood Community College
6301 Kirkwood Blvd. SW
Cedar Rapids, IA 52406
319-398-5665
800-458-4465

Kansas
Existing Industry Division
Department of Commerce
400 SW Eighth Street, 5th Floor
Topeka, KS 66612
913-296-5298

Kentucky
Kentucky Cabinet for Economic Development
Department of Existing Business and Industry
Mr. Bernard L. Williams
500 Mero Street
Capital Plaza Tower, 23rd Floor
Frankfort, KY 40601
800-626-2930

Louisiana
Jefferson Parish Economic Development Commission
The Bid Center
Ms. Phyllis McLaren
1221 Elmwood Park Blvd., Suite 405
Harahan, LA 70123
504-736-6550

Northwest Louisiana Government Procurement Center
Greater Shreveport Economic Development

Ms. Lisa M. Mucker
400 Edwards Street
Shreveport, LA 71120-0074
318-677-2530

Maine
Eastern Maine Development Corporation
Acadia Development Corporation
Mr. Richard L. Allen
One Cumberland Place, Suite 300
Bangor, ME 04401
207-942-6389
800-339-6389 (ME) or 800-955-6549

Maryland
Morgan State University
School of Business and Management
Dr. Otis Thomas
Cold Spring Lane and Hillen Road
Baltimore, MD 21239
301-444-3160

Massachusetts
Small Business Development Center
Metro Boston Regional Office
Boston College
95 College Road, Rahner House
Chestnut Hill, MA 02167
617-552-4091

Michigan
Technical Business Services
Department of Commerce
P.O. Box 30225
Lansing, MI 48909
517-335-2141

Wayne State University
Small Business Development Center
Dr. Raymond M. Genick
2727 Second Avenue
Detroit, MI 48201
313-577-4850

Minnesota
Minnesota Project Innovation Supercomputer Center
Mr. James W. Swiderski
1200 Washington Avenue, South, Suite M-100
Minneapolis, MN 55415
612-338-3280

Mississippi
Mississippi Contract Procurement Center
Mr. Charles W. Ryland
P.O. Box 610
Gulfport, MS 39502
601-864-2961

Central Mississippi Procurement Center
931 Highway 80W, #32
Jackson, MS 39204
601-352-0804

Missouri
Missouri Business Assistance Center
Department of Economic Development
P.O. Box 118
Jefferson City, MO 65102
800-523-1434

Montana
Fort Belknap Indian Community
Mr. James F. Ouldhouse
RR 1, Box 66
Harlem, MT 59526
406-353-2638

State of Montana
Department of Commerce
Mr. Greg DePuydt
1424 Ninth Avenue
Helena, MT 59620
406-444-2750

Nebraska
Nebraska Department of Economic Development
Existing Business Assistance Division
Mr. Jack Ruff
301 Centennial Mall So.
P.O. Box 94666

Lincoln, NE 68509-4666
402-471-3769

Nevada
State of Nevada
Commission on Economic Development
Mr. Ray Horner
Capitol Complex
Carson City, NV 89710
702-687-4325

New Hampshire
Small Business Development Center
University Center, Room 311
400 Commercial Street
Manchester, NH 03101
603-743-3995
800-322-0390 (In NH)

New Jersey
Elizabeth Development Corporation of New Jersey
Elizabeth Procurement Assistance Center
Mr. Arthur Myers
1045 East Jersey Street
P.O. Box 512
Elizabeth, NJ 07207-0512
908-289-0262

New Jersey Institute of Technology
Defense Procurement Technical Assistance Center
Mr. John Mckenna
240 Martin Luther King Blvd.
Newark, NJ 07102
201-596-3105

New Mexico
State of New Mexico
Procurement Assistance Program
Mr. J. Steve Griego
1100 St. Francis Drive, Room 2150
Santa Fe, NM 87503
505-827-0425

New York
Cattaraugus County
Department of Economic Development and Tourism
Mr. David K. Yarnes
303 Court Street
Little Valley, NY 14755
716-938-9111

New York State Department of Economic Development
Division of Small Business
Mr. Raymond R. Gillen
One Commerce Plaza
Albany, NY 12245
518-474-7756

North Carolina
University of North Carolina
Small Business and Technology Development Center
Mr. Scott R. Daugherty
4509 Creedmoor Road
Raleigh, NC 27612
919-571-4154

North Dakota
State Small Business Development Center Office
Economic Development Commission
Business Development Assistance Division
Liberty Memorial Building
Bismarck, ND 58505
701-224-2810

Ohio
Central State University
Developing Nations Center
Mr. James H. Sangster
Wilberforce, OH 45384
513-376-6660

University of Cincinnati
CECE-Extension Unit Small Business Center
Ms. Nancy Rogers
1111 Edison Drive, IAMS Building
Cincinnati, OH 45216
513-948-2082

Oklahoma
Oklahoma Department of Vocational-Technical Education
Business Assistance and Development Division
Ms. Denise Agee
1500 West Seventh Avenue
Stillwater, OK 74074-4364
405-743-5574

Tribal Government Institute
Mr. Marvin E. Stepson
111 N. Peters, Suite 200
Norman, OK 73069
405-329-3840

Oregon
State of Oregon
Economic Development Department
Mr. J. Rick Evans
775 Summer Street NE
Salme, OR 93710
503-888-2595

Pennsylvania
Economic Development Council of Northeastern Pennsylvania
Local Development District
Ms. Karen D. Ostroskie
1151 Oak Street
Pittston, PA 18640
717-655-5581

University of Pennsylvania, PASBDC
Snider Entrepreneurial Center
Nr. Paul A. Fickes
Philadelphia, PA 19104-6374
215-898-1282

Puerto Rico
Commonwealth of Puerto Rico (FOMENTO)
Economic Development Administration
Mr. Pedro J. Acevedo
355 Roosevelt Avenue
Hato Rey, PR 00936
809-753-6861

Rhode Island
Rhode Island Department of Economic Development
Business Development Office
Ms. Stephanie Morris
7 Jackson Walkway
Providence, RI 02903
401-277-2601

South Carolina
University of South Carolina
College of Business Administration
Small Business Development Center
Mr. John Lenti
Columbia, SC 29208
803-777-4907

South Dakota
South Dakota Procurement Technical Assistance Center
School of Business
Mr. Stephen L. Tracy
414 E. Clark
Vermillion, SD 57069
605-677-5498

Tennessee
University of Tennessee
Center for Industrial Services
Mr. T.C. Parsons
226 Capitol Boulevard Bldg., Suite 401
Nashville, TN 37219-1804
615-242-2456

Texas
Panhandle Regional Planning Commission
Economic Development Division
Ms. Perna N. Strickland
P.O. Box 9257
Amarillo, TX 79105-9257
806-372-3381

University of Texas at Arlington
Automation and Robotics Research Institute
Dr. D.H. Liles
P.O. Box 19125

Arlington, TX 76019
817-794-5902

Utah
Utah Department of Community and Economic Development
Utah Procurement Outreach Program
Mr. James F. Odle
324 South State Street, Suite 235
Salt Lake City, UT 84111
801-538-8791

Vermont
State of Vermont
Agency of Development and Community Affairs
Mr. William P. McGrath
109 State Street
Montpelier, VT 05609
802-828-3221

Virginia
George Mason University
Entrepreneurship Center
Dean John O'Malley
440 University Drive
Fairfax , VA 22030
703-993-5137

Southwest Virginia Community College
Ms. Maxine B. Rogers
P.O. Box SVCC
Richlands, VA 24641
703-964-7334

Washington
Economic Development Council of Snohomish County
Ms. C. Grace Brown
913 134th Street SW
Everett, WA 98204
206-743-4567

Spokane Area Economic Development Council
Local Business Assistance
Mr. Ken Olson
221 N. Wall, Suite 310

Spokane, WA 99210-0203
509-624-9285

West Virginia
Mid-Ohio Valley Regional Council
Procurement Technical Assistance Center
Mr. Terrence J. Tamburini
1200B Grand Central Avenue
Vienna, WV 26105
304-295-9312

Regional Contracting Assistance Center, Inc.
Mr. Mick Walker
1116 Smith Street, Suite 202
Charleston, WV 25301
304-344-2546

Wisconsin
Aspin Procurement Institute, Inc.
Mr. Mark F. Wagner
840 Lake Avenue
Racine, WI 53403
414-632-6321

Madison Area Technical College
Small Business Assistance Center
Ms. Wendy L. Lein
211 North Carroll Street
Madison, WI 53703
608-258-2330

Wyoming
Division of Economic Development
Government Marketing Assistance Program
Herschler Building
Cheyenne, WY 82002
307-777-7284

Also, contact the Office of Small and Disadvantaged Business Utilization (OSDBU) to obtain information about the business opportunities available within each government department. Listed below are additional federal departments and agencies.

ARMY CORPS OF ENGINEERS

Part civilian agency and part military agency, the Army Corps of Engineers offers such services as dam, port and water projects, trash and grass collection, real estate appraisal and dredging. The addresses of 10 Army Corps of Engineers offices are listed below.

Lower Mississippi Valley
P.O. Box 80
Vicksburg, MS 39180-0080
(601)634-7135

Missouri River
P.O. Box 103 Downtown Station
Omaha, NE 68101-0103
(402)221-7213

North Atlantic
90 Church St., Rm. 1215
New York, NY 10007-9998
(212)264-7532

North Central
536 South Clark St.
Chicago, IL 60605-1592
(312)353-6397

North Pacific
P.O. Box 2870
Portland, OR 97208-2870
(503)221-3797

Ohio River
P.O. Box 1159
Cincinnati, OH 45201-1159
(513)684-3049

Pacific Ocean
Bldg. 230
Ft. Shafter, HI 96858-5440
(808)438-2481

Southwestern
1114 Commerce St.
Dallas, TX 75242-0216

(214)767-2476

South Pacific
630 Sansome St., Room 1216
San Francisco, CA 94111-2206
(415)556-6998

DEPARTMENT OF AGRICULTURE

The U.S. Department of Agriculture (USDA), which has more than 200 U.S. offices, should have a local listing in your phone book. To receive the pamphlet, "Selling to the United States Department of Agriculture," write to a local USDA office or the main branch at:

USDA
Office of Operations and Finance,
Room 1575, South Building
Washington, DC 20250

Contact the USDA or USDA Office of Small and Disadvantaged Business Utilization to inquire about such USDA service needs as forestry, soil and animal research, road repair, painting, animal care and harbor repair.

DEPARTMENT OF ENERGY

To discover the research and development of energy services the government calls "transportation, guard services, supplies and materials, printing and reproduction, construction and design, material processing and applied research and development," contact the following address to obtain the booklet, "Doing Business with the Department of Energy."
Department of Energy
Technical Information Center
P.O. Box 62
Oak Ridge, TN 37830

DEPARTMENT OF HEALTH AND HUMAN SERVICES

Regional offices of the Department of Health and Human Services (DHHS) are located in Atlanta, Boston, Chicago, Dallas, Denver, Kansas City, New York, Philadelphia, San Francisco and Seattle. To receive the pamphlet, "Doing Business with the DHHS," contact a regional office or write:

Department of Health and Human Services
Division of Contract and Grant Operations

Office of the Secretary
200 Independence Ave., SW, Room 443H
Washington, DC 20201

DEPARTMENT OF HOUSING AND URBAN DEVELOPMENT

For information about furnishings and housing-related products needed by the government and a list of Housing and Urban Development (HUD) regional offices, ask for HUD Form 788 (called "Field Office Jurisdiction") at:

Department of Housing and Urban Development
Program Information Center, Room 1104
451 7th St., SW
Washington, DC 20410
(202)755-6420

DEPARTMENT OF INTERIOR

Contact the following address to inquire about the concessions offered private companies to open businesses on the nation's "public lands."

Concession Management Division
National Park Service
Department of the Interior
1100 L St., NW, Room 3209
Washington, DC 20006
(202)523-5322

NATIONAL PARK SERVICES

Private businesses can operate such services as "park maintenance, including garbage collection, janitor service and security, construction (including buildings, campgrounds, comfort stations, electrical systems, landscaping, parking lots, roads and trails), professional services and many supplies and equipment" on public lands. For more information regarding national park programs, contact:

Business Utilization and Development Specialist
18th and C Sts., NW
Washington, DC 20240
(202)343-5477

Other sectors of the Department of Interior also deal with business agencies. For information, contact:

Office of Public Affairs
Department of the Interior, Room 7211
C St., NW
Washington, DC 20240
(202)343-3171

DEPARTMENT OF STATE

For information about services required by the state department, including equipment maintenance, household goods and packing and storage, messenger and clerical tasks, numerous management needs in personnel, and financial and other administrative needs, contact the State Department Office of Small and Disadvantaged Business Utilization listed at the end of this section.

DEPARTMENT OF TRANSPORTATION

Agencies in the Department of Transportation needing services from the public include the Federal Aviation Administration, the Federal Highway Administration, the Maritime Administration, the Urban Transit Administration and the United States Coast Guard. To find out what the department offers, obtain a copy of "Contracting with the United States Department of Transportation," available from the department's Office of Small and Disadvantaged Business Utilization.

AGENCY FOR INTERNATIONAL DEVELOPMENT

Contracts and grants from this agency allow U.S. firms to export goods to more than 60 countries, including regions in Africa, Asia, Latin America and the Caribbean. "Agriculture, rural development, nutrition, family planning, health, education and human resources, energy, and science and technology" are areas for potential export. For specific information about federal export regulations, contact:
U.S. Agency for International Development,
OSDBU/MRC
Washington, DC 20523

U.S. POSTAL SERVICES

"Let's Do Business" is a pamphlet which explains several contracts offered through post-office programs. Services required by the postal department include "utilities, fuel, vehicle rental, vehicle maintenance, building repairs and services (cleaning, window cleaning, trash removal, snow removal and elevator maintenance) and minor construction requirements." For more information, contact:

Office of Contracts
Documents Processing Branch
Procurement and Supply Department
U.S. Postal Service
475 L'Enfant Plaza, SW
Washington, DC 20260-6232

Or, write to a local postal division:
Northeast Region-New York, NY 10098-0531

Central Region
433 West Buren St.
Chicago, IL 60699-0531

Eastern Region
1845 Walnut St.
Philadelphia, PA 19101-0531

Western Region
850 Cherry Ave.
San Bruno, CA 04900-0531

Southern Region
1407 Union Ave.
Memphis, TN 38166-0531

VETERANS ADMINISTRATION

Three publications, "Doing Business with the Veterans Administration," "Could You Use a Multibillion Dollar Customer?" and "Let's Do Business," are available from the Veterans Administration (VA) by contacting:
Office of Procurement and Supply
Veterans Administration
810 Vermont Ave., NW
Washington, DC 20420
(202)389-2935

For information on VA hospital and cemetery contracts, contact:
Director of the Office of Construction
Veterans Administration
810 Vermont Ave., NW
Washington, DC 20420
(202)389-2935

Chapter 17
DOING BUSINESS WITH THE GOVERNMENT

The federal government negotiates with many types of businesses. To obtain a copy of "Doing Business with the Federal Government," write:

General Services Administration
Office of Real Property, Room 4236
18th and F Sts.
Washington, DC 20405

Contact the General Services Administration (GSA) Business Service Center which covers your state of residence to find out how to sell your service or product to the federal government. While the government may ask you to fill out a Standard Form 129 to be placed on a specific mailing list, they are not demanding any permanent commitment to do business with them.

The GSA Business Service Centers assist in providing a market for your specific products and services or if your small business is "disadvantaged." In addition, the Small Business Administration (SBA) helps small businesses progress beyond their initial stages. When contacting the SBA, talk to the procurement representative and inquire about government contracts available to small businesses.

If you wish to receive daily information about government contracts, read the Commerce Business Daily. Once a government business opportunity is announced, you have at least 30 days to submit a bid.

GSA BUSINESS SERVICE CENTERS

I. District of Columbia and nearby
Maryland and Virginia
7th and D Sts., SW, Room 1050
Washington, DC 20407
(202)472-1804

II. Connecticut, Maine, Massachusetts,
New Hampshire, Rhode Island, Vermont
John W. McCormack Post Office and Courthouse
Boston, MA 02109
(617)223-2868

III. New Jersey, New York, Puerto Rico,
U.S. Virgin Islands
26 Federal Plaza
New York, NY 10278
(212)264-1234

IV. Delaware, Pennsylvania, Maryland,
Virginia, West Virginia
9th and Market Sts., Room 5151
Philadelphia, PA 19107
(215)597-9613

V. Alabama, Florida, Georgia, Kentucky,
Mississippi, North Carolina, South
Carolina, Tennessee
Richard B. Russell Federal Bldg.
and Courthouse
75 Spring St.
Atlanta, GA 30303
(312)353-5383

VI. Illinois, Indiana, Michigan, Minnesota,
Ohio, Wisconsin
230 S. Dearborn St.
Chicago, IL 60604
(312)353-5383

VII. Iowa, Kansas, Missouri, Nebraska
1500 East Bannister Rd.
Kansas City, MO 64131
(816)926-7203

VIII. Arkansas, Louisiana, New Mexico,
Oklahoma, Texas
819 Taylor St.
Fort Worth, TX 76102
(817)334-3284

IX. Colorado, Montana, North Dakota, South Dakota, Utah, Wyoming
Denver Federal Center, Building 41
Denver, CO 80225
(303)236-7409

X. Hawaii, Nevada (except Clark County), Northern California
525 Market St.
San Francisco, CA 94105
(415)974-9000

XI. Arizona, Los Angeles, Clark County, Nevada, Southern California
300 North Los Angeles St.
Los Angeles, CA 90012
(213)894-3210

XII. Alaska, Idaho, Oregon, Washington
440 Federal Building
915 Second Ave.
Seattle, WA 98174
(206)442-5556

Alabama
Birmingham: (205)254-1755
Mobile: (205)690-2371
Montgomery: (205)(832-7310)

Arizona
Phoenix: (602)261-3294
Tucson: (602)792-6301

California
Fresno: (209)487-5069
Sacramento: (916)440-3171

San Diego: (619)293-6640

Colorado
Colorado Springs: (303)635-8911

Connecticut
Hartford: (203)244-3540
Delaware
Wilmington: (302)573-6364

Florida
Jacksonville: (904)791-2791
Miami: (305)350-5751
Tampa: (813)228-2351

Georgia
Savannah: (912)744-4208
Thomasville: (912)226-2716

Hawaii
Honolulu: (808)546-7516

Idaho
Boise: (208)384-1242

Illinois
Springfield: (217)525-4270

Indiana
Indianapolis: (317)269-6234

Iowa
Des Moines: (515)284-4114

Kansas
Topeka: (913)295-2516

Kentucky
Covington: (513)684-1393
Louisville: (502)582-6436

Maine
Augusta: (207)622-6171 ext. 252

Maryland
Baltimore: (301)962-7611

Massachusetts
Andover: (617)681-5504

Michigan
Detroit: (313)226-4910

Minnesota
St. Paul (Ft. Snelling): (612)725-4015

Mississippi
Jackson: (601)960-4449
Tupelo: (601)842-0613

Montana
Billings: (406)449-5285
Helena: (406)449-5285
Missoula: (406)329-3117

Nevada
Las Vegas: (702)385-6444
Reno: (702)784-5302

New Hampshire
Manchester: (603)666-7581

New Jersey
Newark: (201)645-2416
Trenton: (609)989-2082

New York
Albany: (518)472-5447
Brooklyn (NYC): (212)330-7474
Buffalo: (716)846-4588
Plattsburg: (518)563-0860
Rochester: (716)263-6288
Syracuse: (315)423-5424

North Carolina
Asheville: (704)258-2850
Raleigh: (919)755-4680

North Dakota
Bismarck: (701)255-4011 ext. 4316
Fargo: (701)237-5771 ext. 5453

Ohio
Cincinnati: (513)684-2306
Cleveland: (216)522-4220
Columbus: (614)469-6824

Oregon
Eugene: (503)687-6640

Pennsylvania
Erie: (814)452-2903
Harrisburg: (717)782-4457
Pittsburgh: (412)644-3340
Wilkes-Barre: (717)826-6331

Puerto Rico
Hato Rey: (809)753-4370

Rhode Island
Providence: (401)528-4492

South Carolina

Columbia: (803)765-5581

South Dakota
Aberdeen: (605)225-0250 ext. 301
Pierre: (605)224-5852

Tennessee
Memphis: (901)521-3675
Nashville: (615)251-5221

Utah
Ogden: (801)625-6764

Executive Office of the President
Director, OSDBU
Washington, DC 20503
(202)395-3314

Department of Agriculture
Director, OSDBU, Room 127W
Washington, DC 20250
(202)447-7117

Department of Commerce
Director, OSDBU, Room 6411
Washington, DC 20230

Department of Defense
Director, OSDBU, Room 2A340
Washington, DC 20307
(202)694-1151

Defense Logistics Agency Director, OSDBU, Room 4B110
Alexandria, VA 22304-6100
(703)274-6471

OFFICE OF SMALL AND DISADVANTAGED BUSINESS UTILIZATION

Department of the Air Force
Director, OSDBU, Room 4C255
Washington, DC 20330-5040
(202)697-4126

Department of the Army
Director OSDBU, Room 2A712
Washington, DC 20301
(202)695-9800

Department of the Navy
Director, OSDBU, Room 604
Crystal Plaza, Bldg. 6
Washington, DC 20360
(202)692-7122

Department of Education
Director, OSDBU, Room 2141
Washington, DC 20202
(202)245-9582

Department of Energy
Director, OSDBU, Room 2141
Washington, DC 20585
(202)252-8201

Department of Health and Human Services
Director, OSDBU, Room 513D
Washington, DC 20201
(202)245-7300

Department of Housing & Urban Development
Director, OSDBU, Room 10226
Washington, DC 20240
(202)755-1428

Department of the Interior
Director, OSDBU, Room 748, HOLC Bldg.
Washington, DC 20530
(202)724-6271

Department of State
Director, OSDBU, Room 513 (SA-6)
Washington, DC 20520
(202)235-9579

Department of Transportation
Director, OSDBU, Room 10222
Washington, DC 20590
(202)426-1930

Department of the Treasury
Director, OSDBU, Room 127W
Washington, DC 20520
(202)447-7117

Agency for International Development
Director OSDBU, Room 648 SA14
Rosslyn, VA 22209
(703)235-1720

Environmental Protection Agency
Director, OSDBU, Room 1108
CM No. 2 Code A149C
Washington, DC 20460
(202)557-7777

Export-Import Bank of the United States
Director, OSDBU, Room 1031
Washington, DC 20571
(202)566-8111

Federal Home Loan Bank Board
Director, OSDBU, Room G-3, 4th Floor
Washington, DC 20552
(202)377-6245

Federal Trade Commission
Director, OSDBU, room 850
Washington, DC 20580
(202)523-5552

General Services Administration
Director, OSDBU, Room 6017
Washington, DC 20405
(202)566-1021

National Aeronautics Administration
Director, OSDBU, Headquarters, Coke K
Washington, DC 20504
(202)453-2088

National Credit Union Administration
Director, OSDBU
1776 G St., NW, Room 6630
Washington, DC 20456
(202)357-1025

National Science Foundation
Director, OSDBU
1800 G St., NW, Room 511A
Washington, DC 20550
(202)357-5000

Nuclear Regulatory Commission
Director, OSDBU
Maryland National Bank Bldg., Room 7217
Washington, DC 20555
(202)492-4665

Railroad Retirement Board
Director, OSDBU
844 North Rush St., Room 1230
Chicago, IL 60611
(312)751-4565

Tennessee Valley Authority
Director, OSDBU
1000 Commerce Union Bank Bldg.
Chattanooga, TN 37401
(615)751-2624

U.S. Information Agency
Director, OSDBU
400 6th St., SW, Room 1719
Washington, DC 20457

U.S. Postal Service
Director, OSDBU
475 L'Enfant Plaza West, SW, Room 1340
Washington, DC 20260-6201
(202)268-4633

Veterans Administration
Director, OSDBU
810 Vermont Ave., NW, Room 005C
Washington, DC 20420
(202)376-69962

Chapter 18
FEDERAL GOVERNMENT AUCTIONS

U ncle Sam has a secret that most people don't know about because, of course, he doesn't advertise it. But, you can get great bargains on everything from animals and rugs to businesses and other properties. Lots of agencies within the federal government, such as the IRS and the U.S. Postal Service, sell merchandise that has been seized, unclaimed, or has become obsolete. To get your share, write to the various agencies listed below to see what they are currently offering at their auctions.

Burros And Horses: Bureau Of Land Management

Division of Public Affairs
Bureau of Land Management
U.S. Department of the Interior
Room 5600, 18th & C Streets, NW
Washington, DC 20240
Wild Horse and Burros Program Office
202-208-5717 or 202-653-9215

You can purchase a wild horse for $125 or a burro for $75. Its under the "Adopt-A-Horse" program that is aimed at keeping wild herds of these animals under control. You also need to pay shipping for the animals that usually have all of their shots. Individuals living west of the Mississippi, should contact the Program Office above to find out which of the 12 satellites they are closest to. Individuals who live east of the Mississippi should call 703-461-1365 for information on adoption. To adopt one of these beautiful animals, you must have proper shelter for the animal, be of legal age in your state, and have no prior offenses against animals. You will not receive title of ownership of the animal until one year after adoption. This is to ensure that the animal is not used for exploitive purposes. Contact the office above for more information.

FHA Money May Be Waiting For You

DHUD-Distributive Shares Division
541 7th Street, SW
Washington, DC 20410
HUD Locator
DHUD-Insurance Operation Division
202-708-1422
703-235-8117

You may be receiving a "Mutual Mortgage Dividend" check if you have paid off the mortgage on your home. Every year, the FHA estimates how many people will default on their mortgages and, based on that estimate, calculates how much mortgage insurance home buyers will purchase. If the estimate was more than the actual outcome of loan defaults, you will receive a check for money that is owed to you. Call 703-235-8117 for more information if you think you are due an insurance premium refund or distributive share.

You may also qualify for a refund check if you have paid the entire FHA insurance premium on your mortgage, up front, instead of in installments. You must however, carry a loan for at least 7 years to qualify for a check. Your lender should tell you, if you have paid your insurance premium up front, if you are eligible to receive a Mutual Mortgage Dividend check upon fulfillment of the mortgage agreement. When you are finished paying off your loan agreement, the bank should notify the HUD of this, which in turn will notify you if you have a refund coming.

Be careful of "bounty hunters" who claim that they can locate the money from HUD for you, when all it takes is a phone call. They may charge you up to 50% of the refund amount, that can be several thousands of dollars, that you can locate yourself. Just call 703-235-8117 for a list of individuals who are due a refund check. That is exactly what these bounty hunters do. By contacting this number, you will receive a free information package with a list of mortgagors in your state and the necessary forms to apply for the refund. You will need the loan number and an FHA case number (From the Recorded Deed Of Purchase) to apply for your refund. Good luck!

Chapter 19
INEXPENSIVE CRIME INSURANCE FROM THE GOVERNMENT

f you reside in one of the following states with expensive theft insurance, the federal government will insure your home or business against theft. Call the Federal Crime Insurance program at (800)638-8780 if your state of residence is not on the list.

Alabama, Arkansas, California, Colorado, Connecticut, Delaware, the District of Columbia, Florida, Georgia, Illinois, Iowa, Kansas, Louisiana, Maryland, Massachusetts, Missouri, New Jersey, New York, North Carolina, Ohio, Pennsylvania, Puerto Rico, Rhode Island, Tennessee, Virgin Islands or Virginia.

To receive an application for this two-part program (one for business insurance against burglary and robbery and, two, for home insurance), contact:

Federal Crime Insurance Program
P.O. Box 6301
Rockville, Maryland 20850
(800)638-8780

RESIDENTIAL COVERAGE

This insurance policy, which can be purchased for $1,000, $3,000, $5,000, $7,000 or $10,000, protects your home against robbery and burglary.

To qualify for this insurance, your home must have dead bolt or dead-latch locks on all windows and doors.

While there is a $100 or 5 percent deductible on the insurance policy, the government will recover up to $1500 for lost jewelry, gold, silver, furs, arts, antiques, coin and stamp collections and up to $200 for lost cash. Every other item will be covered, up to the amount of your policy.

Contact the police and your insurance company if you are robbed, or call the government toll-free at (800)526-2662. The following are yearly premiums for home or apartment coverage.

BUSINESS INSURANCE

Business insurance can cover either a robbery or burglary, or both. Commercial insurance can include every $1,000, from $1,000 to $15,000.

The premiums for business coverage vary according to the class of business, company income, and the amount and type of insurance coverage. Businesses are grouped into six classes, depending on the type of operation. A business can receive both burglary and robbery coverage by adding the premiums of the two types and subtracting 10 percent from the total. Order the Federal Crime Insurance Program's "Commercial Coverage Rate Tables" by calling toll-free (800)638-8780 or writing:

Federal Crime Insurance Program
P.O. Box 6301
Rockville, Maryland 20850

As with a residence, your business must have all windows, doors and openings securely locked to be eligible for this insurance policy. In addition, up to a 40- percent insurance discount can be obtained by installing burglar alarms in your business offices.

When applying for this insurance policy, your business will be thoroughly inspected for proper maintenance. If the building is not satisfactory, you will be given a certain date to meet the required standards. You may obtain an "exception" if meeting every standard is too expensive or unreasonable.

If the company's receipts are less than $300,000, the insurance policy deductible will be $250 or five percent, whichever is greater. If the business's income is between $300,000 to $499,999, the deductible is $350 or five percent, whichever is higher. If the company's earnings are over $500,000, the deductible is $500 or five percent, whichever is more.

Chapter 20
FEDERAL MONEY
FOR YOUR BUSINESS

The following is a descriptive list of the various money sources for small businesses, entrepreneurs, inventors, and researchers. This partial listing was obtained from the "Catalog of Federal Domestic Assistance," published by the U.S. Government Printing Office in Washington, D.C. The number listed next to the title description is the official government reference for the program. Contact the address listed below for further details. The following types of assistance are available;

LOANS: Money borrowed from a federal agency for a specific period of time with the expectation of repayment.

LOAN GUARANTEES: If the borrower of a loan defaults on repayment to a private lender, then the federal agency agrees to pay back part or all of that loan.

GRANTS: Money given for a fixed period of time by a federal agency without repayment.

DIRECT PAYMENTS: Funds that are given to individuals or businesses for restricted or unrestricted use.

INSURANCE: Coverage that assures reimbursement in the case of losses sustained.

- Economic Injury Disaster Loans (EIDL) - 59.002
    Office of Disaster Assistance
    Small Business Administration
    409 3rd Street SW
    Washington, DC 20416
    202-502-6734

Assistance provided for business concerns that have suffered economic injury because of specific Presidential, SBA, or Department of Agriculture disaster declarations. Loans available. Estimated annual funds available = $60,000,000.

- Loans For Small Business (Business Loans 7(a)(11)) - 59.003
Director
Loan Policy and Procedures Branch
Small Business Administration
409 3rd Street SW
Washington, DC 20416
202-205-6570

Assistance provided for small businesses owned by low-income persons or small businesses located in high unemployment areas. Loans and Loan Guarantees available. Estimated annual funds available = $17,000,000.

- Physical Disaster Loans (7(b) Loans (DL)) - 59.008
Office of Disaster Assistance
Small Business Administration
409 3rd Street SW
Washington, DC 20416
202-205-6734

Assistance provided to victims of designated physical-type disasters for uninsured loans. Loans and Loan Guarantees available. Estimated annual funds available = $ 290,000,000.

- Veterans Loan Program (Veterans Loans) - 59.038
Director
Loan Policy and Procedures Branch
Small Business Administration
409 3rd Street SW
Washington, DC 20416
202-205-6570

Assistance provided for small businesses owned by Vietnam-era and disabled veterans. Loans available. Estimated annual funds available = $17,000,000.

- Small Business Innovation Research (SBIR Program) - 10.212
SBIR Coordinator
Office of Grants & Program Systems

Cooperative State Research Service
Department of Agriculture
Room 323, Aerospace Building
14th & Independence SW
Washington, DC 20250-2200
202-401-6852

Assistance provided to stimulate technological innovation in the private-sector, strengthen small businesses in meeting Federal research and development needs, and to increase minority and disadvantaged participation in technological innovation. Grants available. Estimated annual funds available = $4,887,045.

- Farm Operating Loans - 10.406
Director
Farmer Programs Loan Making Division
Farmers Home Administration
Department of Agriculture
Washington, DC 20250
202-382-1632

Assistance provided to enable operators of family farms to make efficient use of their resources. Loan Guarantees available. Estimated annual funds available = $ 3,498,109,000.

- Farm Ownership Loans - 10.407
Administrator
Farmers Home Administration
Department of Agriculture
Washington, DC 20250
202-382-1632

Assistance provided to farmers, ranchers, and aquaculture operators to become owner-operators of not larger than family farms. Loans and Loan Guarantees available. Estimated annual funds available = $ 1,081,500,000.

- Industrial Development Grants (IDG) - 10.424
Director
Community Facilities Loan Division
Farmers Home Administration
Department of Agriculture
Washington, DC 20250
202-382-1490

Assistance provided to facilitate the development of private, small businesses for improving the economy in rural communities. Grants available. Estimated annual funds available = $20,750,000.

- Minority Business Development Centers (MBDC) - 11.800
Assistant Director
Office of Program Development
Room 5096, Minority Business Agency
Department of Commerce
14th & Constitution Ave NW
Washington, DC 20230
202-377-5770

Assistance provided to minority firms and individuals interested in entering or expanding their interests in business. Grants available. Estimated annual funds available = $25,437,000.

- American Indian Program (AIP) - 11.801
Assistant Director
Office of Program Development
Room 5096, Minority Business Development Agency
Department of Commerce
14th & Constitution Ave NW
Washington, DC 20230
202-377-5770

Assistance provided to American Indians and individuals interested in entering or expanding their interests in business. Grants available. Estimated annual funds available = $1,495,000.

- Mortgage Insurance-Hospitals (242 Hospitals) - 14.128
Insurance Division
Office of Insured Multifamily Housing Development
Department of Health and Human Services
Washington, DC 20410
202-708-3000

Assistance provided for the financing of hospitals. Loan Guarantees available. Estimated annual funds available = $388,234,000.

- Rent Supplements - Rental Housing For Lower Income Families - 14.149
Chief
Program Support Branch

Office of Multi-Family Housing Management
Department of Health and Human Services
Washington, DC 20410
202-708-2654

Assistance provided to low-income families who require good quality rental housing at a cost they can afford. Direct Payments Available. Estimated annual funds available = $51,957,000.

GET FREE HELP WITH YOUR TAXES

Contact a regional Internal Revenue Service branch to receive assistance in filling out your tax return.

Community Outreach Tax Help

This program offers seminars to inform the public about tax laws and rules.

Small Business Tax Workshops

These programs educate the small businessman about all the tax laws and rules which apply to him.

Student Tax Clinics

Check with a local Internal Revenue Service agent or business college to receive free income-tax return information and assistance from experienced law and accounting students.

Tax Counseling for Senior Citizens

Government subsidies allow local organizations to offer free tax help to citizens at least 60 years of age through a program called, "Tax Counseling for the Elderly." Contact a local IRS office for further details.

Volunteer Income Tax Assistance

This government program offers free tax advice to elderly, handicapped, non-English speaking and underfinanced citizens. For additional information, contact:

Taxpayer Information and Education Branch
Taxpayer Service Division
Internal Revenue Service
Department of the Treasury

The Department of Labor provides grants, training programs and information to help you find a new job. For details, call a local job information service office listed in the state or federal government section of your phone book.

In addition, the government offers the following programs to help you search and train for a job.

ADULT EDUCATION FOR WOMEN
A booklet entitled, "How to Get Credit for What You Know: Alternative Routes to Educational Credit," explains how working women with children can attend college part-time or at home. For information, contact:

Women's Bureau, Department of Labor
200 Constitution Avenue, NW, Room S3005
Washington, DC 2021
(202)523-6668

NOTES

_____

_____

_____

_____

_____

_____

_____

_____

Chapter 21
LET THE GOVERNMENT HELP YOU FIND A JOB

APPRENTICESHIP PROGRAMS

For details on working with veterans and members of the military, contact:

Bureau of Apprenticeship and Training
Employment and Training Administration
Department of Labor
601 D St., NW, Room 6308
Washington, DC 20213
(202)376-2570

EMPLOYMENT AND TRAINING ASSISTANCE

To find out information on employee training programs, contact:

Employment and Training Administration
Department of Labor
601 D Street, NW
Washington, DC 20213
(202)376-6093

JOB CORPS

Students ages 16-21 receive room and board, supplies and money, and job counseling when they join the Job Corps. They learn such skills as machine and large equipment operation, car repair and mechanics, painting, carpentry and test-taking. For information, contact:

Employment and Training Administration

Department of Labor
601 D Street, NW, Room 6414
Washington, DC 20213
(202)376-7139

JOB INFORMATION SERVICE

This information is provided by your local Job Service center listed in the U.S. government offices section of your phone book. Or, you can contact:

Division of Planning and Operations
Office of Program Services
Employment and Training Administration
Department of Labor

OFFICES OF SMALL AND DISADVANTAGED BUSINESS UTILIZATION

601 D Street, NW, Room 8028
Washington, DC 20213
(202)376-6185

JOB PROTECTION

Special government protections for workers include employee rights, pension programs, retraining programs and others. Transit, hospital, railroad and airport employees, among others, are covered by these protection laws. For details, contact:

Division of Employee Protections
Bureau of Labor-Management Services and Cooperative Programs
Department of Labor
200 Constitution Ave., NW, Room N5639
Washington, DC 20210
(202)523-6495

JOB SERVICE

For information about Job Service centers listed under "government offices" in your phone book, contact:

Employment Service Office
Employment and Training Administration
Department of Labor
601 D Street, NW, Room 8100
Washington, DC 20213
(202)376-6750

JOB TRAINING PROGRAMS

Contact the following address to obtain job training information available through the government:

National Commission for Employment Policy
1522 K Street, NW, Room 300
Washington, DC
(202)724-1550

VETERANS TRAINING PROGRAMS

Outreach Program for Disabled and Other Veterans

For details on state job assistance for all veterans, contact:

Veterans Employment and Training Service
Office of the Assistant Secretary for Veterans Employment and Training
Department of Labor, Room S-1316
200 Constitution Ave., NW
Washington, DC 20210
(202)523-9110

PART-TIME WORK FOR SENIORS

The Senior Community Service Employment Program provides part-time jobs to seniors 55 years or older. For information, contact:

Division of Older Worker Programs
Employment and Training Administration
Department of Labor
601 D Street, NW
Washington, DC 20213
(202)376-7287

WORK INCENTIVES

For details on this program that helps families with children find jobs, contact:

Office of Work Incentive Programs
Employment and Training Administration
Department of Labor
601 D Street, NW, Room 8028
Washington, DC 20213
(202)3376-6890

For a complete list of job publications released by the Department of Labor, contact:

Superintendent of Documents
United States Government Printing Office
Washington, DC 20402
(202)783-3238

COMPARISON OF PAY AT DIFFERENT JOBS

"Profiles of Occupational Pay" is a publication comparing the pay rates of similar jobs throughout the country. It may be obtained by contacting:

Office of Publications
Bureau of Labor Statistics
Department of Labor
441 G Street, NW, Room 2029
Washington, DC 20212
(202)523-1239

Chapter 22
VALUABLE GOVERNMENT PUBLICATIONS

DICTIONARY OF OCCUPATIONAL TITLES

This publication lists skills and requirements needed for more than 25,000 different jobs. It can be purchased for about $25 or checked out from any public library. Another book, "Selected Characteristics of Occupations," explains the physical requirements of certain jobs.

Exploring Careers

"Exploring Careers," a book detailing career opportunities for junior high and high school students, can be obtained by contacting:

Superintendent of Documents
Government Printing Office
Washington, DC 20402
(202)783-3238

HOW TO FIND A SUMMER JOB

To receive this free publication, contact:

Employment Service
Employment and Training Administration
Department of Labor
601 D Street, NW, Room 8100
Washington, DC 20213
(202)376-6750

JOB REQUIREMENTS

These government studies reveal the experience and knowledge needed to obtain a job in more than 150 different fields. For information, contact:
Office of Economic Growth
Bureau of Labor Statistics

Department of Labor
601 D Street, NW, Room 4000
Washington, DC 20213
(202)272-5381

Labor Market Information
For details on job availability and employment throughout the country, contact:

Division of Labor Market Information
Office of Policy Evaluation and Research
Employment and Training Administration
Department of Labor
601 D Street, NW, Room 9304
Washington, DC 20213
(202)376-6263

Occupational Outlook
The books "Occupational Outlook" and "Occupational Outlook for College Graduates" can be obtained by contacting:

Superintendent of Documents
Government Printing Office
Washington, DC 20402
(202)783-3238

DISABILITY INSURANCE
Disabled persons who are unable to work may be eligible for up to $1,400 per month in government benefits. For more information, contact a local social security office or:

Social Security Administration, Room 4100, Annex
6401 Security Blvd.
Baltimore, MD 21235
(301)592-3000

BENEFITS FOR PERSONS 72 YEARS AND OLDER
Contact the above address to find out if seniors who were formerly without social security protection are eligible to receive as much as $138 per month in social security benefits.

Chapter 23
SOCIAL SECURITY PROGRAMS AND BENEFITS

RETIREMENT INSURANCE

Contact a local social security office listed in your phone book for information on how direct retirement payments as high as $1,000 per month may be obtained.

SURVIVORS INSURANCE

Upon the death of a principal money maker in a family, contact a local social security office to discover how survivors insurance can be obtained.

"BLACK LUNG BENEFITS"

Disabled coal miners suffering from lung disease can receive up to $609 per month in "black lung" benefits. Their disabled dependents also are eligible for this program.

SUPPLEMENTAL SOCIAL SECURITY

This program provides benefits up to $169 per month to help disabled persons 65 years and older who receive limited government subsidies

The Farmers Home Administration (FmHA) provides valuable benefits to farmers and non-farming country dwellers who want to purchase homes.

MONEY FOR RENTING

The FmHA will pay your rent if (1) you earn less than $25,000 per year and reside outside a city, and if (2) you live in a rural area and forfeit more than 25 percent of your income toward rent. To find out your eligibility status, contact:

Administrator, Farmers Home Administration
Department of Agriculture
Washington, DC 20250
(202)447-7967

LITTLE-KNOWN
SOCIAL SECURITY BENEFITS

SOCIAL SECURITY AND EDUCATION

Students are eligible for social security benefits until: (1) they graduate from high school; or (2) they reach the age of 19 plus one month. To be eligible a student must be enrolled full time at a high school, trade school or college.

Go to a nearby social security office with your social security card and pertinent enrollment information to apply. If you marry, turn 22, drop out of school or fail to meet the minimum attendance requirements, your benefits will stop. You must periodically ask the school attendance office or admission and records office to fill out a form to prove your continuing enrollment. In addition, find out from the social security office if your benefits may be reduced or eliminated through employment.

SOCIAL SECURITY AND THE DISABLED

To receive disability payments, doctors must conclude that you have been unable to do any substantial work for the past 12 months or more. However, those who are blind (with vision worse than 20/200) should contact a local social security office to find out if they are exempt from these rules.

BENEFITS FOR THE SPOUSE OF DISABLED PERSONS

Disabled widows and widowers can receive social security checks if they have been unable to do any meaningful work for the previous 12 months or more.

SOCIAL SECURITY FOR DISABLED PERSONS UNDER AGE 22

Disabled children under 22 receive social security checks based on: (1) the income of their parents; (2) whether their parents receive social security benefits; and (3) whether their parents have died.

BENEFITS BEFORE AGE 65

If you have paid a large amount in social security taxes, you may receive retirement checks by age 62. You may work while receiving these checks, but your benefits will be reduced. Once you are 70, however, these checks will not be reduced or stopped regardless of employment income.

Chapter 24
MONEY FOR NON-FARMERS FROM THE FARMERS HOME ADMINISTRATION

MONEY FOR SAVING FUEL

The FmHA can weatherize your home if (1) you reside in a rural town of no more than 20,000 people; (2) your electricity originates from a rural co-operative; and (3) you make less than $15,000 per year.

Contact a local Rural Electric office to arrange the service. They will add slightly to your electric bill to pay for your $500 to $1,500 loan. The loan can be used to insulate, weather strip and install storm doors and windows in your house.

FARM LOANS

Two notable programs the FmHA offers farmers are the Economic Emergency Loan program and the farm ownership loan.

The emergency loan program provides up to $400,000 to assist framers and ranchers who are unable to obtain farm credit. For additional information on emergency loans, contact:

Administrator of the Farmers Home Administration
U.S. Department of Agriculture
Washington, DC 20250

Farm ownership loans are for low-income individuals who hope to successfully operate small or family-oriented farms. For more information, contact:

Farmers Home Administration
U.S. Department of Agriculture
Washington, DC 20520

HELP FOR THE UNEMPLOYED

The U.S. Department of Labor's Trade Adjustment Assistance Program provides compensation for those who have been laid off from their jobs because of excessive imports. Contact a local union representative to determine if your company has applied for assistance. Even if you were laid off from a certified company and currently receive unemployment benefits, visit a nearby state unemployment office and ask to fill out a petition for Trade Adjustment Assistance.

If your unemployment benefits have expired and you are still without work, many options are available.

First, a local unemployment office should help you find a job if your company is under a TAA program because it was affected by imports. Second, the state government pays to retrain you for a new job in your area. Third, state and federal governments may offer up to $800 in living expenses if you are forced to relocate to find a new job. Fourth, the government will pay 90 percent of your moving expenses when this occurs. Fifth, the government will provide a lump sum of $800 upon your move.

Before you receive any compensation, you must prove to the local unemployment office that you were laid off.

TRA benefits, like TAA programs, are offered to laid-off individuals employed by companies adversely affected by imports. In addition, your unemployment benefits must have expired to become eligible. TRA benefits are essentially an extension of unemployment benefits.
Nevertheless, apply for re-employment services, training, job search allowance, relocation allowance and the job search program even if you fail to qualify.

If the government determines that your company has not been affected by imports, inquire at your local union about appealing the decision. You have 60 days to complete the appeal.

For more information from the government, contact:
Office of Trade Adjustment Assistance,
Employment and Training Administration
U.S. Department of Labor
601 D Street, NW, Room 6434
Washington, DC 20213
(203)376-6896

In addition, the State Employment Security Agency may be able to answer your questions. The 10 regional employment and training administration offices are listed below.

Region 1
John F. Kennedy Building
Room 1700-C
Boston, MA 02203
(617)223-4684

Region 2
1515 Broadway, Room 3612
New York, NY 10036
(212)944-2990

Region 3
3535 Market St., Room 12220
Philadelphia, PA 19104
(215)596-6301

Region 4
1371 Peachtree St., NE, Room 632
Atlanta, GA 30309
(404)881-3178

Region 5
230 S. Dearborn St., 5th Floor
Chicago, IL 60604
(312)353-0313

Region 6
555 Griffin Square Building, Suite 403
Dallas, TX 75202
(214)767-2567

Region 7
Federal Office Building
911 Walnut St., Room 1100
Kansas City, MO 64106
(816)374-3661

Region 8
Federal Building

1961 Stout St., Room 1680
Denver, CO 80202

Region 9
450 Golden Gate Ave., Room 9477
San Francisco, CA 94102
(415)556-8545

Region 10
Federal Office Building, Room 1131
909 First Ave.
Seattle, WA 98174
(206)442-1133

NOTES

_____

_____

_____

_____

_____

_____

_____

_____

Chapter 25
HOUSING
GRANTS & LOANS

T he following HUD programs assist the buyer in receiving money for renting and owning mobile homes, houses, etc. The Farmers Home Administration also provides financial assistance for those interested in rural housing.

LOW-INCOME RENTAL GRANTS

The federal government offers this program to those living in urban and rural areas. If you reside in a city and pay 25 percent of your income on rent, you may qualify for these free grants. Contact the Farmers Home Administration or a local HUD office to obtain information regarding low cost, country housing. If you wish, you may contact the national office:

Public Housing and Indian Programs
Department of Housing and Urban Development
Washington, DC 20410
(202)755-6522

HOUSING PROGRAMS
REDUCED-INTEREST HOMES FOR LOW-INCOME FAMILIES

With this program, the government pays up to $1,000 of the interest per year on a home loan. For an application and information, contact the HUD or:

Director, Single Family Development Division
Office of Single Family Housing
Department of Housing and Urban Development
Washington, DC 20410
(202)755-6720

REHABILITATION MORTGAGE INSURANCE

This HUD program helps families restore homes in poor condition. Because the government guarantees your repayment of the loan and reduces your interest rate, it is not difficult to obtain an HUD loan. For further information, contact a regional HUD office or the above address.

LOANS FOR PURCHASING OF LAND TITLES

If a person wants to buy the land which his/her house occupies, a loan of up to $10,000 can be arranged through the HUD. Contact a local HUD office or the above address for additional information.

LOANS FOR PURCHASING CONDOS

If you want to purchase a condominium, a guaranteed loan can provide you with more than $67,000. Contact a regional HUD office or the above address for information and applications.

LOANS FOR SPECIAL CREDIT RISKS

For information about low-interest loans for small- to moderate-income families, contact a HUD office or the above address.

GRADUATED PAYMENT MORTGAGE
Section 245 Graduated Payment Mortgages

Loans of more than $67,000 can be guaranteed through the government as you pay off your home with increasing payments to correspond with your current income. Contact a local HUD office or the above address for detailed information.

MORTGAGE LOANS FOR MOBILE HOMES AND LOTS

For information regarding the guaranteed purchase of mobile homes and their lots, contact an HUD office or the above address.

MONEY TO BUY A MOBILE HOME

To obtain an application for a loan of up to $22,500 to purchase a mobile home, contact an area HUD office or the above address.

CONDOMINIUM MORTGAGE INSURANCE

For information on government loans of up to $36,000 for building condominiums, contact a local HUD office or the above address.

This guaranteed government loan offers $39,400 to aid families in purchasing homes or refinancing any debts. Contact an HUD office for further information.

MORTGAGE LOANS FOR VETERANS

Any veteran can apply for a home loan of up to $107,000 by contacting any HUD office.

MORTGAGE LOANS FOR LOW- AND MODERATE- INCOME FAMILIES
This loan assists those who have been forced out of their homes by government action, as well as low- and moderate-income families who need low-interest loans. Contact a nearby HUD office for more information.

MORTGAGE INSURANCE FOR HOMES IN OLDER AREAS
Contact an HUD office to receive information about a guaranteed loan to repair houses in the older areas of poorer cities.

OTHER HOUSING HELP
The FmHA offers loans from $1,000 to $60,000 to those who wish to own a rural home. Individuals 62 and over with a limited income can also receive grants to repair their homes.

Persons younger than 62 can obtain long-term, low- interest loans to purchase homes and their accompanying property.

Those who are poor and residing out of the city can also receive free grants as well as repayable loans. Contact the FmHA at the above address for additional information.

CASH FROM THE FEDERAL GOVERNMENT
In addition to grants made by government agencies, you may be able to obtain a Small Business Administration (SBA) loan. If your loan request has been rejected by a commercial lender and you are able to obtain collateral for the loan, then you are probably eligible for an SBA loan. Repayment terms for SBA loans range from 7 to 25 years. Also, with Small Business Investment Company financing, you can get start-up and expansion capital through a loan or equity position in the company.

LOW-INCOME-HOUSING REPAIR LOANS AND GRANTS
Administrator, Farmers Home Administration
Department of Agriculture
14th Street & Independence Avenue, S.W.
Washington, D.C. 20250
(202) 447-4323

Information: Grants allow rural homeowners to make essential repairs

on their homes' foundation, roof, basic structure, as well as water and waste disposal systems and weatherization.
Amounts: Grants ranging from $400 to $5,000 over a homeowner's lifetime.

BUSINESS EMPLOYMENT

Employment and Training Administration
Department of Labor
200 Constitution Avenue, N.W.
Washington, D.C. 20210
(202) 635-0672

Information: Grants support studies, new approaches and research and development for the employment and training of the nation's workforce.
Amounts: Grants ranging from $1,000 to $1 million.

MINORITIES

Minority Business Development Agency (MBDA)
Department of Commerce
14th Street and Constitution Avenue, N.W.
Room 5073
Washington, D.C. 20230
(202) 377-1936

Information: Grants provide money to businesses which will provide free financial, management and technical assistance to disadvantaged individuals wishing to start a business.
Amounts: Grants ranging from $10,000 to $2,145,000; average is $213,000.

REAL ESTATE

Office of Real Property
Federal Property Resource Service
General Services Administration
Washington, D.C. 20405
(202) 535-7084
Information: Grants provide for disposal of surplus real property, which may be used for public works or recreation and public health or educational purposes.
Amounts: Sale, exchange or donation of property.

REAL ESTATE: PERSONAL PROPERTY

Office of Personal Property
Federal Property Resources Service

General Services Administration
Washington, D.C. 20405
(202) 535-7000

Information: Grants provide for selling of unneeded government property in a manner that would obtain the maximum net return from sales.
Amounts: Sale, exchange or donation of property and goods.

**REAL ESTATE:.RENTAL HOUSING FOR
LOWER-INCOME FAMILIES**
Department of Housing and Urban Development
Elderly and Handicapped Division
451 Seventh Street, S.W.
Washington, D.C. 20410
(202) 755-5216

Information: Grants make quality rental housing available to elderly or handicapped low-income families.

URBAN HOMESTEADING

State and local governments receive titles from the federal government to certain houses in need of repair. They offer these homes to any person who would be willing to repair the home and live in it once it is fixed up. Although anyone who does not own a home can apply, priority is given to those who forfeit 30 percent of their income to living expenses and would be unable to own a home if this program did not exist.

The addresses and phone numbers of HUD regional and field offices are listed at the end of this section. Contact them if you are willing to repair a home you intend to own.

When you purchase a home from the government, you must repair the home and reside in it for at least five years. "Certain" repairs must be completed within one year, but you have three years to make "other" repairs. You become the official owner of the home after three years, and you can even sell it after five years. Incredibly, the home's initial cost is a mere $1 plus some repairs.

U.S. DEPARTMENT OF HOUSING
AND URBAN DEVELOPMENT
REGIONAL AND FIELD OFFICES

Alaska
710 C St., Box 64
Anchorage, AK 99513
(907)271-4183

Arizona
One North First St., 3rd Floor
P.O. Box 13468
Phoenix, AZ 85004
(602)261-4754

Arkansas
320 West Capitol, Suite 700
Little Rock, AR 72201
(501)378-6375

California
1615 W. Olympic Blvd.
Los Angeles, CA 90015
(213)251-7261

California and Nevada
450 Golden Gate Ave.
San Francisco, CA 94102
(415)556-3317

Colorado, Utah, Wyoming,
Montana, North and South Dakota
Executive Tower
1405 Curtis St.
Denver, CO 80202
(303)844-5121
Connecticut
One Hartford Square West
Hartford, CT 06106
(203)722-2445

District of Columbia
451 7th St., SW
Washington, DC 20410
(202)453-4527

Florida
325 West Adams St.

Jacksonville, FL 32202
(904)791-3912

Georgia
Richard B. Russell Federal Building
75 Spring St., SW
Atlanta, GA 30303
(404)331-4005

Hawaii
300 Ala Moana Blvd, Room 3318
Honolulu, HI 96850
(808)546-3132

Illinois
547 West Jackson Blvd.
Chicago, IL 60606
(312)353-0116

Indiana
151 North Delaware St.
P.O. Box 7047
Indianapolis, IN 46207
(317)269-5177

Kentucky
601 W. Broadway
Louisville, KY 40201
(502)582-6141

Louisiana
1661 Canal St.
New Orleans, LA 70112
(504)569-2325

Maryland
Equitable Building
10 North Calvert St.
Baltimore, MD 21202
(301)962-3723

Michigan
Patrick McNamera Federal Building
477 Michigan Ave.

Detroit, MI 48226
(313)226-7194

Minnesota
220 South Second St.
Minneapolis-St. Paul, MN 55401
(612)349-3025

Mississippi
Federal Building, Suite 1016
100 W. Capitol St.
Jackson, MS 39269
(601)960-4765

New Jersey
Military Park Building
60 Park Place
Newark, NJ 07102
(201)877-1750

New York
Statler Building, Messanine
107 Delaware Ave.
Buffalo, NY 14202
(716)846-4164

New York
26 Federal Plaza
New York, NY 10278
(212)264-0187

North Carolina
415 N. Edgewood St.
Greensboro, NC 27401
(919)333-5374

Ohio
New Federal Building
200 N. High St.
Columbus, OH 43215
(614)469-5557

Oklahoma
200 NW 5th St.

Oklahoma City, OK 73102
(614)231-4803

Oregon and Idaho
Cascade Building
520 Southwest 6th Ave.
Portland, OR 97204
(503)221-7014

Pennsylvania
105 S. 7th St.
Philadelphia, PA 19106
(215)597-2228

Puerto Rico
Federico Degetau/Federal Building
U.S. Courthouse, Room 428
Carlos Chardon Ave, Hato Rey
San Juan, PR 00918
(809)753-4544

South Carolina
Strom Thurmond Federal Building
1835 Assembly St.
Columbia, SC 29201
(803)765-5918

Tennessee
One Northshore Building
1111 Northshore Dr.
Knoxville, TN 37919
(615)558-1426
Texas
Washington Square
800 Dolorosa
San Antonio, TX 78285
(512)229-6784

Virginia
701 E. Franklin St., Room 420
Richmond, VA 23219
(804)771-2853

Chapter 26
STATE FUNDS
FOR HOUSING
AND REAL ESTATE

B
ecause of the many budget cutbacks that the federal government has been facing in recent years, many housing responsibilities have been turned over to the state governments. What was created was housing finance agencies (HFAs) designed to finance mortgages for lower-income first-time home buyers and to aid in the development of multi-family housing. There are several programs that have been developed at the state level that were designed for all facets of the housing and real estate markets including buying, selling, building, rehabilitating, and improving current structures. Funds are available for almost any type of housing situation. Check with the addresses below for their various programs.

Alabama
Alabama Housing Finance Authority
P.O. Box 230909
Montgomery, AL 36123-0909
205-242-4310

Alaska
Alaska Housing Finance Corp.
P.O. Box 101020
235 East 8th Avenue
Anchorage, AK 99510
907-561-1900

Arizona
Arizona Department of Commerce
Office of Housing Development
1700 West Washington
Phoenix, AZ 85007
602-280-1365

Arkansas
Arkansas Development Finance Authority
P.O. Box 8023
100 Main Street, Suite 200
Little Rock, AR 72203
501-682-5900

California
California Housing Finance Agency
1121 L Street, 7th Floor
Sacramento, CA 95815
916-322-3991

California Department of Housing and Community Development
P.O. Box 952050
Sacramento, CA 94252-2050
916-322-1560

Colorado
Colorado Housing & Finance Authority
1981 Blake Street
Denver, CO 80202
303-297-7427

Connecticut
Connecticut Housing Finance Authority
40 Cold Spring Road
Rocky Hill, CT 06067
203-721-9501

Delaware
Delaware State Housing Authority
Division of Housing and Community Development
18 the Green
P.O. Box 1401
Dover, DE 19901
302-739-4263

District of Columbia
DC Housing Finance Agency
1401 New York Avenue, NY
Suite 540
Washington, DC 20005
202-408-0415

District of Columbia Department of Housing and Community
Development
51 N Street, NE
Washington, DC 20002
202-535-1353

Florida
Florida Housing Finance Agency
2571 Executive Center Circle East
Tallahassee, FL 32399
904-488-4197

Georgia
Georgia Residential Finance Authority
60 Executive Parkway South, Suite 250
Atlanta, GA 30329
404-679-4840

Hawaii
Hawaii Housing Authority
1002 North School Street
P.O. Box 17907
Honolulu, HI 96817
808-848-3277

Idaho
Idaho Housing Agency
760 W. Myrtle
Boise, ID 83702
208-336-0161

Illinois
Illinois Housing Development Authority
401 N. Michigan Avenue, Suite 900
Chicago, IL 60611
312-836-5200
800-942-8439

Indiana
Indiana Housing Finance Authority
One North Capitol, Suite 515
Indianapolis, IN 46204
317-232-7777

Iowa
Iowa Finance Authority
100 East Grand Avenue, Suite 250
Des Moines, IA 50309
515-281-4058

Kansas
Kansas Office of Housing
Department of Commerce
400 SW 8th, 5th Floor
Topeka, KS 66603
913-296-3481

Kentucky
Kentucky Housing Corporation
1231 Louisville Road
Frankfort, KY 40601
502-564-7630
800-633-8896

Louisiana
Louisiana Housing Finance Agency
5615 Corporate, Suite 6A
Baton Rouge, LA 70808-2515
504-925-3675

Maine
Maine State Housing Authority
P.O. Box 2669
295 Water Street
Augusta, ME 04330
207-626-4600
800-452-4668

Maryland
Department of Housing and Community Development
45 Calvert Street
Annapolis, MD 21401
301-974-2176

Massachusetts
Massachusetts Housing Finance Agency
50 Milk Street
Boston, MA 02190
617-451-3480

Executive Office of
Communities and Development
Commonwealth of Massachusetts
100 Cambridge Street, Room 1804
Boston, MA 02202
617-727-7765

Michigan
Michigan State Housing Development Authority
Plaza One, Fourth Floor
401 South Washington Square
P.O. Box 30044
Lansing, MI 48909
517-373-8370
800-327-9158

Minnesota
Minnesota Housing Finance Agency
400 Sibley Street
St. Paul, MN 55101
612-296-9951
612-296-7608
800-652-9747

Missouri
Missouri Housing Development Commission
3770 Broadway
Kansas City, MO 64111
816-756-3790

Montana
Montana Board of Housing
2001 Eleventh Avenue
Helena, MT 59620
406-444-3040

Nebraska
Nebraska Investment Finance Authority
1033 O Street, Suite 218
Lincoln, NE 68508
402-434-3900

Nevada
Department of Commerce, Housing Division
1802 N. Carson Street, Suite 154
Carson City, NV 89710
702-687-4258

Nevada Rural Housing Authority
2100 California Street
Carson City, NV 89701
702-687-5797

New Hampshire
Housing Finance Authority
P.O. Box 5087
Manchester, NH 03108
603-472-8623

New Jersey
New Jersey Housing Agency
3625 Quakerbridge Road
Trenton, NJ 08650-2085
609-890-1300
800-NJ-HOUSE

New Mexico
New Mexico State Housing Authority
1100 St. Francis Drive
Santa Fe, NM 87503
505-827-0258

Mortgage Finance Authority
P.O. Box 2047
Albuquerque, NM 87103
505-843-6880
800-444-6880

New York
State of New York
Executive Department
Division of Housing and Community Renewal
One Fordham Plaza
Bronx, NY 10458
212-519-5700

New York State Housing Authority
250 Broadway
New York, NY 10007
212-306-3000

North Carolina
North Carolina Housing Finance Agency
3300 Drake Circle, Suite 200
Raleigh, NC 27611
919-781-6115

North Dakota
Housing Finance Agency
P.O. Box 1535
Bismarck, ND 58502
701-224-3434

Ohio
Ohio Housing Finance Agency
775 High Street, 26th Floor
Columbus, OH 43266
614-466-7970

Oklahoma
Oklahoma Housing Finance Agency
P.O. Box 26720
Oklahoma City, OK 73126-0720
405-848-1144
800-256-1489

Oregon
Oregon Housing Agency
Housing Division
1600 State Street, Suite 100
Salem, OR 97310
503-378-4343

Pennsylvania
Pennsylvania Housing Finance Agency
2101 North Front Street
Harrisburg, PA 17105
717-780-3800

Rhode Island
Rhode Island Housing and Mortgage Finance Corporation
60 Eddy Street
Providence, RI 02903
401-751-5566

South Carolina
South Carolina State Housing Financing and Development Authority
1710 Grevais Street, Suite 300
Columbia, SC 29201
803-734-8836

South Dakota
South Dakota Housing Development Authority
P.O. Box 1237
Pierre, SD 57501
605-773-3181

Tennessee
Tennessee Housing Development Agency
700 Landmark Center
401 Church Street
Nashville, TN 37219
615-741-4979

Texas
Texas Housing Agency
P.O. Box 13941 Capitol Station
Austin, TX 78711
512-472-7500

Utah
Utah Housing Finance Agency
177 East 100 South
Salt Lake City, UT 84111
801-521-6950

Vermont
Vermont Housing Finance Agency
One Burlington Square
P.O. Box 408
Burlington, VT 05402
802-864-5743
800-222-VFHA
Vermont State Housing Authority

P.O. Box 397
Montpelier, VT 05601-0397
802-828-3295

Virginia
Virginia Housing Development Authority
601 S. Belvedere Street
Richmond, VA 23220
804-782-1986

Washington
Washington State Housing Finance Commission
111 Third Avenue, Suite 2240
Seattle, WA 98101-3202
206-464-7139

West Virginia
West Virginia Housing Development Fund
814 Virginia Street, East
Charleston, WV 25301
304-345-6475

Wisconsin
Wisconsin Housing and Economic Development Authority
P.O. Box 1728
Madison, WI 53701
608-266-7884
800-362-2767

Wyoming
Wyoming Community Development Authority
123 S. Durbin Street
P.O. Box 634
Casper, WY 82602
307-265-0603

Chapter 27
MAKING MONEY WHILE PROTECTING THE ENVIRONMENT

People have said that we must stop destroying the environment before it destroys us. Well, why not make this task profitable with some help from the government. They can provide you with lots of information on how to improve the environment around you and make some money while doing it. They can provide you with information on everything from starting your own energy conservation business to how to recycle effectively.

Government Loans To Start Your Own Energy Conservation Business

Contact: Your state Economic Development Office in your state capitol or your local Small Business Administration Office.

If you have ever been interested in providing energy production and conservation services to others, then the Small Business Administration can assist you financially with direct loans or loan guarantees for up to $750,000. Call the office above for more information on Energy Business Loan Guarantees.

Free Government Study Shows That Plants Eliminate 90% Of Office Pollution

NASA Library
Building 1100, Room 517A
Stennis Space Center, MS 39529
601-688-3244

Your house plants is actually cleaning the chemicals in the air for you. A recent study conducted by NASA titled Interior Landscape

Plants For Indoor Air Pollution Abatement, proves that indoor plants can be beneficial to the environment and reduce indoor air pollution up to 90%.

Buying Fuel Efficient Company Cars

Public Information Center
Environmental Protection Agency
401 M Street, SW
Washington, DC 20460
202-260-7751

Find out if the cars you're using for your company are fuel efficient with the EPA's annual Mileage Guide.

Help Your Employees Carpool: It's The Law

Traffic Operations Division
Federal Highway Administration
U.S. Department of Transportation
400 7th Street, SW, TV-31
Washington, DC 20590
202-366-4069
   or
Association for Commuter Transportation
808 17th Street, NW
Washington, DC 20006
202-223-9669

Carpooling can cut down on the number of cars, fuel, and pollutants used in commuting to help the air in our environment stay cleaner. Both offices above can provide you with information regarding how to increase the rate of carpooling withing your company, since it is the law.

Low Interest Loans To Buy Energy Saving Equipment

Contact: Your state Office of Economic Development located in your state capitol

Small businesses can obtain low interest loans to purchase energy saving equipment. California, for example, offers up to $150,000 at 5% for a 4 year term.

Employees Get A Tax Break For Using Public Transportation

Taxpayer Services
Internal Revenue Service
U.S. Department of the Treasury
1111 Constitution Avenue, NW, Room 2422
Washington, DC 20224
800-829-3676
   or
Your Local IRS Office

Employees can receive (at the time of publication) $15 a month for using public transportation to work, and not be taxed for the amount. Legislation is currently attempting to increase the monthly amount. For more information, contact the office above for IRS publication #535 that will explain the tax break in more detail.

Save Money Recycling Office Paper

National Technical Information Service
5285 Port Royal Road
Springfield, VA 22161
703-487-4650

Office Paper Recycling: An Implementation Manual (PB90199431) was published to assist office paper recovery programs. The cost of this guide is $19 and explains everything from setting up a recovery program to finding a market for paper.

Free Help For Your Employees With Cholesterol, High Blood Pressure or Smoking Problems

National heart, Lung, and Blood Institute
National Institutes of Health
Building 31, 4A-21
9000 Rockville Pike
Bethesda, MD 20892
301-496-4236

A free Workplace Information Pack is offered by this office that provides literature on educating your employees on the risks of cholesterol, high blood pressure, and smoking.

Free Consultants Make Your Company A Safe And Healthy Place To Work

Occupational Safety and Health Administration
U.S. Department of Labor
200 Constitution Avenue, NW
Washington, DC 20210
202-523-8151

OSHA is an agency that was created to encourage companies to reduce the hazards of being in a particular work environment. They can assist your company with any problems or situations that you may need information on, and they have an extensive list of publications from which any company may benefit from. These publications include *Controlling Electrical Hazards; Asbestos Standards For The Construction Industry; Hand and Power Tools; Hearing Conservation; Respiratory Protection; Working Safely With Video Display Terminals*; and *Workplace Health Programs*. Contact the office above for more information.

NOTES

_____

_____

_____

_____

_____

_____

_____

_____

Chapter 28
GIFTS AND BOOKS FROM UNCLE SAM

CONSUMER INFORMATION CATALOGS

This quarterly catalog lists free or almost free ($.50 to $1) booklets dealing with such diverse topics as child care, diets and food, health and drugs, housing, money management and business, travel, etc. To order a free Consumer Information Catalog, send your name, address, city, state and zip code to:

Free Consumer Information Catalog, S. James
Consumer Information Center-B
P.O. Box 100
Pueblo, Colorado 81002

Government Service Administration Publications

For information on GSA booklets, pamphlets, publications, etc., contact:

General Services Administration
Publications Division (XSP)
Washington, DC 20405

GOVERNMENT PRINTING OFFICE

The GPO, which distributes most government publications, sells more than 15,000 technical and non-technical government books, booklets, papers and pamphlets. For details contact the above address or:

Superintendent of Documents
Government Printing Office
Washington, DC 20402
(202)783-3238

GETTING GIFTS

Many unusual and inexpensive gifts are available in the following catalogs sold through the Smithsonian Museum, the National Gallery of Art and the National Archives.

Bureau of the Mint (announcements of new coins)
55 Mint Street
San Francisco, CA 94175

Cooper-Hewitt Museum (annual catalog)
Smithsonian Institution
National Museum of Design
2 East 91st St.
New York, NY 10128
(212)860-6868

The Freer Gallery of Art (annual publication)
Sales Catalog
Smithsonian Institution
Washington, DC 20560
(202)357-1432

Library of Congress (annual card and gift catalog)
Information Office, Box A
Washington, DC 20540
(202)287-5112

Library of Congress (annual catalog)
Selected Publications
Publishing Office
Washington, DC 20540
(202)287-5112

National Archives (microfilm publications on a variety of topics)
National Archives Books
NEPS, Room 505
Washington, DC 20408

National Gallery of Art (annual catalog; send a $1 check to the "Publications Fund")
Smithsonian Institution, Publications Service
Washington, DC

Smithsonian Institution Traveling Exhibition Service (annual catalog)
Smithsonian Institution
P.O. Box 1949
Washington, DC 20013
(202)357-3168

The Smithsonian Institution (Quarterly Gift Catalog, Annual Collection of Recordings Catalog, Annual Smithsonian Book Catalog)
Pubic Inquiry Mail Service
Washington, DC 20560
(202)357-2700

United States Capital Historical Society (annual catalog)
200 Maryland Ave., NW
Washington, DC 20560
(202)543-8919

White House Historical Association (annual catalog)
740 Jackson Place, NW
Washington, DC 20506
(202)737-8292

Federal Regulatory Directory
This information is published by the Congressional Quarterly and contains news about the agencies which regulate business and other aspects of our lives.

Congressional Directory
This directory offers an in-depth phone list to connect you to staff members in Congress who may be able to answer your questions.

Government Depositories
More than 1,300 government depository libraries possess specific government documents on certain topics.

> # Chapter 29
> # VIDEOS FROM THE GOVERNMENT TO HELP YOUR BUSINESS

I f you own a business, you know that you just can't walk down to the video store and rent videos like "How To Protect The Information In Your Company" or "How To Start A Home-Based Business." These kinds of videos are only available through government agencies. Although many are offered on a free loan-basis with the option to buy, some require a nominal fee unless you are part of a non-profit organization.

How To Find Customers For Your Products Overseas

International Trade Administration (ITA)

U.S. Department of Commerce

14th & Constitution Avenue, NW

Washington, DC 20230

202-377-0332

Learn all about selling abroad and foreign trade shows with these videos that are offered on a free loan basis.

The $ and Sense of Exporting (You Can Sell Them) (18m, free loan) - U.S. companies show how they became successful in the overseas market.

Finding Buyers for Your Products (14m, free loan) - Explains how the Commerce Department assists businesses in selling abroad with their trade promotion programs.

Bring the World Top Your Fingertips (14m, free loan) - Explains the Commerce Department's Commercial Information Management System that is an international marketing retrieval database.

Advertising Strategies, And Future Markets For Your

Products And Services

Modern Talking Picture Service

5000 Park Street, North

St. Petersburg, FL 33709

800-243-MTPS

This service provides many great videos on a free-of-charge loan basis with postage paid. Anyone can qualify.

The Many Faces of Marketing: Changing American Lifestyles and Social Trends (26m, free loan) - Contains a presentation by Florence Skelly, a marketing research expert, to the Federal Trade Commission.

The More Creative the Ad, The Harder it Works (2 parts) (21m/27m, free loan) - Learn from top advertising agency executives successful marketing strategies.

Today and Tomorrow (VTOO2, 23m, $15) - U.S. and world crops are analyzed, as well as forecasts of supplies and prices are included in this video.

How You Can Use Government Research For Business Opportunities

Sales Desk

National Technical Information Service (NTIS)

U.S. Department of Commerce

5285 Port Royal Road

Springfield, VA 22161

703-487-4650

Your business can profit from the results of government-sponsored research and development projects. So find out how by contacting this office for a free information video.

NTIS--The Competitive Edge (#PR-858/827, 8m, free loan) - Presents the services offered by the National Technical Information Service.

Free Services To Expand Your Markets

Office of Public Affairs

U.S. Department of Commerce

14th & Constitution Avenues, NW

Washington, DC 20230

202-377-3263

Get information on how to use the Department of Commerce's resources to maintain your business' edge in the market.

Show Business is Good Business: How U.S. Manufacturers Expand Their Markets Through Experts (18m, free loan) - Explains how American businesses can benefit from the different agencies within the Commerce Department.

Help In Selling Your Products Overseas
Office of Public Affairs
Bureau of Export Administration (BEA)
U.S. Department of Commerce
14 & Constitution Avenues, NW
Washington, DC 20230
202-377-2721

Learn about the policies and procedures of exporting to other countries and how to apply for an exporting license.

Keep America Strong, Keep America Competitive (18m, free loan) - Introduces the Bureau of Export Administration and its services.

How To Help Your Employees With Drug Or Alcohol Problems

Division of Applied Research
National Institute on Drug Abuse
5600 Fishers Lane, Room 10A53
Rockville, MD 20857
01-443-0802

The National Institute of Drug Abuse has developed some videos to help you in helping your employees deal with their drug problems, especially if it is affecting their work habits.

Drugs At Work (employee/employer version) - Describes the scope and nature of drug problems within the workplace and how the Federal government is attempting to reduce this problem.

Getting Help (employee/employer version) - Describes an effective employee assistance program with comments from professional and EAP professionals.

Drug Testing: Handle With Care (employee/employer version) - Explains the options available to employers in drug-testing as a part of the hiring and firing process.

Finding Solutions - The solutions are presented in a personal, employment, and community-wide responsibility format.

Chapter 30
HOW TO PREPARE AND MARKET A BUSINESS PLAN

I f you are trying to develop marketing and promotional business plans, as well as a general plan, then the SBA has three videos that can help you. They are offered on a free loan basis with the option to purchase within 30 days.

Office of Business Development & Marketing
Small Business Administration
409 3rd Street, SW
Washington, DC 20416
202-205-6665

Marketing: Winning Customers With A Workable Plan ($30.00) - Describes a step-by-step plan on how to develop an effective marketing plan including identifying competitors and determine customer needs.
The Business Plan: Your Roadmap To Success ($30.00) - Describes how to develop an effective business plan that will promote growth and profitability.
Promotion: Solving The Puzzle ($30.00) - Shows how to develop an effective marketing strategy that targets new customers and increases sales.

Home Based Business Basics
Oklahoma State University
Agricultural Communications
111 Public Information Building
Stillwater, OK 74078
405-744-3737

This video demonstrates how to do market research, handle legal problems and financial dilemmas, and cope with business and family relationships. The video is available on a free loan basis from your local county cooperative extension service or, it can be purchased for $30 from the address above.

How To Inspect A Home Before You Invest

University of Illinois Film Center
1324 South Oak Street
Champagne, IL 61820
800-367-3456

This video was designed to help the home buyer know what to look for in a home. *From Roof To Foundation* is the title of this release and it follows an inspection expert through a home tour. The video is available on a free loan basis from your local county cooperative extension service or, it can be purchased for $45 (Or, rent it for $10 for 10 days) from the address above.

Free Video On How To Start A Business In Your Home

Office of Business Development & Marketing
Small Business Administration
409 3rd Street, SW
Washington, DC 20416
202-205-6665

Home-Based Business: A Winning Blueprint demonstrates the steps necessary to starting and maintaining a home-based business. The video is offered on a free loan basis for 30 days from the address above. Or, you may purchase it for $39 from SBA, "Success," Department A, P.O. Box 30, Denver, CO 80202-0030.

Video On Starting A Child Care Business

Contact: Your County Cooperative Extension Service
(Under county government in phone book)
    or
Video Production
Texas A & M University
107 Reed McDonald Building
College Station, TX 77843
409-845-2840

If you are planning to open a day care, then don't miss out on the valuable information offered by the Texas Agricultural Extension Service.

Better Kid Care - Family Day Care Training is a 4 part video program that covers child development, nutrition, health and safety, and business management. Contact one of the offices above to find out how you can get a copy of this video.

Mortgage Rates, Bankruptcy and Credit
Satellite Programming
Virginia Cooperative Extension Service
217 Hutcheson Hall
Blacksburg, VA 24061
703-231-6941

There are three videos to help you deal with these situations; 1) *Choosing Adjustable Rate Mortgages*, 2) *Avoiding Bankruptcy*, and 3) *Problems With Credit*. The videos are available on a free loan basis only to residents of Virginia, but may be obtained through your local County Cooperative Extension Service. Copies are available from the office above for $20 to $30.

FEDERAL
INFORMATION CENTERS

Florida
Ft. Lauderdale - (305)522-8531
Jacksonville - (904)354-4756
Miami - (305)350-4155

Iowa
(800)532-1556

Kansas
(800)432-2934

Kentucky
Louisville - (502)582-6261

Louisiana
New Orleans - (504)589-6696

Maryland
Baltimore - (301)962-4980

Massachusetts
Boston - (617)223-7121

Michigan
Detroit - (313)226-7016
Grand Rapids - (616)451-2628

Minnesota
Minneapolis - (612)349-5333

Missouri
St. Louis - (314)425-4106 or (800)392-7711

Nebraska
Omaha - (402)221-3353 or (800)624-8363

New Jersey
Newark - (201)645-3600
Trenton - (609)396-4400

New Mexico
Albuquerque - (505)766-3091

New York
Albany - (518)463-4421
Buffalo - (716)846-4010
New York - (212)264-4464
Rochester - (716)546-5075
Syracuse - (315)476-8545

North Carolina
Charlotte - (704)376-3600

Ohio
Akron - (216)375-5638
Cincinnati - (513)684-2801
Cleveland - (216)522-4040
Columbus - (614)221-1014
Dayton - (513)223-7377
Toledo - (419)241-3223

Oklahoma
Oklahoma City - (405)231-4868
Tulsa - (918)584-4193

Oregon
Portland - (503)221-2222

Pennsylvania
Philadelphia - (215)597-7042
Pittsburgh - (412)644-3456

Rhode Island
Providence - (401)331-5565

Tennessee
Chattanooga - (615)265-8231
Memphis - (901)521-3285
Nashville - (615)242-5056

Texas
Austin - (512)472-5494
Dallas - (214)767-8585
Fort Worth - (817)334-3624
Houston - (713)229-2552
San Antonio - (512)224-4471

Utah
Salt Lake City - (801)524-5353

Virginia
Norfolk - (804)441-3101
Richmond - (804)643-4928
Roanoke - (703)982-8591

Washington
Seattle - (206)442-0570
Tacoma - (206)383-5230

Wisconsin
Milwaukee - (414)271-2273

FREE
BONUS REPORTS

FREE BONUS REPORT #1
FEDERAL JOBS

There are over 1,000 federal occupations, not only in the United States, but all over the world. The different fields range anywhere from education to technology. Typically, people think a federal occupation is located in Washington D.C. and deals only with political issues. However, the federal government offers various types of jobs in many diverse locations.

Only about 12 percent of all federal jobs are located in Washington D.C. The rest of the United States is divided into 10 regions each having their own federal agencies that represent the United States: Boston, New York City, Philadelphia, Atlanta, Chicago, St. Louis, Dallas, Denver, San Francisco, and Seattle. There are also many federal overseas jobs, currently about <u>55,000</u> civilians and <u>500,000</u> military personnel work overseas.

THE ADVANTAGES

Generally, federal pay rates are competitive with the rates for the same type of work done outside of the government. In some cases, the rising rate of pay increases has not kept up with the rising rate of inflation. However, federal jobs offer greater benefits than most other work places. First, new federal employees earn 13 days of vacation time each year. After three years, they earn 20 days annually. This is significantly more than the vacation policies offered by most companies outside of the government. Second, federal pension benefits for retired employees exceed the benefits of pension plans from most other companies. A fair pay rate combined with excellent benefits is the highest advantage of federal employment.

Another important benefit federal jobs offer is mobility. Spouses of civilian or military personnel who relocate are eligible for government jobs in the area of relocation. They can find positions available at military installations,consulates, or overseas embassies. Lastly, all federal agencies are strictly regulated by federal laws and regulations. Employees and applicants are guaranteed fair treatment. Employment discrimination, harassment, or on-the-job difficulties are dealt with in accordance to the law.

HOW TO APPLY

-Visit a federal job information and testing center (FJI/T) to gather information about federal employment.

-Decide which Office of Personnel Management (OPM) listing to apply under. Read the descriptions available in the FJI/T . For example, "Typists", "Professional and Administrative Positions, or "Social Workers" are each separate listings.

-After determining your interest, refer to the *United States Government Manual* to identify offices that work with your interests. Write, call, or visit these agencies and the individuals who run them. Inquire about their function, their ongoing activities, and their plans for the future. You can receive an abundance of information about the positions from the agencies themselves.

-To find specific employment opportunities, look at bulletin boards and job listing reference books in the personnel offices of the agencies you are interested in. Read publications that list federal job openings. For example, *Federal Times* and *Federal Career Opportunities* list both domestic and overseas employment opportunities.

-List all of the contacts you have in government agencies. Give them copies of your SF171 (the application for federal employment). Ask them to keep an eye out for job openings and to distribute your SF171 to the appropriate agencies. Increase your contacts by arranging opportunities to talk with people in your field of interest. The *Federal Yellow Book* and the *Federal Executive Telephone Directory* can provide you with telephone numbers and mailing addresses of many important contacts.

APPLICATION PROCEDURES

The Office of Personnel Management (OPM) is the federal government's personnel agency for positions in the competitive civil service. OPM provides information about application procedures and federal job openings. The FJI/T is the section of this office that handles preliminary testing. OPM examines applicant's qualifications, determines applicant's eligibility, and refers them to specific agencies for employment consideration. OPM has a centralized inventory of applicants called registers.

Most federal organizations are included in this competitive civil service system. The organizations not included are called excepted service. They have their own hiring system which exempts applicants from passing an OPM examination. It is best to contact the agency directly about their application procedures. Some of these agencies include, the Federal Bureau of Investigation and the U.S. Postal Service. A complete listing of these agencies can be obtained from the OPM in a pamphlet entitled "U.S. Government Establishments with Positions Outside the Competitive Service"

The first step when applying for a civil service position is to submit a federal application for employment (SF171) to the OPM office. Some positions, such as clerical positions, require a written test in addition to the application. The content you provide in the SF171 is critical in obtaining the position you want. It should be high-quality. OPM reviews the application to determine if you meet the requirements for the positions you applied for. They will evaluate your experience and training described on the application. Your chances of being hired not only depend on your qualifications, but also on how well you describe them and correlate them to the positions requirements. You may also be asked to provide additional information.

Once OPM has thoroughly reviewed your qualifications, they will notify you if you are eligible for the position you applied for. This notification could be in the form of a GS rating, a test score, or some other notice. Federal white-collar jobs are classified in the General Schedule (GS) pay system. The system starts with GS-1 and goes to GS-18. The higher the grade, the higher the responsibilities, the duties, and the salary. GS-9 to GS-12 are middle level;GS-13 to GS-15 are senior grades. Federal blue-collar positions are classified in the Wage Grade pay system. These pay rates are determined by the rates paid in industry outside of the government for similar work. Rates vary according to location and compatibility with outside rates.

OPM has a limit of candidates it accepts, when this limit is reached OPM closes the specific register and stops accepting applications. However, OPM will accept your application if you were in a federal overseas job at the time of the closing date, providing you submit it within 120 days of your return along with proof of your overseas employment. Veterans can also take advantage of this provision. Contact OPM for details to apply for these privileges.

OPM's purpose is to examine applications and provide qualified applications to agencies at their request. Their purpose is not to locate a job for the applicant. Applicants must seek their own positions.

THE SELECTION PROCESS

To qualify for most federal positions, you must be a U.S. citizen. You must also have the education and experience required for the position you choose. For some jobs, you have to show you have the abilities and skills to perform a certain type of work. Your eligibility is determined on the information you present and the qualifications you describe on your federal application form (SF171). Other factors include, the number of qualified applicants who apply, and the frequency of vacancy in your field of interest.

The selection process begins when OPM receives a request from a federal agency that has a position to be filled. OPM then sends the agency the names of the three highest applicants on the register who meet the requirements. The agency's hiring department then chooses from these three. The names not selected by the agency are returned into the register. Some agencies have direct hiring. They do not go through OPM, but hire on their own. This is frequent in specialized positions or temporary positions.

THE HIRING PROCESS

Once you are hired by the federal government, you are offered an appointment. The three types of appointments are career-conditional, temporary, or term. A career-conditional appointment enables you to be eligible for all the fringe benefits of federal employment. You are also eligible for transfer and promotional privileges. There is a one-year probation period that the employee must complete to secure a career-conditional appointment. The employee receives a career appointment, tenure, and a permanent civil service status after three years of service. One of the advantages of a career-conditional appointment is that the employee may leave a federal agency for up to three years without having to go through appointment procedures again. If the employee is gone for longer than three years he has to be revaluated by OPM. Some exceptions are granted to spouses of federal employees. Or depending on the position you are applying for, you may be able to take a written test in place of a reevaluation.

A term appointment is assigned to an employee who is hired to work on a specific project. A term is from between one and four years. These employees can be transferred and promoted only within the project they were hired for. If they plan to transfer to outside positions or move to a career-conditional appointment, they must resubmit their name to the civil service register of the OPM agency.

Temporary appointments are assigned for one year or less. Temporary employees cannot transfer or move to career-conditional appointments. They also cannot be promoted. The only way they can be eligible for these variations, is to reapply to the OPM agency.

DIRECT APPOINTMENT ELIGIBILITY FOR SPOUSES OF GOVERNMENT EMPLOYEES

You can get direct appointments from federal agencies, bypassing the OPM, if you meet the conditions of Executive Order 12585. These are the conditions:

-You are a U.S. citizen when you apply for the position in the United States. You may also be eligible if you become a citizen by the time you apply for employment in the United States.

-If you were working overseas, you must have been a family member of one of the following overseas employment positions: a civilian employee, a nonappropriated fund employee, a member of a uniformed service member. You do not necessarily have to be a dependent of one of the above at the time you apply for employment. As long as you were a dependent while you were working overseas, you are eligible.

-You must meet qualifications for the position you are applying for. You must also receive a performance rating that states your overseas service was successful.

You must prove your previous service by obtaining a SF50 (Notification of Personnel Action) or other documentation.

-You have up to three years to exercise your direct appointment eligibility after returning from overseas. OPM may approve a longer time period.

AN OVERSEAS FEDERAL EMPLOYEE

The U.S. Federal Government employs many citizens in a variety of foreign countries. There are positions in the U.S. military and in varying federal agencies.To obtain specific information of federal employment openings overseas contact the U.S. Office of Personnel Management. On the West coast: San Francisco Area Office P.O. Box 7405, San Francisco, CA 94120. They are located at 211 Main St., room 235. IOn the East coast: Washington Area Office, 1900 East St., N.WW., Washington D.C. 20415. Some overseas federal agencies include the following:

Economic-Assistance Agencies: Department of Defense, Agency for International Development, Peace Corps, African Development FOundation, Overseas Private Investment Corporation, and Export-Import Bank

Diplomatic Agencies: Department of State, and United States Information Agency

Agencies in Developing Countries: Department of Agriculture, Federal Highway Administration, National Oceanic and Atmospheric Administration, United States Travel and Tourism Administration, and Central Intelligence Agency.

The overseas federal employment system operates differently from the civil service system in the United States. Most overseas hiring is handled by local personnel offices in the overseas area. Since OPM offices are located in the United States, they cannot handle a lot of the hiring procedures. When vacancies occurs in an overseas Federal Government office, there are a variety of options to fill the position.

Many employees are transferred overseas from the United States. Others might be a spouse or dependent of a citizen who is stationed or a civilian who is employed in the area. Others might be U.S. citizens who are residing or traveling in the area when a vacancy occurs. Other vacancies might be filled by native residents.

Some countries have regulations to ensure a certain number of native residents are employed by foreign government offices. Many of these policies restrict hiring dependents of employees to leave positions open for native residents. However in some countries, positions restricted to native residents can be offered to the spouses or dependents of U.S. federal employees. Most overseas jobs available to dependents are temporary appointments. These appointments can lead to eligibility for career appointments in the future.

GETTING AN OVERSEAS JOB
(WHEN YOUR SPOUSE HAS ONE)

You can gather information about employment opportunities in the overseas country where your spouse is employed while you are living in the country. Federal government employment does not have to begin at an OPM agency in the United States. Local civilian personnel offices, community service centers, and local newsletters in the overseas country provide useful information. Most of the time your application will not be considered until after you and your spouse are actually overseas. This occurs because most overseas jobs available for spouses are "local hire" positions. As soon as you arrive overseas, submit an application for employment with the local civilian employment office. It is important to do this as soon as you arrive because applicants are often considered by the order of their application date.

The procedures at local personnel offices vary. Usually after the offices receive the application, they review the qualifications of the applicant. Then, they inform the applicant what types of positions and what grade level they qualify for. Their name is entered on a register of eligible applicants. Visit the local personnel office as soon as you arrive to inquire about any special procedures.

TYPES OF OVERSEAS EMPLOYMENT ARRANGEMENTS

-Dependent Hire Appointment: Most spouses who work in the overseas Defense Department are in a dependent hire appointment. This type of appointment can be used to later obtain a direct hire appointment using the EO 12585 (previously mentioned).

-Part-time/Intermittent/Temporary (PIT) and American Family Member (AFM) Appointments: United States citizens who are family members of U.S. Government employees are eligible for both PIT and AFM appointments. PIT appointments are used for seasonal work, to fill in gaps between filling vacant positions, or to fill vacancies due to unusual circumstances. AFM appointments originally were established to staff native employees in the foreign service. But, some are made available to American family member who are overseas.

Most PIT positions are clerical, but it varies according to the location of the position. In areas where there is a low level of education, natives who are qualified for high-level vacancies are often hard to find. In this case, more openings would be available to family members. PIT and AFM appointments are eligible to direct hiring appointment under EO 12585.

-Nonappropriated Fund (NAF) Appointments: NAF jobs are funded by independent organization funds, membership fees, or club proceeds. They are not considered federal jobs because they are not funded by the federal government. This type of appointment does not lead to eligibility for a direct hire appointment under EO12585.

-Department of Defense Dependents Schools (DODDS) Appointments: There are two types of DODDS appointments. The first is as support personnel under a variation of the dependent hire appointment. The second is as an educator hired on a non-permanent basis. An appointment is issued for the time period of the school year. Appointments can be assigned for future school years. Only dependent hire appointments can be used as eligibility for direct hire appointments under EO 12585.

-Overseas Limited Appointments: These appointments are for temporary overseas positions above the level of GS-8. Personnel offices select candidates from among U.S. residents in the area of the vacancy. They can be credited toward EO 12585 eligibility.

-Berlin Tariff Agreements: This employment agreement is used by the Allied Forces in the territory of Berlin. Employees are hired from the local area. Employment is eligible towards EO 12585.

-Individual Employment Contracts: In addition to the Department of Defense and State, many federal agencies have overseas positions available. They hire employees under individual employment contracts. Overseas federal agencies like to hire spouses or dependents because most of their living allowances are already paid for. An example of an agency with many open possibilities for spouses is the Agency of International Development located in various developing countries. An agency may contract an individual for services in their field of expertise or special interest for a special project. Employment under contract is not considered federal employment, so it cannot count towards EO12585 eligibility.

-Other Employment Opportunities: Some agencies hire particular employees for their offices. This type of employment is credited towards EO12585 requirements if the employment meets specific criteria. FIrst, the position must be a nonpermanent appointment. Second, the position must have been filled by an applicant who was residing overseas (local hire). Third, the U.S. Congress must have funded the position.

RETURNING FROM OVERSEAS EMPLOYMENT

When you return to the United States, make sure you obtain copies of your complete record of your overseas federal government job. Personnel offices in the United States will need to verify your overseas employment.

How do you begin looking for federal employment once you have returned to the United States? Determine if your overseas position enables you to meet the eligibility requirements of the EO12585 for direct appointment. If it does, you do not have to go through OPM, but may apply directly to the agencies you are interested in.. You can obtain direct career-conditional appointments through the agencies. If you obtain this type of appointment, you will serve a one-year probation period that does not include you previous overseas employment. After three years, you will receive a career appointment along with permanent status and tenure. If you do not meet the requirements of EO12585, you will have to process through OPM. Your application will be evaluated and submitted to the competitive hiring procedures.

Alabama
Office of Personnel Management
Building 600 suite 341
3322 Memorial Parkway
Huntsville, AL 35801
Phone 205-544-5802

Alaska
Office of Personnel Management
Federal Building 701 C Street
PO Box 22
Anchorage, AK 99513
Phone 907-271-5821

Arizona
Office of Personnel Management
United States Postal Service Building
522 North Central Avenue Room 120
Phoenix, AZ 85004
Phone 602-261-4736

Arkansas
200 North West Fifth Street Second Floor
Oklahoma City, OK 73102
Phone 405-231-4948

California
Office of Personnel Management
Linder Building, Third Floor
845 South Figueroa
Los Angeles, CA 90017
Phone 213-894-3360

Office of Personnel Management
1029 J Street, Second Floor
Sacramento, CA 95814
Phone 916-551-1464

Office of Personnel Management
Federal Building, Room 4 s-9
880 Front Street
San Diego, CA 92188
Phone 619-557-6165

Office of Personnel Management
PO Box 7405
211 Main Street, Second Floor Room 235
Phone 415-974-9725

Colorado
Office of Personnel Management
PO Box 25167
12345 West Alameda Parkway
Lakewood, CO 80225
Phone 303-236-4160

Connecticut
Office of Personnel Management
Federal Building, Room 613
450 Main Street
Hartford, CT 06103
Phone 203-240-3263

Delaware
Office of Personnel Management
Wm. J Green, Jr. Federal Building
600 Arch Street Room 1416
Philadelphia, PA 19106
Phone 215-597-7440

District Of Columbia
Office of Personnel Management
1900 East Street North West
Washington, DC 20415
Phone 202-653-8468

Florida
Office of Personnel Management
Commodore Building Suite 150
3444 McCrory Place
Orlando, FL 32803
Phone 407-648-6148

Georgia
Office of Personnel Management
Richard B. Russell Federal Building, Room 960
75 Spring Street, South West
Atlanta, GA 30303
Phone 404-331-4315

Guam
Office of Personnel Management
Pacific Daily News Building
238 O'Hara Street Room 902
Agana, GU 96910
Phone 671-472-7451

Hawaii
Office of Personnel Management
Federal Building Room 5216
300 Ala Moana Buelivard
Honolulu, HI 96850
Phone 808-541-2791

Idaho
Office of Personnel Management
Federal Building
915 Second Avenue
Seattle, WA 98174
Phone 206-442-4365

Illinois
Office of Personnel Management
175 West Jackson Room 530
Chicago, IL 60604
Phone 312-353-6192

Indiana
Office of Personnel Management
Minton-Capehart Federal Building
575 North Pennsylvania Avenue
Indianapolis, IN 46204
Phone 317-269-7161

Iowa
Office of Personnel Management
Federal Building Room 134
601 East 12th Street
Kansas City, MO 64106
Phone 816-426-5702

Kansas
Office of Personnel Management
One-Twenty Building Room 101
120 South Market Street
Wichita, KS 67202
Phone 316-269-6794

Kentucky
Office of Personnel Management
Federal Building
200 West Second Street Room 506
Dayton, OH 45402
Phone 513-225-2720

Louisiana
Office of Personnel Management
1515 Poydras Street Suite 608
New Orleans, LA 70112
Phone 504-589-2764

Maine
Office of Personnel Management
Thomas J. McIntyre Federal Building Room 104
80 Daniel Street
Portsmouth, NH 03801
Phone 603-431-7115

Maryland
Office of Personnel Management
Garmatz Federal Building
101 West Lombard Street
Baltimore, MD 21202
Phone 301-962-3833

Massachusetts
Office of Personnel Management
Thomas P. O'Neil Federal Building
10 Causeway Street
Boston, MA 02222
Phone 617-565-5900

Michigan
Office of Personnel Management
477 Michigan Avenue Room 565
Detroit, MI 48226
Phone 313-226-6950

Minnesota
Office of Personnel Management
Federal Building
Ft. Snelling
Twin Cities, MN 55111
Phone 612-725-3430

Mississippi
Office of Personnel Management
Building 600 suite 341
3322 Memorial Parkway
Huntsville, AL 35801
Phone 205-544-5802

Missouri
Office of Personnel Management
Federal Building Room 134
601 East 12th Street
Kansas City, MO 64106
Phone 816-426-5702

Office of Personnel Management
Old Post Office Room 400
815 Olive Street
St. Louis, MO 63101
Phone 314-539-2285

Montana
Office of Personnel Management
PO Box 25167
12345 West Alameda Parkway
Lakewood, CO 80225
Phone 303-236-4160

Nebraska
Office of Personnel Management
One-Twenty Building Room 101
120 South Market Street
Wichita, KS 67202
Phone 316-269-6794

Nevada
Office of Personnel Management
1029 J Street, Second Floor
Sacramento, CA 95814
Phone 916-551-1464

New Hampshire
Office of Personnel Management
Thomas J. McIntyre Federal
80 Daniel Street
Portsmouth, NH 03801
Phone 603-431-7115

New Jersey
Office of Personnel Management
 Federal Building
970 Broad Street
Newark, NJ 07102
Phone 201-645-3673

New Mexico
Office of Personnel Management
Federal Building
421 Gold Avenue South West
Albuquerque, NM 87102
Phone 505-766-5583

New York
Office of Personnel Management
Jacob K. Javits Federal Building
26 Federal Plaza
New York City, NY 10278
Phone 212-2640422

Office of Personnel Management
James M. Hanley Federal Building
100 South Clinton Street
Syracuse, NY 13260
Phone 315-423-5660

North Carolina
Office of Personnel Management
4565 Fall Neuse Road PO Box 25069
Raleigh, NC 27609
Phone 919-856-4361

North Dakota
Office of Personnel Management
Federal Building
Ft. Snelling
Twin Cities, MN 55111
Phone 612-725-3430

Ohio
Office of Personnel Management
Federal Building
200 West Second Street Room 506
Dayton, OH 45402
Phone 513-225-2720

Oklahoma
Office of Personnel Management
200 North West Fifth Street
Oklahoma City, OK 73102
Phone 405-231-4948

Oregon
Office of Personnel Management
Federal Building Room 376
1220 South West Third Street
Portland, OR 97204
Phone 503-221-3141

Pennsylvania
Office of Personnel Management
Federal Building Room 168
PO Box 761
228 Walnut Street
Harrisburg, PA 17108
Phone 717-7824494

Office of Personnel Management
Wm. J Green, Jr. Federal Building
600 Arch Street Room 1416
Philadelphia, PA 19106
Phone 215-597-7440

Office of Personnel Management
Federal Building
1000 Liberty Avenue Room 119
Pittsburgh, PA 15222
Phone 412-644-2755

Puerto Rico
Office of Personnel Management
Frederico Degetau Federal Building
Carlos E. Chardon Street
Hato Rey, PR 00918
Phone 809-766-5242

Rhode Island
Office of Personnel Management
 Federal Building Room 310
Providence, RI 02903
Phone 401-528-5251

South Carolina
Office of Personnel Management
Federal Building
4565 Fall Neuse Road
Raleigh, NC 27609
Phone 919-856-4361

South Dakota
Office of Personnel Management
Federal Building
Twin Cities, MN 55111
Phone 612-725-3430

Tennessee
Office of Personnel Management
200 Jefferson Avenue Suite 1312
Memphis, TN 38103
Phone 901-521-3956

Texas
Office of Personnel Management
Room 6B12
1100 Commerce Street
Dallas, TX 75242
Phone 214-767-8035

Office of Personnel Management
643 East Durango Buelivard
San Antonio, TX 78206
Phone 512-229-6600 or 229-6611

Utah
Office of Personnel Management
PO Box 25167
12345 West Alameda Parkway
Lakewood, CO 80225
Phone 303-236-4160

Vermont
Office of Personnel Management
Thomas J. McIntyre Federal Building
80 Daniel Street,Room 104
Portsmouth, NH 03801
Phone 603-431-7115

Virginia
Office of Personnel Management
Federal Building Room 220
200 Grandby Street
Norfolk, VA 23510
Phone 804-441-3355

Washington
Office of Personnel Management
915 Second Avenue
Seattle, WA 98174
Phone 206-442-4365

West Virginia
Office of Personnel Management
200 West Second Street Room 506
Dayton, OH 45402
Phone 513-225-2720

Wisconsin
Office of Personnel Management
Federal Building
Ft. Snelling
Twin Cities, MN 55111
Phone 612-725-3430

Wyoming
Office of Personnel Management
PO Box 25167
12345 West Alameda Parkway
Lakewood, CO 80225
Phone 303-236-416

FREE BONUS REPORT #2
HOW TO ESTABLISH
YOUR CREDIT

Take your initial investment of $500.00 and go to a bank in your neighborhood and open a regular savings account. Go back to the same bank after one week and ask to borrow $500.00. There will be no hesitation on the part of the loan officer to lend you the money as this is a 100% risk-free proposition. The bank will use your savings account of $500.00 as collateral. Your investment of $500.00 is drawing interest but cannot be withdrawn as it is held by the bank as collateral. Take the $500.00 you borrowed from the first bank and go to another bank in your neighborhood. Open a savings account. Come back to the same bank and ask to borrow $500 against your passbook.

Repeat this procedure of opening new accounts and borrowing in three more banks. Now you have five bank accounts totalling $2,500.00. They are all earning interest. You will also be paying interest on the borrowed money. Remember that you are involved in this activity for only one purpose -- to get an AAA credit rating so that you can borrow large sums of money.

The next step is to go to the sixth bank and open a checking account with your $500.00. Now you are ready to play the credit game. Write a check for the loan payment one week earlier than the due date. Now keep making payments to all the banks you have a loan. Once you have made three payments to the banks, you can be sure that you have built your credit rating.

The next step is to open a retail account with any of the following:

CAR DEALER
FURNITURE STORE
JEWELRY STORE
CLOTHING STORE
APPLIANCE STORE

If you do not need any of the merchandise and would like to start the chain of building your credit so that you can borrow other people's money, you should go to several department stores and open an instant charge account. Most of the time, these stores will grant you credit on the spot. Some may want to take a week or 10 days for checking your credit references. If you have good credit references with three banks you should receive the charge accounts without any problems.

Let us assume that you have several department store credit cards. Since you have not charged anything on your cards, they are all inactive. You have decided not to purchase anything as your purpose for opening these accounts was to establish credit. What you would do now is buy items which could easily be returned. Buy one or two items from these stores and after a few days return them. Making a purchase makes your account active. When you return the merchandise, it will be registered on your bill as CREDITS. The billing system of stores does not usually differentiate between payments and returns. You can repeat this procedure with all the stores. This will make your account very active and you won't be spending any money.

AN ALTERNATIVE METHOD OF GETTING CREDIT

There is another way to begin establishing credit. There is a credit program offered by the Key Federal Savings & Loan Association, which will grant you a Mastercard even though you do not have any credit references. The address and phone numbers are given at the end of this section.

Under this program, you are asked to submit a Timesaver application with the Key Financial Services and also open a savings account of $300.00. They will issue you a Visa card against the security of your savings account. The credit limit will be equal to the amount of your deposit. Your savings account is federally insured and earns interest. Your credit card account is reviewed every twelfth month to determine whether your credit limit can be increased and/or your savings account returned to you with interest. There is a service fee of $25.00 for each card that will be billed to your credit card statement. Key Financial Service charges a one-time processing fee of $25.00 which is payable at the time you submit your application and is refunded if your application for any reason is declined.

Write to the following address for an application:
Timesaver Inc.
12276 Wilkins Avenue
Rockville, Maryland 20852
Phone: 800-368-2800

This is the fastest way to establish your credit. The charges and requirements given above were in effect at the time of publication of this kit. Write to them for current information.

OTHER BANK CREDIT CARDS

Once you have active credit with department stores or clothing stores, you are ready to apply for your own Visa or Mastercard through your local banks. You can still apply for the Visa card even though you have already obtained one from the Timesaver Inc. Fill out an application for a bank credit card at the bank you maintain your checking account. It is relatively easy to get the card at the bank where you have your checking account. However, you can apply to any and all banks in your area or in the entire state. Applying and getting a bankcard can be compared to playing a number game. If you were to apply to several banks for credit, some would refuse and some would send you the credit cards. This is due to the fact that all banks have different requirements for granting credit. Your strategy should be to apply at as many banks as possible.

INSIDE INFORMATION
-- WHAT DO BANKS CHECK?

Banks, finance companies and other financial institutions are involved in different operations. They have one person working as a loan officer whose job is to approve or disapprove credit applications, and they do not time to evaluate each application in detail. A point system is used to "grade" your application. If the data you give them "earns" a certain number of points, the application is approved. If the points fall short of the requirement, the application for credit is declined. If you knew beforehand what the bankers are looking for and if your application met this point requirement, you would get the loan. The following factors are assigned different points by the banks.

1. Age
2. Marital Status
3. Phone
4. Number of dependents
5. Number of years at residence
6. Years at present job
7. Credit Rating
8. Wife's Employment
9. Monthly/weekly income
10. Payment records

The most important factors in the above list are your total family income, years at present residence, years at present job, and credit references.

APPLYING FOR A PERSONAL LOAN:

When you have the references of several department stores and bankcards, it will not be hard to get a personal loan of $5,000 (for example). The scoring and point system given above will help you in understanding what the banks expect you to have. You should also have good reasons for requesting the personal loan. Your chances of getting this loan are greatly diminished if you state that you want to pay your taxes. Tax is a recurring liability which you will incur every year. The most popular reasons that will be quickly accepted are:

Medical expenses
Furniture purchases
Vacation
Dental Expense
Home Repairs
College tuition; fees for children
Funeral Expenses

Many people who do not know the workings of a bank will walk into the bank and ask for a business loan assuming that it will be the easiest to get. On the contrary, the application for a business loan is the one scrutinized in most detail. As soon as the loan officer will hear of the business loan, he will refer you to the commercial loan department. They will require you to submit your balance sheet and the income tax returns for the past two years. To keep it simple and to get quick action on your application, you should apply for a personal loan.

HOW TO GET THE CREDIT OF OTHERS:

Let us suppose you wanted to borrow $5,000 as a personal loan and the bank turns you down because you do not have many credit references. You can immediately propose to your bankers, "What if I get a cosigner?" As soon as you mention the cosigner, the attitude of your banker will become very positive and he will be more than cooperative in arranging the loan for you. The people who know the inside workings of banks know that the credit and income of your cosigner are not so thoroughly scrutinized. The banks will accept just about anybody as your cosigner. It could be your brother, sister, mother, cousin, friend or even a stranger.

WHERE TO BUY THE CREDIT OF OTHERS

If you do not want to trouble your relatives with cosigning your loan, you can always pay someone to do it for you. Ask your friends about cosigning the loan for you for a "Finder's Fee." It sounds more professional to say that you are going to pay him the "Finder's Fee" than to say that you will simply pay him. Everyone is aware that businesses pay huge fees to brokers, agents and others for finding property, businesses, machinery and other items or inventions. The "Finder's Fee" could be anywhere from 1%-5% of the loan amount.

GET ALL THE CREDIT CARDS YOU WANT!

Once you have received your first credit card using any of the methods outlined above, the major hurdle in borrowing other people's money is over. Now, you can pick the bank credit card applications from your choice of banks. Apply to as many banks as possible. Now, you are on your way to riches by acquiring large sums of money on your signature alone and using it to make more money -- just like the wealthy do. With this money, you can start a business, send your children to college or get started in the lucrative real-estate business.

HOW TO BORROW $20,000 INSTANTLY

Most banks and savings and loan associations have "overdraft protection" or "ready reserve accounts" for the convenience of their checking account customers. This is a pre-approved amount of money ready for your use whenever your checking account is depleted. It is not uncommon for banks to give a credit limit of $3,000 to $5,000 to its customers. What you have to do is open checking accounts at banks and savings and loan associations which offer this service. Before you go to a bank to open a checking account, phone and find out if indeed they have the "overdraft" protection for their clients.

If you needed, $40,000 (for example), you would then open checking accounts at 10 different banks. Apply for "overdraft protection" at all of them. Once your application is approved, the money is there for you to withdraw. If you needed $20,000 instantly, you would write five checks for $5,000. The pre-approved "overdraft protection" will cover your checks. You can borrow more or less depending on the number of banks to which you apply for the "overdraft protection."

YOU CAN KEEP THIS AMOUNT AS LONG AS YOU WANT. All banks require, is that you make their monthly payments.

FREE BONUS #3
FEDERAL MONEY PROGRAM

TELEPHONE NUMBERS: The phone numbers given in this guide were current at the time of publication. But, however, phone numbers do change frequently even for government agencies. If you find that you are not able to contact the particular agency by phone, just write a letter to them at the address provided.

40 FREE MONEY PROGRAMS, 56 LOAN PROGRAMS

Business Loans to Low-Income Entrepreneurs, Loans for Small Business; loans and loan guarantees; amount of loans previously given out: $11,728,000; estimated amount of loans to be given out in the future: $17,000,000; amount of guarantees given out: $32,892,000; estimated amount of guarantees to be given out: $40,000,000.

Contact: Director,
Office of Business Loans
Small Business Administration
1441 L St., NW, Washington, DC 20416
(202) 653-6470

Loans to Investors in Overseas Projects, Foreign Investment Guarantees; loan guarantees previously given out: $200,000,000; estimated loan guarantees to be given out: $175,000,000.

Contact: Information Officer,
Overseas Private Investment Corp.Washington, DC 20527
(202) 457-7093

Loans to Provide Long-Term Financing for Fixed Assets to Small Businesses, Certified Development Company Loans; loans previously given out: $293,104,000; estimated loans to be given out: $330,000,000.

Contact: Office of Economic Development
SBA, Room 720
1441 L St., NW ,Washington, DC 20416
(202) 634-7750

Free Money to Airlines Which Service Smaller Towns, Payments for Essential Air Services; direct payments previously given out: $28,393,000; estimated payments to be given out: $25,140,000.

Contact: Director
Office of Essential Air Service, S-60
Dept. of Transportation
400 Seventh St., SW, Washington, DC 20590
(202) 366-1030

Grants to Provide Technical Assistance to Small Businesses, Small Business Development Center (SBDC); grants previously given out: $39,610,000; estimated grants to be given out: $45,000,000.

Contact: SBA
Small Business Development Center
1441 L St., NW, Room 317, Washington, DC 20416
(202) 653-6768

Loans to Minority Businesses to Help Prepare Government Proposals, Office of Minority Economic Impact Loans; loans previously given out: $850,000; estimated loans to be given out: $850,000.

Contact: Minority Business Loan Program Office
U.S. Dept of Energy
1333 Broadway, Oakland, CA 94612
(415) 273-6403

Grants to Train and Counsel Potential and Existing Small Businesses, Service Corps of Retired Executives and Active Corps of Executives; grants previously given out: $999,000; estimated grants to be given out: $900,000.

Contact: SBA
1441 L St., NW , Washington, DC 20416
(202) 653-6634

Special Services to Help Owners of Disadvantaged Companies Become Competitive, Minority Business Development Procurement Assistance; amount in special services previously given out:

$$22,988,000; estimated amount in special services to be given out: $$23,541,000.

Contact: Office of AA/MSBDCOD
Small Business Administration
1441 L St., NW, Washington, DC 20416
(202) 653-6407

Loans to Guarantee Surety Bonds for Small Contractors, Bond Guarantees for Surety Companies; loans previously given out: $1,050,977,000; estimated loans to be given out: $$1,250,000,000.

Contact: Director
Office of Surety Guarantees
Small Business Administration
4040 North Fairfax Dr., Arlington, VA 22203
(703) 235-2900

Free Money to Investors of Energy-Related Projects, Energy-Related Inventions; grants previously given out: $4,890,000; estimated grants to be given out: $4,850,000.

Contact: Director NBS Office of Energy-Related Inventions
National Bureau of Standards
Gaithersburg, MD 20899
(301) 975-5500

Insurance for U.S. Investments in Foreign Countries, Foreign Investment Insurance (Political Risk Insurance); insurance previously provided: $2,250,000,000; estimated amount of insurance to be provided: $2,470,000,000.

Contact: Information Officer
Overseas Private Investment Corp.
Washington, DC 20527
(202) 457-7093

Training to Help Small Business Managers Operate Their Businesses, Business Development Assistance to Small Business; amount in training and counseling previously provided: $18,408,000; estimated amount in training and counseling to be provided: $17,745,000.

Contact: Associate Administrator for Business Development

Small Business Administration
1441 L St., NW , Washington, DC 20416
(202) 653-6881

Grants to Provide Assistance to Economically or Disadvantaged Businesses, Management and Technical Assistance for Disadvantaged Businesses; grants previously given out: $8,427,000; estimated amount of grants to be given out: $8,080,000.

Contact: Associate Administrator for Minority Small Business
1441 L St., NW, Room 602
Washington, DC 20416
(202) 653-6475

Grants to Determine Minority Energy Consumption and Usage Patterns, Socioeconomic and Demographic Research, Data and Other Information; grants previously given out: $769,000; estimated grants to be given out: $769,000.

Contact: Department of Energy
Forrestal Building, Room 5B-110, Washington, DC 20585
(202) 586-1593

Grants to Improve Public Health Protection Against Toxic Environmental Agents, Characterization of Environmental Health Hazards; grants previously given out: $28,335,000; estimated grants to be given out: $24,622,000.

Contact: Associate Director for Extramural Program
National Institute of Environmental Health Sciences
P.O. Box 12233
Research Triangle Park, NC 27709
(919) 541-7723

Loans to Purchase Replacement, Additional or Reconstructed Vessels, Capital Construction Fund; direct payments previously given out: $268,000; estimated payments to be given out: $251,000.

Contact: Associate Administrator for Maritime Aids
Maritime Administration
Department of Transportation
Washington, DC 20590
(202) 366-0364

Loans to Rehabilitate and Improve Irrigation Facilities, Irrigation Systems Rehabilitation and Betterment; loans previously given out: $2,100,000; estimated amount of loans to be given out: $650,000.

Contact: Commissioner
Bureau of Reclamation
Department of the Interior, Washington, DC 20240
(202) 343-5471

Money Not to Produce Wheat, Wheat Production Stabilization; direct payments previously given out: $2,926,704,332; estimated amount of payments to be given out: $641,480,000.

Contact: Commodity Analysis Division
Agricultural Stabilization and Conservation Service
U.S. Dept. of Agriculture
P.O. Box 2415, Washington, D.C. 20013
(202) 447-4146

Grants to Business Interested in Improving Forests and Rangelands, Competitive Research Grants for Forest and Rangeland Renewable Resources; grants to be given out: $2,844,000.

Contact: Director
Competitive Research Grants
U.S. Dept of Agriculture, Room 112
J.S. Morrill Bldg., SW , Washington, DC 20251
(202) 475-5022

Loans to Small Farmers, Resort Operators, and Teenage Entrepreneurs, Farm Operating Loans; loan guarantees previously given out: $1,792,079,160; estimated loan guarantees to be given out: $3,498,109,000.

Contact: Director,
Farm Real Estate and Production Division
Farmers Home Administration
U.S. Dept. of Agriculture, Washington, DC 20250
(202) 382-1632

Loans to Venture Capital Companies, Small Business Investment Companies; loans and loan guarantees; loans previously given out: $35,900,000; estimated loans to be given out: $36,000,000; loan guarantees previously given out: $117,505,000; estimated loan guarantees to be given out: $118,000,000.

Contact: Director,
Office of Investment
Small Business Administration
441 L St., NW, Washington, DC 20416
(202) 653-6584

Money to Landowners to Improve Water Quality, Rural Clean Water Program; direct payments: estimated amount to be given out: $316,000.

Contact: Conservation and Environmental Protection
Agricultural Stabilization and Conservation Service
U.S. Dept. of Agriculture
P.O. Box 2415
Washington, DC 20013
(202) 447-6221

Loans to Businesses Injured by Disasters, Economic Injury Disaster Loans; loans and loan guarantees; amount previously given out: $5,028,972; estimated amount to be given out: $5,796,960.

Contact: Disaster Assistance Division
Small Business Administration
1441 L St., NW, Washington, DC 20416
(202) 653-6879

Emergency Loans to Farmers, Ranchers and Aquaculture Operators, Emergency Loans; loan guarantees previously given out: $29,890,570; estimated amount to be given out: $600,000,000.

Contact: Administrator,
Farmers Home Administration
U.S. Dept. of Agriculture, Washington, DC 20250
(202) 382-1632

Loans to Small Business That Are Damaged by Physical Disasters, Physical Disaster Loans; loans and loan guarantees previously given out: $245,655,000; estimated amount to be given out: $280,000,000.
Contact: Disaster Assistance Division
Small Business Administration
1441 L St., NW, Washington, DC 20416
(202) 653-6879

Free Money to Study Reasons for Unemployment, Research and Evaluation Program; grants previously given out: $4,120,000; estimated amount to be given out: $1,210,000.

> Contact: David H. Geddes,
> Room H7317
> EDA Dept. of Commerce, Washington, DC 20230
> (202) 377-4085

Loans to Farmers and Ranchers to Improve Irrigation, Water Supplies, Or Grazing Conditions. Soil and Water Loans; loan guarantees previously given out: $4,718,810; estimated amount to be given out: $11,000,000.

> Contact: Administrator,
> Farmers Home Administration
> U.S. Dept. of Agriculture, Washington, DC 20250
> (202) 382-1632

Loans for Handicapped to Start Business, Handicapped Assistance Loans; loans and loan guarantees; direct payments previously given out: $11,728,270; estimated payments to be given out: $12,000,000; loan guarantees previously given out: $170,000; estimated guarantees to be given out. $5,000,000.

> Contact: Director,
> Office of Business Loans
> Small Business Administration
> 1441 L St., NW
> Washington, DC 20416
> (202) 653-6470

Money to Wool and Mohair Producers, National Wool Act Payments; direct payments previously given out: $128,154,875; estimated amount to be given out. $83,800,000.

> Contact: Commodity Analysis Division
> Agricultural Stabilization and Conservation Service
> U.S. Dept of Agriculture
> P.O. Box 2415, Washington, DC 20013
> (202) 475-4645

Loans to Businesses That Create Jobs, Economic Development - Business Development Assistance; estimated loan guarantees to be given out: $20,000,000.

> Contact: Deputy Assistant Secretary for Loan Programs
> Finance Directorate
> Economic Development Administration
> Herbert Hoover Bldg., Room H7844
> Washington, DC 20230
> (202) 377-5067

Free Money to Fishermen Whose Vessels Are Damaged Because of Foreign Fishermen, Fishing Vessel and Gear Damage Compensation Fund; direct payments previously given out: $857,000; estimated payments to be given out: $947,000.

> Contact: Chief, Financial Services Division
> National Marine Fisheries Service,
> Department of Commerce
> 1825 Connecticut Ave., NW , Washington, DC 20235
> (202) 673-5421

Money to Grain Producers, Grain Reserve Program; direct payments previously given out: $832,364,835; estimated payments to be given out. $498,229,000.

> Contact: Cotton, Grain and Rice Price Support Division
> Agricultural Stabilization and Conservation Service
> U.S. Dept of Agriculture
> P.O. Box 2415, Washington, DC 20013
> (202) 382-9886

Loans to Small Businesses That Cannot Get Financing Elsewhere, Small Business Loans; loan guarantees previously given out: $2,419,725,100; estimated loan guarantees to be given out: $2,621,000,000.

> Contact: Director,
> Office of Business Loans
> Small Business Administration
> 1441 L St., NW, Washington, DC 20416
> (202) 653-6470

Money for Not Growing Cotton, Cotton Production Stabilization; Direct Payments previously given out: $922,434,133; estimated payments to be given out: $1,469,526,000.

> Contact: Commodity Analysis Division
> Agriculture Stabilization and Conservation Service
> P.O. Box 2415
> U.S. Dept of Agriculture, Washington, DC 20013
> (202) 447-6734

Free Money and Loans to Do Business in Economic Declining Areas, Special Economic Development and Adjustment Assistance Program; grants previously given out: $24,672,605; estimated amount of grants to be given out: $24,657,000.

> Contact: Director Economic Adjustment Division
> Economic Development Administration
> Herbert Hoover Bldg., Room H7217
> Washington, DC 20230
> (202) 377-2659

Loans to Businesses Providing Telephone Service to Rural Areas, Rural Telephone and Loan Guarantees; estimated loan guarantees to be given out: $119,625,000; insured loan guarantees previously given out: $193,411,000; estimated amount to be given out: $239,250,000.

> Contact: Administrator
> Rural Electrification Administration
> U.S. Dept of Agriculture, Washington, DC 20250
> (202) 382-9540

Loans to Businesses with Investments Overseas, Direct Investment Loans; loans previously given out: $23,000,000; estimated loans to given out: $23,000,000.

> Contact: Information Officer
> Overseas Private Investment Corp. ,
> Washington, DC 20527
> (202) 457-7093

Loans to Vietnam-Era Veterans to Start Businesses, Veterans Loan Program; loans previously given out: $16,997,000; estimated loans to be given out: $17,000,000.

Contact: Director,
Office of Business Loans
Small Business Administration
1441 L St., NW , Washington, DC 20416
(202) 653-6470

Money for Landowners with Migratory Waterfowl Nesting, Breeding and Feeding Areas, Water Bank Program; direct payments previously given out: $9,230,000; estimated payments to be given out: $10,409,000.

Contact: Conservation and Environmental Protection
Division
Agricultural Stabilization and Conservation Service
U.S. Dept. of Agriculture
P.O. Box 2415
Washington, DC 20013
(202) 447-6221

Loans to Investors in Rental Housing in Rural Areas, Rural Rental Housing Loans; loan guarantees previously given out: $554,935,629; estimated loan guarantees to be given out: $554,900,000.

Contact: Administrator
Farmers Home Administration
U.S. Dept. of Agriculture, Washington, DC 20250
(202) 382-1604

Loans to Small Businesses Through Local Governments, State and Local Development Company Loans; direct loans and loan guarantees; guarantees previously given out: $39,096,000; estimated guarantees to be given out: $35,000,000.

Contact: Office of Economic Development
Small Business Administration
1441 L St., NW
Washington, DC 20416
(202) 653-6470

Loans and Purchases for Producers of Feed Grains, Wheat, Rice, Rye, Soybeans, Honey, Upland Cotton, Extra-Long Staple Cotton, Dairy Products, Peanuts, Tobacco, and Sugar, Commodity Loans and Purchases; Purchases: $1,573,717,964; estimated purchases to be given out. $995,610,000; loans previously given out: $13,301,528,946; estimated loans to be given out: $6,094,773,000.

Contact: Agricultural Stabilization and Conservation Service
U.S. Department of Agriculture
P.O. Box 2415 , Washington, DC 20013
(202) 447-7641

Loans to Small Businesses in Energy-Related Businesses, Small Business Energy Loans; estimated loan guarantees to be given out: $5,000,000.

Contact: Office of Business Loans
Small Business Administration
1441 L St., NW, Washington, DC 20416
(202) 653-6470

Money to Farmers and Ranchers for Rehabilitation Due to Erosion, etc.; Emergency Conservation Program; Direct Payments previously given out: $5,927,826; estimated payments to be given out: $13,021,000.

Contact: Conservation and Environmental Protection
Division
Agricultural Stabilization and Conservation Service
U.S. Dept. of Agriculture
P.O. Box 2415
Washington, DC 20013
(202) 447-6221

Money for Not Growing Feed Grains, Feed Grain Production Stabilization; Direct Payments previously given out: $8,128,467,102; estimated payments to be given out: $5,016,696,000.

Contact: Commodity Analysis Division
Agricultural Stabilization and Conservation Service
U.S. Dept. of Agriculture
P.O. Box 2415
Washington, DC 20013
(202) 447-4417

Money to Prevent Erosion of Cropland, Conservation Reserve Program; direct payments previously given out: $267,024,141; estimated payments to be given out: $736,316,000.

Contact: Conservation and Environmental Protection
Division
Agricultural Stabilization and Conservation Service
U.S. Dept. of Agriculture
P.O. Box 2415
Washington, DC 20013
(202) 447-6221

Loans to Businesses in Towns with Less Than 50,000 People,
Business and Industrial Loans; loan guarantees previously given out:
$95,415,000; estimated loan guarantees to be given out: $95,700,000.

Contact: Administrator
Farmers Home Administration
U.S. Dept. of Agriculture, Washington, DC 20250
(202) 447-7967

**Money to Farmers and Ranchers for Pollution Control and Water
Conservation**, Agricultural Conservation Program; direct payments previously given out: $198,788,000; estimated payments to be given out:
$228,479,000.

Contact: Conservation and Environmental Protection
Division
Agricultural Stabilization and Conservation Service
U.S. Dept. of Agriculture
P.O. Box 2415, Washington, DC 20013
(202) 447-6221

Free Money for Small Business Research, Small Business Innovation
Research; grants previously given out: $3,798,022; estimated grants to
be given out: $3,942,178.

Contact: SBIR Coordinator
Competitive Research Grants
Office of Grants and Program Systems
U.S. Dept. of Agriculture, Room 112
J.S. Morrill Bldg., SW
Washington, DC 20251
(202) 447-7002

Premium Subsidy for Crop Insurance, Crop Insurance; insurance previously given out: $548,980,246; estimated insurance to be given out: $1,670,500,333. Premium subsidy previously given out: $135,743,000; estimated subsidy to be given out: $228,523,000.

> Contact: Manager
> Federal Deposit Insurance Corporation
> U.S. Dept. of Agriculture
> Washington, DC 20250
> (202) 447-6795

Free Money to Coal Operators for Cleaning Up Coal Mines, Rural Abandoned Mine Program; grants previously given out: $10,041,380; estimated amount of grants to be given out: $4,594,000.

> Contact: Deputy Chief of Programs
> Soil Conservation Service
> Dept. of Agriculture
> P.O. Box 2890
> Washington, DC 20013
> (202) 447-4527

Money for Small Forest Land Owners, Forestry Incentives Program; direct payments previously given out: $11,814,226; estimated payments to be given out: $14,203,000.

> Contact: Conservation and Environmental Protection
> Division
> Agricultural Stabilization and Conservation Service
> U.S. Dept. of Agriculture
> P.O. Box 2415, Washington, DC 20013
> (202) 447-6221

Grants and Loans for Farmers to Build Housing and Recreation Facilities for Employees, Farm Labor Loans; loans previously given out: $11,372,385; estimated loans to be given out: $11,480,000; grants previously given out: $11,297,304; estimated grants to be given out: $9,513,000.

> Contact: Multi-Family Housing Processing Division
> Farmers Home Administration
> U.S. Dept. of Agriculture, Washington, DC 20250
> (202)382-1604

Money to Rice Producers, Rice Production Stabilization; direct payments previously given out: $467,857,524; estimated payments to be given out: $733,550,000.

> Contact: Commodity Analysis Division
> Agricultural Stabilization and Conservation Service
> U.S. Dept. of Agriculture
> P.O. Box 2415, Washington, DC 20013
> (202) 447-5954

Loans to Small Farmers, Ranchers, Forest Businesses, and Resort Operators to Purchase Real Estate, Farm Ownership Loans; loan guarantees previously given out: $477,066,000; estimated loan guarantees to be given out: $819,000,000.

> Contact: Administrator
> Farmers Home Administration
> U.S. Dept. of Agriculture
> Washington, DC 20250
> (202) 382-1632

Loans to Businesses Providing Power to Rural Communities, Rural electrification loans and loan guarantees; loan guarantees previously given out: $774,672,000; estimated loan guarantees to be given out: $813,450,000; insured loans previously given out: $622,050,000; estimated insured loans to be given out: $622,050,000.

> Contact: Administrator
> Rural Electrification Administration
> U.S. Dept. of Agriculture, Washington, DC 20250
> (202) 382-9540

Free Money to Fishermen Who Lose Money Due to Off-Shore Oil Drilling, Fishermen's Contingency Fund; direct payments previously given out: $721,000; estimated payments to be given out: $726,000.

> Contact: Chief
> Financial Services Division
> National Marine Fisheries Service
> 1825 Connecticut Ave., NW , Washington, DC 20235
> (202) 673-5421

Loans to Businesses to Improve Telephone Service to Rural Areas, Rural Telephone Bank Loans; loans previously given out: $80,139,000; estimated loans to be given out: $177,045,000.

> Contact: Governor
> Rural Telephone Bank
> U.S. Dept. of Agriculture, Washington, DC 20250
> (202) 382-9540

Loans for Fishing Boats, Fishing Vessel Obligation Guarantees; guaranteed loans previously given out: $97,400,000; estimated loans to be given out: $130,000,000.

> Contact: Chief
> Financial Services Division
> National Marine Fisheries Service
> 1825 Connecticut Ave., NW
> Washington, DC 20235
> (202) 673-5424

Free Money to Landowners to Prevent Erosion or Improve Recreation, Great Plains Conservation; direct payments previously given out: $8,740,705; estimated payments to be given out: $8,245,000. Grants previously given out: $11,812,106; estimated grants to be given out: $12,286,000.

> Contact: Deputy Chief for Programs
> Soil Conservation Service
> U.S. Dept of Agriculture
> P.O. Box 2890
> Washington, DC 20013
> (202) 447-4527

Loans to Investors and Builders of Nursing Homes, Mortgage Insurance-Nursing Homes, Intermediate Care Facilities and Board and Care Homes; mortgages insured: $174,577,950.

> Contact: Insurance Division
> Office of Insurance Multifamily Housing Development
> Dept. of Housing and Urban Development
> Washington, DC 20410
> (202) 755-6223

Free Money for Small Business Research, Small Business Innovation Research; grants previously given out: $4,754,000; estimated grants to be given out: $6,350,000.

Contact: Office of Innovation Research and Technology
Small Business Administration
1441 L St., NW, Washington, DC 20416

Loans for Land Developers, Mortgage Insurance-Land Development; loan guarantees previously given out: $73,080,930; estimated loan guarantees to be given out: $43,572,000.

Contact: Director
Single Family Development Division
Office of Insured Single Family Housing
Dept. of Housing and Urban Development
Washington, DC 20410
(202) 755-6720

Loans for Investors, Builders or Developers of Rental Housing for the Elderly, Mortgage Insurance-Rental Housing for the Elderly; mortgages previously insured: $8,419,600; estimated mortgages to be given out: $15,561,000.

Contact: Insurance Division
Office of Insured Multifamily Housing Development
Dept. of Housing and Urban Development
Washington, DC 20410
(202) 755-6223

Free Money to Real Estate Investors Who Rent to Elderly or Handicapped, Interest Reduction Payments; direct payments previously given out: $627,996,000; estimated payments to be given out: $625,651,000.

Contact: Director
Office of Multifamily Housing Management
Dept. of Housing and Urban Development
Washington, DC 20410
(202) 426-3968

Loans for Investors, Builders or Developers of Rental or Coop Housing for Moderate Income Families, Mortgage Insurance-Rental and Cooperative Housing for Moderate Income Families, Market Interest Rate; mortgages previously insured: $353,786,000.

Contact: Insurance Division
Office of Insured Multifamily Housing Development
Dept. of Housing and Urban Development
Washington, DC 20410
(202) 426-3968

Loans to Condominium Developers, Mortgage Insurance-Construction or Substantial Rehabilitation of Condominium Projects; mortgages previously insured: $2,678,000.

Contact: Insurance Division
Office of Insured Multifamily Housing Development
Dept. of Housing and Urban Development
Washington, DC 20410
(202) 755-6223

Loans for Investors, Builders or Developers of Rental Homes, Mortgage Insurance-Rental Housing; estimated mortgages to be insured: $9,337,000.

Contact: Insurance Division
Office of Insured Multifamily Housing Development
Dept. of Housing and Urban Development
Washington, DC 20410
(202) 755-6223

Loans to Real Estate Investors Who Want to Improve or Purchase 1-4 Unit Dwellings, Rehabilitation Mortgage; insured loans previously given out: $22,848,995; estimated loans to be given out: $21,365,000.

Contact: Director
Single Family Development Division
Office of Insured Single Family Housing
Dept. of Housing and Urban Development
Washington, DC 20410
(202) 755-6720

Loans for Investors, Builders or Developers of Rental Housing for Moderate Income Families, Mortgage Insurance-Rental Housing for Moderate Income Families; mortgages previously insured: $527,474,300; estimated mortgages to be given out: $233,419,000.

Contact: Insurance Division
Office of Insured Multifamily Housing Development
Dept. of Housing and Urban Development
Washington, DC 20410
(202) 755-6223

Free Money to Shippers and Shipbuilders, Construction-Differential Subsidies; direct payments previously given out: $1,252,000; estimated payments to be given out: $464,000.

Contact: Associate Administrator for Maritime Administration
Dept. of Transportation
400 Seventh St., SW, Washington, DC 20590
(202) 366-0364

Loans to Investors, Builders or Developers of Rental Housing in Urban Renewal Areas, Mortgage Insurance-Rental Housing in Urban-Renewal Areas; estimated mortgages to be given out: $24,898,000.

Contact: Insurance Division
Office of Insured Multifamily Housing Development
Dept. of Housing and Urban Development
Washington, DC 20410
(202) 755-6223

Free Money for Employees Who Lose Their Job Because of Imports, Trade Adjustment Assistance Workers; TRA payments previously given out: $192,680,000; estimated payments to be given out: $276,000,000. Reemployment Services previously given out: $50,388,000; estimated amount of services to be given out: $80,000,000.

Contact: Director
Office of Trade Adjustment Assistance
Employment and Training Administration
Dept. of Labor
601 D St., NW, Room 6434, Washington, DC 20213
(202) 376-2646

Free Money to Investors, Builders, and Developers of Rental Housing for Lower-Income Families, Rent Supplements-Rental Housing for Lower-Income Families; direct payments previously given out: $46,643,000; estimated payments to be given out: $34,460,000.

Contact: Management Information Chief
Program Support Branch
Office of Multifamily Housing Management
Dept. of Housing and Urban Development
Washington, DC 20410
(202) 755-5654

Free Money to Indian-Owned Businesses, Indian Grants-Economic Development; grants and direct payments previously given out: $6,895,814; estimated amount of grants and payments to be given out: $7,000,000.

Contact: Director
Office of Indian Services
Bureau of Indian Affairs
18th & C Streets, NW, Room 4600
Washington, DC 20240
(202) 343-1400

Loans to Home Builders Who Use Experimental Housing Construction Techniques, Mortgage Insurance-Experimental Homes; loan guarantees; average mortgage previously given out was about $65,000.

Contact: Assistant Secretary for Policy Development and Research
Div. of Innovative Technology and Special Projects
Dept. of Housing and Urban Development
Washington, DC 20410
(202) 755-5904

Loans to Investors to Improve Rental Apartment Buildings, Supplemental Loan Insurance-Multifamily Rental Housing; estimated loans to be given out: $31,123,000.
Contact: Insurance Division
Office of Insured Multifamily Housing Development
Dept. of Housing and Urban Development
Washington, DC 20411
(202) 755-6223

Loans for Indians and Native Alaskans To Be Used for Business and Industry, Indian Loans-economic development loans previously given out: $8,053,145; estimated loans to be given out: $12,500,000. New loan guarantees previously given out: $38,158,047; estimated loan guarantees to be given out: $45,000,000.

Contact: Director
Office of Indian Services
Bureau of Indian Affairs
18th and C Streets, NW, Room 4600
Washington, DC 20245
(202) 343-3657

Loans for Investors Who Purchase, Repair or Refinance Rental Apartment Buildings, Coinsurance for the Purchase or Refinancing of Existing Multifamily Projects; loan guarantees previously given out: Section 223(f) $1,392,020,000; estimated guarantees to be given out: $1,773,986,000; Section 221(d) $$599,491,800; estimated guarantees to be given out: $$855,870,000; Section 232: estimated guarantees to be given out: $77,806,000.

Contact: Director
Office of Insured Multifamily Housing Development
Coinsurance Branch
Dept. of Housing and Urban Development
Washington, DC 20410
(202) 426-7113

Loans to Investors, Builders, and Developers of Rental Housing Using Experimental Construction Techniques, Mortgage Insurance-Experimental Rental Housing; loan guarantees previously given out: $2,314,814 (average).

Contact: Assistant Secretary for Policy Development and Research
Div. of Innovative Technology and Special Projects
Dept. of Housing and Urban Development
Washington, DC 20410
(202) 755-0640

Free Money for Investors in Rental Apartment Buildings Who Are in Financial Trouble, Operating Assistance for Troubled Multifamily Housing Projects; grants and direct payments previously given out: $32,342,000; estimated grants and payments to be given out: $38,150,000.

> Contact: Chief
> Program Support Branch
> Management Operations Division
> Office of Multifamily Housing Management
> Dept. of Housing and Urban Development
> Washington, DC 20420
> (202) 755-5654

Loans to Investors to Purchase or Refinance Rental Apartment Buildings, Mortgage Insurance for the Purchase or Refinancing of Existing Multifamily Housing Projects; mortgages previously insured: $11,719,000.

> Contact: Office of Insured Multifamily Housing Development
> Dept. of Housing and Urban Development
> Washington, DC 20410
> (202) 755-6223

Loans for Shippers to Buy Vessels, Federal Ship Financing Guarantees; loan guarantees previously given out: $26,500,000.

> Contact: Associate Administrator for Maritime Aids
> Maritime Administration
> Dept. of Transportation, Washington, DC 20590
> (202) 366-0364

Money to Dairy Farmers and Manufacturers Who Suffer a Loss from Contamination, Dairy Indemnity Program; direct payments previously given out: $440,000; estimated payments to be given out: $545,000.

> Contact: Emergency Operations and Livestock Division
> Agricultural Stabilization and Conservation Service
> Dept. of Agriculture
> P.O. Box 2415, Washington, DC 20013
> (202) 447-7673

Free Money to U.S. Shippers Who Compete with Foreign Operators, Operating-Differential Subsidies; direct payments previously given out: $222,918,000; estimated payments to be given out: $218,100,000.

> Contact: Associate Administrator for Maritime Aids
> Maritime Administration
> Dept. of Transportation
> 400 Seventh St., SW , Washington, DC 20590
> (202) 366-0364

Special Services to Assist Small Business Obtain Government Contracts, Procurement Assistance to Small Businesses; specialized services previously given out: $15,659,000; estimated amount of services to be given out: $16,644,000.

> Contact: Associate Administrator for Procurement
> Assistance
> Small Business Administration
> 1441 L St., NW , Washington, DC 20416
> (202) 653-6635

NOTES

_____

_____

_____

_____

_____

_____

_____

_____

_____

_____

_____

"Are you all right, dear? Is something wrong?"

"I'm fine, Mama, but . . . Grampa died. And I need to tell Daddy."

"Oh, my! . . . All right, dear. Here's your father."

My dad's a big man, built like Uncle Hank. I love hearing his deep voice.

"Hey, it's my big city girl. How're you doing up there?"

"Daddy? It's Grampa. He's . . . passed on. I'm sorry to be the one who has to tell you."

My dad is quiet, and I can picture him as he gets all still and serious. And I remember all the stories Daddy told me about him and Grampa, about hunting and fishing together. And how Grampa almost cried the day Daddy left for Vietnam.

But my dad is also the brave one. He clears his throat and says, "Was it . . . there at home? It wasn't an accident or anything, was it?"

"No, not an accident, I don't think. But it's . . . unusual, Daddy. Because Grampa's in the big freezer, the one in the utility room. And I don't know . . . how it happened. So it's . . . unusual. I had to call the police. I'm sorry to have to tell you this."

A second of silence, then, "Did you say in the freezer? You sure about that?"

"You can't make a mistake about something like this, Daddy."

I hear the intercom buzzer at the front door.

My dad says, "Well, I'm coming up there tonight if I can—tomorrow, for sure. Are you all right until then? Do you want me to call Uncle Hank for you?"

"No, don't do that, Daddy. I have a friend here who's helping me. And I called Grampa's lawyer, too. So I'm okay. I've got to go now, Daddy. The police are here. I love you."

"I love you, too, Gwennie. And I'll be there right away. And I'll call. Here's your mama again."

"Gwennie? Now don't you be afraid. Everything'll work out. You just tell everybody the truth, and then trust it all to God, you hear? You're bein' watched over, same as always."

"I know, Mama. Thank you. I have to go now. I'll call back in a bit. I love you."

"I love you too, sweetheart."

I put the cell phone in my pocket, and the intercom buzzes again. And Robert and I walk out to open the door for the police.

Except when I open the door, it's not the police.

chapter 13

TOO MUCH

Before I can react, Uncle Hank pushes past me into the front hall, brushes Robert aside and walks through the open parlor door.

"Lawrence?"

I'm inside now, and Uncle Hank's in the study.

"Robert! In here!" He follows me at a dead run into Grampa's bedroom, and I slam the door and lock it.

"Lawrence!" His big fist shakes the door in its frame. "Are you in there? Tell Gwennie to open the door. I need to talk to you, right now."

Robert and I have our shoulders against the door. And I can see Robert beginning to make his old man face, and he takes a breath: He's about to start talking like Grampa again.

So I poke him in the side, and I shout through the door. "Just go away. This isn't a good time. So just leave." Because in the back of my mind I guess I think I can keep Uncle Hank out of all this for another day or so. There's already too much to deal with.

Uncle Hank bangs the door again. "I want to see him. And who's that kid in there with you? That your boyfriend or something? What's going on around here, Gwennie? Open this door, or I'm going to give it a good kick and come in anyway."

"Hold it, mister! Police! Hands on the wall, and don't turn around!"

"What the—? Oh, great! Nice going, Gwennie. You had to go and be stupid and call the police."

I open the bedroom door, and there are two officers, both men, one with a hand on his pistol. The second officer has his left hand against Uncle Hank's back, and he's patting around with the other to check for weapons.

It takes all my courage to speak. "I'm Gwendolyn Page. I'm the one who called 911."

The officer finishes with Uncle Hank and says, "What's the yelling about?" And to me he says, "You know this man?"

I nod. "He's my uncle."

Still talking to me, he says, "And you live here?"

I nod. "With my grampa. It's his house."

Uncle Hank snarls, "And it's my house too."

The second officer says to Hank, "Just keep it quiet unless someone asks you a question, okay?" Then to me he says, "And you're the one reported the dead body, right? You want to show me now?"

I nod at the officer, but I'm watching my uncle's face. The anger drains away. Seconds later I'm looking at a different man, more like a boy. Somebody's little brother. "Body?" he says. "What body?"

Hank turns from the officer and locks eyes with me. "Gwennie? Is it . . . it's Lawrence?"

My eyes fill with tears, and I nod.

The crumpled face, the pain in his eyes. And I cross Uncle Hank off the list of suspects. Because I believe his sadness and shock, believe it completely.

The officer nods at Robert and asks me, "Who's he?"

"A friend of mine. He found it first . . . the body."

Uncle Hank moves to the couch and slumps into the cushions, face in his hands.

"Okay, then," the officer says. "Why don't you two lead the way."

The next ninety minutes feel like a dream. After Robert and I show the policeman the freezer, he calls for an evidence team. Fingerprint dusting, dozens of photographs, a medical examiner from the coroner's office, a body bag, an ambulance.

Robert and Uncle Hank each spend about fifteen minutes in the study giving their statements to the man in charge, Detective Keenan. Jason the tenant shows up, and he gets questioned too. And a technician takes fingerprint samples from all of us, "for the process of suspect elimination," he says.

By the time it's my turn to give a statement, Kenneth

Grant arrives, and he comes into the study with me. I start with how I came home from my violin lesson on Thursday. I play Grampa's message, and after it rewinds, the detective takes the whole answering machine and puts it into a plastic evidence bag. I tell the entire story, right up to calling Mr. Grant and the police and my parents, and then Uncle Hank pushing his way into the parlor.

When I'm done, Mr. Grant says, "Detective Keenan, I've got some information that may or may not be important. Thursday was the last day my client was seen alive, and it was also the day he left a message on my office voice mail. He told me that an envelope was on its way to me, and he asked me not to open this envelope except in the event of his death. He also asked me to call on Friday and check to see if his granddaughter was all right, which I did."

"Where is it, this envelope?" It's clear the detective doesn't care much for lawyers.

"In a safe at my office. I haven't opened it. It's registered mail."

"I'll send an officer to get it."

The lawyer pauses. "Actually, since I am the addressee, the contents are privileged client information. And there's nothing that automatically links this envelope to your case." The detective stiffens, and Mr. Grant quickly adds, "But I want to cooperate in every way, so I'll be happy to bring the envelope wherever you'd like me to, and I'll open it in your presence. Then we can determine together if any of the contents are relevant."

The detective's not completely happy, but he says, "Three P.M. tomorrow at the Twenty-fourth Precinct house—100th Street between Amsterdam and Columbus. We'll have a probable cause of death by then." Turning to me, the officer says, "I want you to be there, and your boyfriend too. And neither of you leaves the city until this is settled."

"Oh . . . he's not my boyfriend."

"Just tell him not to go anywhere, okay?"

As quickly as the craziness began, it ends. The patrolmen, the technicians, the detective, Mr. Grant, Jason from the third floor—everyone just leaves. Uncle Hank too. He trudges away to find a cab, looking ten years older. In a matter of five minutes they're gone, and it's Robert and me sitting by ourselves in the parlor.

It feels like a long time before either of us talks. Then Robert says, "I hate to mention it, but I'm still really hungry. You?"

I nod. I hate to admit it too. It seems disrespectful to eat, to do something so normal right here in Grampa's house, right where he'll never be again.

Then, for the first time, I understand why there's always food after a funeral, at least in my family. Food and eating are all about life, about keeping up the strength to go on. And Grampa would want that. He truly would.

I feel drained, but I get to my feet and move toward the kitchen. "How about a ham and cheddar omelette? Maybe with some mushrooms?"

Robert smiles. "That'd be great."

I turn the corner and bend down to get the frying pan from the cabinet below the cooktop. And I hear, "If you don't mind, I'd like an omelette as well. And some toast with jam. Sounds quite delicious."

It's an almost perfect British accent, and I know Robert means well, trying to lighten things up. But I'm not in the mood. So I say, "Please, no joking, not now."

"Awfully sorry—though I must say that merely requesting sustenance can hardly be construed as humour."

The idiot's still being British, so I put my head around the corner. "I'm serious, Robert, not now."

Then I see his face. It's chalky white, and Robert's eyes are wide, locked, staring at the space in front of the fireplace. So I look there too.

And there it is. Just like at the Nike store.

It's the shadow man.

chapter 14

UNINVITED

ear is an excellent cure for fatigue. It even dulls my grief. I'm instantly alert, looking at the vague, wavy shadow of an invisible person, a man, standing in the parlor.

And then I remember what Robert said about being out in public: No clothes. There's a naked man standing twenty feet away from me. A shiver grabes my spine and shoots all the way to my toes. I know I have legs and arms, but I can't seem to move them. I'm paralyzed.

Robert's not much better. At least he can talk. And he can think too, because he begins looking wildly around the room, and he says, "What's going on? Who's that talking?" He's pretending he doesn't know what's happening. And I don't really understand why.

The man chuckles. "Nice try, my good fellow. But you see, I heard you talking to the young lady on the subway this afternoon. It's Gwen, and I assume that's short for Gwendolyn, right? You were telling Gwendolyn about your experiences two years ago. So please, don't pretend to be confused."

Robert adjusts instantly. His face is still pale, but in a conversational tone, he says, "How come you followed us?"

"Curiosity, at first. I could tell you saw me. Which is nothing new. A person in my condition becomes sensitized to being noticed. This is at best a limited form of invisibility, and people are always catching glimpses of me."

"And how about dogs?" says Robert, and I can tell he's pulled that question from his own experience, his own time in the same condition. And it strikes me that my two guests, one invited and the other not, have a link, a strange bond that I can only imagine. But I'm learning fast.

The man laughs, and even his laughter has a British tone to it. "I have had to nearly throw myself in front of speeding taxicabs in order to avoid the teeth and claws of the city's canine residents. I have never seen so many ill-mannered four-footed creatures in my life. And, frankly, the two-footed New Yorkers are not much better.

"But getting back to your question, Robert: I followed you because you not only saw something—me—but you reacted in a way no one ever has before. You seemed to know *what* you were seeing. And when you began to practically run away, I knew I'd best investigate. I managed to catch up just as you got to Columbus

Circle. I didn't get to hear everything you said to Gwendolyn on the train—too many people about, and I had to keep retreating so as not to be trampled. But I heard enough to know that you and I should talk.

"So why don't we all sit at the table together? I often cook for myself, and I often nibble at some of the finest restaurants and delicatessens in the world. But a simple meal, cooked to order, is a luxury I've been craving for almost three years. Gwendolyn, are you planning to step over here and knock me senseless with that skillet, or may I prevail upon you to continue with your previously announced dinner preparations?"

The direct address wakes me up. I look down, and I'm still holding the frying pan.

"No, I'll cook. Omelettes. I'm ready."

"Excellent."

And as I dig around for ingredients in the refrigerator, the man says, "So tell me about your experience, Robert. And please, leave nothing out. I'm certain I shall know if you try to hold anything back."

It's the tone of his voice. Something unpleasant, almost threatening. I'm cracking eggs into a bowl, and from my position at the stovetop, I can see Robert on the couch, facing the fireplace. He gets this wonderfully simple look on his face and says, "Why would I hold anything back? Besides, there's not that much to tell. I woke up one morning at my house in Chicago and I was invisible. And I was that way for almost a month. I stayed at home with my parents, and we kept it a secret.

And then one morning I woke up, and I was back. I had some fun, and I missed a lot of school. And I learned more about what I want in life. Because that time changed the way I look at myself. And other people. But that's about it."

So Robert's holding back, telling as little as possible. I don't blame him.

The man makes a clucking sound, and I can imagine him shaking his head. "No, no, no—that's far too simplified. I want details, young man, all the details. After a month in the shadow world, you went to bed invisible one night, and then you woke up normal again? Is that what you're saying?"

Robert nods his head. "That's what happened. Was it different for you? I mean, like, at the start? And, who are you?"

"Call me William, please. I was employed as a rather undistinguished assistant professor of English literature at a university some distance north of here. Three winters ago I awoke at four in the morning needing a drink of water, and I went to the kitchen in my flat and reached for a glass, and—no hand. No hand, no arm, nothing visible beneath my pyjamas. I had been divorced for two years, living on my own, writing literary criticism when not teaching. So, unlike you, I faced my predicament alone. And that night my former life came to an abrupt end. I simply disappeared, which I must say I found quite invigorating. Rather like being reborn. No debts, no more whining from my ex-wife, no more

alimony or child-support payments—quite delightful."
He chuckles and then adds, "I even got to settle a few
old scores at the university before I left."

Warning bells go off in my head, because I've never
liked the kind of person who holds a grudge. And again,
I feel a dark undercurrent—something almost cruel.
Something dangerous.

Robert has to be feeling the way I do, but he's nodding, playing along. He says, "But now you want to get
back to normal again."

The man pauses, considering Robert's statement. "I
would at least like the option. I'd like to know how this
happened. Which is why you, young man, are of such in-
tense interest to me. You see, being in this state has en-
abled me to develop a way to make quite a lot of money.
However, at some point it would be good to become my
former self so I can spend that money in more conven-
tional ways than I'm currently able to. It does one little
good to be stinking rich if one cannot purchase a villa in
a sunny climate and then live at that villa without
alarming the local population. A person who looks like
me cannot speed about in an expensive motorcar without being covered with clothes from head to toe, and of
course, that takes all the fun out of owning a convert-
ible. So I'm keenly interested in how you returned to or-
dinary life." He pauses, then adds, "And I think you are
not telling me all you know about it."

With a look of confused innocence, Robert says,
"There's nothing more to tell. It's not like I planned for

it to happen, and I didn't plan for it to stop, either. It happened, and then it stopped."

Robert may be the best actor I know. And now I understand exactly why he's holding back like this. The goal is to say good-bye to this man as soon as possible. But what if he decides he wants to stick around? What happens then?

I've got the first omelette almost ready, so I put two pieces of bread in the toaster. "William, do you want some orange juice with your omelette? Or milk? Or coffee? And what do you want on the toast? There's orange marmalade, strawberry preserves, and grape jelly." It's strange to be talking to someone I can't see, because the man isn't in front of the mantel anymore, and it's exactly like Robert told me: If you're in that state, no one can see you unless you're right up against another background.

And when the man answers, I jump, because William's just opposite me, right on the other side of the island where I'm cooking. Close enough to reach across the stovetop and touch me. Another shiver.

"Orange juice will be perfect, and strawberry preserves. No coffee, thanks. And you do not have to shout in my direction, Gwendolyn. I am presently invisible, but my hearing is unimpaired."

And the smile in the man's voice tells me that he enjoyed seeing me jump.

By the time the toaster pops, I've got three places set at the table, and then I serve the first meal. "All ready."

I've moved my daffodils, and I place William's food on the table so he's facing me as I cook the second omelette. I don't want to miss anything. Robert can be matter-of-fact about this, but it's all new to me, and I want to see—or not see—the whole magic act. And then I want this man to leave.

I have to admit that mealtime is quite a show. The knife floats, slices off a tab of butter, and then spreads it onto the toast. The salt and pepper rise into the air and take turns shaking above the omelette. The juice glass goes up, tips, and the liquid seems to spill into midair and disappear. The fork is in almost constant motion, cutting, spearing, ferrying back and forth between plate and mouth.

And I'm overcooking the second omelette.

Robert's at the table now, and between mouthfuls the man keeps talking. I wish he'd talk with his mouth open so I could see the food floating there before he swallows. But he has proper English table manners.

"As I followed you here, I was hoping to walk indoors behind you so we'd have a quiet moment to begin our conversation. And then I saw that large man, Henry Carlton Page, as I recall the name, who began pounding on the door. You two made such a dash that I couldn't slip into the house with you, and I had to stay outside for most of the afternoon. I didn't think it wise to ring the bell."

Robert says, "Weren't you freezing?"

"It was not pleasant, but unless it's bitterly cold, I

have trained myself to ignore bodily discomfort. Then the police arrived and opened all the doors, and I've been admiring your home ever since, Gwendolyn. And I must say, this is quite a ripping little drama you've got going here. After my initial tour of the premises, I took up residency in the library, since that seemed to be the police command center. And I listened to all of the statements taken by that dreadful chief inspector. And I shall be quite interested to see what he makes of the case. And, of course, Gwendolyn, I am truly sorry about the loss of your grandfather. He has a kindly face. The police were very respectful of him—which is more than they've ever been to me. It was fascinating to watch them do their work. Real life is far more interesting than television, don't you think?"

After a sip of orange juice, the glass hangs in midair, and he says, "I just *adore* nosing about in other people's business, don't you? In fact, I often think I should start my own private detective agency. Because sometimes I'll just choose a person who's walking down the street, someone who looks interesting to me, and I'll follow along for days and days—home, office, gym, restaurants, even business trips, and those quiet evenings with friends and family. It's fascinating to learn so much about another human being, all those little secrets. Of course, I snoop mostly because it's amusing, just because I can. But I'm certain I would be paid handsomely for the information I could discover. But it's not a job for the faint of heart. I've had some rather close calls as an amateur. So it's probably just as well that I've found . . . other work."

Robert's omelette is served, and as I pour out the egg mixture to start cooking mine, I notice my hands are shaking. But I'm curious, and I say, "So, what is this other work?" It's a casual question, but right away I feel like I shouldn't have asked.

The juice glass descends. Then a napkin lifts slowly off the table, dabs the air, and returns to its place. And his voice says, "I'd rather not go into that. But I can tell you that it's an endeavour that has a kinship with the grand old English tradition of Robin Hood."

I flip my omelette. And even though the man scares me, I'm still curious. So I ask another question. "Do you just sleep in stores . . . like, anywhere it's warm?"

"Do you mean, am I a homeless person? No, I rent a comfortable flat north of Fourteenth Street, situated above what used to be a meat-cutting plant. It's a one floor walk-up, and I have my own door at street level with an electronic entry pad—which saves me the trouble of keeping track of a key. I come and go whenever I wish, and my neighbors do not seem to notice or care when my door opens and closes at odd hours. New York is a lot like London in that way, everyone basically minding his own business. I have groceries delivered to my entryway once a week. I did have a break-in last September, but the burglar took an unfortunate tumble down my stairs—I waited until he had a television in his arms. Poor lad thought no one was home. And as he lay at the bottom of the stairs with a broken ankle, sharp things like forks and pencils began to mysteriously float through the air and then suddenly jab into his arms and legs. Quite a lot of howling. The fellow finally managed to flee with relatively minor injuries, but I am certain that neither he nor any of his colleagues will ever be back. He had a *frightening* experience."

I'm having the same experience, right now. I flinch as the last of William's omelette disappears, followed by the final few bites of toast. And I can imagine the flexing of his jaw muscles as he chews, imagine him reaching up with a long fingernail to pick a scrap of food from his teeth. There's a smirky sneer on his face. I don't have to see it to know it's there. Maybe he was a decent person back in his former life, but not anymore, and I don't want him in my home, or in my life, or anywhere near me. Compared to this man, my uncle Hank is a teddy bear. Yes, Uncle Hank's been a bully. But William—if that's even his name—William is doing stuff that's really nasty, and he's doing it on purpose. And he's smirking because he knows he can get away with anything he wants to. And if I could, I'd push him out the door right now, this instant.

I'm at the table now, and I take a drink of orange juice. It tastes sour. Everything seems to have turned sour. Sour and surreal.

"Something wrong, Gwen?" There's a mock-caring tone in William's voice.

I shake my head and turn my attention to my plate, angry that I let my thoughts show on my face.

He goes on, his voice oozing sarcasm. "You look as if you're disturbed about something. Ahh, of course—your grandfather. Poor dear. How insensitive of me. And here I am, intruding on your grief, even making you cook for me. I should be ashamed of myself, I really should. I'm afraid I haven't made a very good first impression."

His chair scoots back from the table, and Robert gets to his feet as well.

"I must be going now. Robert, if you'll escort me to the door, that would be grand. And when I'm standing on the front steps, we shall shake hands like gentlemen, and that way you'll know for certain that I'm outside. And that way you'll both sleep better tonight—knowing that I'm actually gone. Or at least, actually . . . outside."

Again, the smirk. His voice has moved across the parlor and the hallway door opens. Robert follows, and then the street door opens. And watching from beside the table, I see Robert put out his hand, and there's a shake, and then Robert's inside again, fast, shutting both doors. "And put the bar in place," I say, but Robert's ahead of me, already fitting the bottom of the brace rod into its floor socket.

He walks back to the table and sits across from me. "That is one creepy guy."

I nod and then shiver. "He's awful. And I'm sorry I doubted what you told me earlier. But until it's right there, it's just too . . . unbelievable."

Because this afternoon on the subway when I dropped Robert's story into the same bucket with Belinda's alien adventures, I couldn't see how this invisibility stuff would ever affect my own little story.

And now William has changed that. My story has been picking up a lot of passengers recently. Too many.

I say it again. "So I'm sorry I doubted you."

Robert waves my apology aside. "But now what do I do?" he asks. "Because no way am I going to tell this guy how to reverse the process. He shouldn't have that information. He's a crook—you heard him. He's Robin Hood. That means he steals from rich people, which has to be why he likes it here in New York. Except I bet he doesn't give a cent to the poor—or anyone else. But I already figured that out."

I stare at Robert. "What do you mean? Figured what out?"

"It was in yesterday's newspaper. There's a big story in the *Times* about more than a dozen unsolved robberies. Van Cleef and Arpels, Bulgari, Harry Winston—all the top jewelry stores in the city. A salesperson and a customer will be sitting across from each other, and the customer is looking at some rings or necklaces—things that cost two or three hundred thousand dollars each—and suddenly, one or two of the items is missing. Just missing. It's not the salesperson stealing, and it's not the rich customer. So guess who's taking the stuff? William reaches over, closes his hand around a nice chunk of jewelry, and it disappears. Then he walks out the door and probably makes a phone call to somebody who can sell it for him. And the same sort of shoplifting has been happening at all the big diamond wholesalers on Forty-seventh Street. Our new friend is a major thief. And the most recent store was Tiffany and Company—three robberies in the last two weeks. And do you know where Tiffany's is? Right at Fifty-seventh and Fifth Avenue. Which is just around the corner from Niketown. It has to be him."

I'm quiet a minute, trying to sort through everything. I can't, so I ask, "So what should we do? We have to do *something*, don't we? Shouldn't we tell the police?"

Robert shakes his head. "Because what happens if it becomes this huge news story—because it would—and suddenly everyone knows there's a way to make a person disappear? The FBI and the CIA would get on the case, I'm sure of that. And they'd figure it out. They would. Because the first thing that guy would do is tell them about me. And then my parents would be involved. And then Alicia and her parents. Because this process is dangerous technology, especially if it gets into the wrong hands. And it would all come out. It would all come out. . . ."

His thoughts trail off, and he looks tired and confused.

I look at my watch, and it's almost seven-thirty. It

feels more like three A.M. I'm beyond tired, beyond drained, beyond exhausted. I'd like to go to bed, or at least take a nap. Then I think about my bedroom.

I'm not a superstitious person, but I don't want to go downstairs to my bedroom. Downstairs is where Grampa was.

And while I'm wondering if Robert is bothered by stuff like that, he says, "Are you going to think I'm terrible if I tell you that I want to stop thinking about all this and go down to the basement and practice awhile?"

So that answers that. He's not only fine about going downstairs, he's going to walk right up to the yellow crime scene tape stretched across the back hall, take a right turn, walk down into the dim basement, and then play his trumpet.

I shake my head. "No, that's fine. You need to. I'm just going to stretch out here on the couch and try to calm down. It's a lot to deal with in one day."

"Yeah it is," he says. Then a very sweet smile. "And you've been incredible, really. And it's my turn to do the dishes, okay?"

Before I can say thanks, he comes over and he's giving me a hug. And it makes me feel like I'm eight years old, sitting in the pickup, snuggled between my mom and dad on that long drive we took to Memphis, just the three of us, safe and warm on a country road with the wipers slapping rain from the windshield. I could stay folded against him like this for hours.

And then suddenly we're both embarrassed. We separate, and I say, "Thanks. For doing the dishes."

"Sure. No problem. Happy to help out," and he picks up his trumpet and goes down the stairs.

I take the dark green fleece blanket off the back of Grampa's recliner. I sit on the couch and try to make the room stop spinning. And it does.

Then I lie down. I spread out the blanket and curl up, pulling it around my shoulders. My mind wants to review the day, spin back through every detail, sort and file and categorize and judge every event, every person, every moment. But I don't allow it. I do what my mom told me to when I called home. She said I could trust it all to God. She said I was being watched over. And I reach out, because that's all I want, to be watched over. And I'm almost at peace, and then I'm crying. Because of Grampa.

It's the blanket. It smells like his aftershave.

But I calm myself again, and I trust Grampa to God as well. Because, honestly, there's nothing else I can do.

And sometimes trust has to be enough.

chapter 15

REINFORCEMENTS

C ell phone. My ring.

Morning light is coming through the shutters, and I'm tangled in the green blanket on the couch, trying to get the phone out of my pocket.

"Hello?"

"Hello, sweetheart—how're you doin' there?"

"Hi, Daddy. I'm fine. Are you coming?"

"I'm already in Newark, be at Penn Station in about an hour. I wanted to call last night, but your mama said you'd be in bed early after such a hard day. How'd everything go, with the police and everything?"

"It was okay. After about two hours everybody left. Except for Robert. He's a friend from the music camp at Tanglewood last summer. He's in the city for auditions, same as me. And I didn't want to be alone. Uncle Hank was here for a while too. So he knows about Grampa. And Mama was right. I fell asleep on the couch around eight o'clock."

I tell Daddy about the meeting at the police station

in the afternoon, and then he has to go get on his train. "See you soon, Gwennie."

Grampa's bedroom door is shut, and I'm thinking Robert is still asleep. Daylight makes the house more cheerful, so I walk downstairs to my room.

After I shower and dress, I go back upstairs and there's a note from Robert.

Have to run errands. Be back about noon. Practice!
Robert

I know it's good advice, to practice. And before, no one would have needed to remind me. But I can't. Daddy's coming, and the place needs to be tidied up. Robert did load the dirty dishes into the dishwasher, but he cleans up the way my big brothers do. The kitchen and dining area are still a mess.

I start to open all the shutters, and then I remember William. For all I know, he's right outside, trying to see into the house. It's a bad feeling, and I leave the windows covered.

After I finish the dishes, I walk to the table, pick up the chair William sat on, and put it over in the corner. I don't want to use that chair again. It should probably be reupholstered. Or burnt.

Then I move the daffodils back to the center of the table, and they're still as bright and fresh as ever, *Tossing their heads in sprightly dance.* Thank you, Mr. Wordsworth.

Robert's back a few minutes before my dad arrives, and I'm glad, because I want my dad to meet him. But as the front buzzer sounds, Robert smiles at me and then disappears down the stairs with his trumpet.

"Hey, there she is!"

In the middle of my dad's bear hug, I remember how much I love my family, remember how much it means to have that love, always there. But even during this sweet moment in the doorway, at least half my mind is watching, on high alert, making sure there's not room for someone to slip past us into the house. The William thing is making me completely paranoid. Robert made me promise not to tell my dad or anyone else about that situation.

But there are plenty of other things to talk about, and we do, for almost an hour, and during that time neither of us says anything about Grampa. And as we talk, my dad does a good job of hiding how sad he is that his own dad is gone now. But I can still tell he's torn up about it. Because I know how I would feel.

When Robert comes back upstairs, right away my dad grabs his hand and says, "I want to thank you for taking care of my little girl last night. Means a lot to me."

Robert's sort of embarrassed, but he smiles back and says, "Sure, no problem. I mean, it's not like she wasn't doing great on her own. But I was glad to be here."

"So," Daddy says, "what d'you think's gonna happen at the meeting, at the police? Got any clues?"

It's hard to remember that my dad grew up in Queens. His accent sounds like pure West Virginia. Which I think is actually much nicer.

I shrug. "There's that letter Grampa sent to his lawyer. That's got to be important, don't you think?"

Robert nods his head. "Probably. Has to be important."

My dad says, "Well, we're all gonna know soon enough, I guess."

And he's right about that. We have time to eat some soup and sandwiches, and I get Daddy moved into Grampa's bedroom, with the sheets all changed and everything, and then it's time to walk to Broadway and hail a cab for the ride to the police station.

The Twenty-fourth Precinct station is on 100th Street next to a playground in the middle of the block. It's also close to an apartment complex called the Frederick Douglass Houses, more than a dozen buildings that fill most of the area between 100th and 104th streets. West Side High School is close too, and I get a quick look at the public school I'd attend if I actually lived around here. And if I didn't have a scholarship at Latham Academy. And if my family and my grampa hadn't helped me become a classical musician. So many ifs.

Mr. Grant is already inside the station waiting for us, and shortly after Detective Keenan takes us up a short flight of stairs to a conference room, Uncle Hank walks in. He and my dad have a quick hug. Both men are genuinely happy to see each other.

With a big smile, still holding my dad at arm's length, he says, "I don't think I've seen you since that summer before you went into the army."

My dad nods and says, "That was a real camping trip. Great memories, great memories."

And my perception of Uncle Hank shifts again. Because I can see how narrow a view I've had of the man. He really is someone's uncle, and someone else's little brother. I'm sorry it took something like this to make me figure that out.

I look around the room, and that's when I notice it's got one of those mirrored glass walls. And right away I get the feeling I'm being watched.

The detective takes charge, pointing at chairs for everyone, including a court stenographer, who moves to a corner facing us, sets up his portable keyboard, and then nods at the officer.

"Okay. First, let's see this letter you brought, Mr. Grant. And everyone, please speak clearly for the stenographer."

The lawyer reaches into his briefcase, pulls out a tan envelope, and passes it to the detective who's sitting across the table.

Detective Keenan says, "I am examining the postmark, which is Thursday of last week. This is a stamped and sealed registered mail envelope, and it has not been opened since received at the offices of Kenneth Grant, Attorney-at-Law."

He passes the envelope back to Mr. Grant. "Mr.

Grant will now open the envelope in clear view, and we'll determine together if any of the contents are relevant to the case at hand, that being the suspicious death of Lawrence Page, former resident of West 109th Street, New York City."

The lawyer tears open the envelope flap and pulls out three smaller sealed envelopes. Mr. Grant says, "There are three standard number-ten envelopes here, each sealed. One is addressed to me, Kenneth Grant. One is addressed to Henry Page, care of Kenneth Grant, and the third is addressed to Gwendolyn Page, also care of Kenneth Grant. And now I am opening the envelope addressed to me."

He does, and he takes out two handwritten pages, and reads them each silently. No one is talking, so the stenographer's fingers are still. Looking around the table, I'm the only one not trying to read the lawyer's face. Except Robert. He seems uncomfortable, and he's glancing around the conference room. Maybe the two-way mirror makes him jumpy. Then Robert notices I'm looking his way, and he flashes me a tense smile.

Clearing his throat, Mr. Grant passes the letter to the detective and says, "After you take a look at this, if there are no objections, I'll read each page aloud into the record. While this includes some personal business of the deceased, I believe it is relevant to these circumstances."

Detective Keenan scans the pages, says "I agree with that," and then hands the letter back.

Mr. Grant says, "For the record, I am reading from a

handwritten page, and am confident that the handwriting can be proven beyond all doubt to be that of my client, Lawrence Page." He adjusts his glasses and begins, first reading the date at the top of the page.

I am Lawrence Page, and I am writing this of my own free will, sitting alone in my own home.

Whoever's reading this knows that I'm gone now. I want anybody who's concerned, and I'm sure that's a number of people, to know one thing for certain: No one but me had any part in getting me into the freezer chest that's located on the ground floor of this home. This was my idea, and I put myself in there.

I'm sorry for the way it looks, and I'm sorry for the fright it must have given someone when I was found.

As I'm writing this, I'm at that point in my life where I know what's going to happen next. And I don't want anybody but me to feel responsible about making decisions—what to do, or what not to do for me—during my final days. So I have made my own decision.

Folks might disagree with what I've done, or the way I've done it, and I expect some will. But there it is. The people who know me and love me will understand, and they're the only ones I care about.

Lawrence Daniel Page

My dad wipes a tear from the corner of his eye, and Uncle Hank blows his nose into a handkerchief. And I'm crying too. I can hear Grampa's voice so clearly. I don't really understand why he did this. But I know that I'm one of the people who loves him. And Grampa says that I'll understand. So I will. I hope I will.

Detective Keenan pushes a box of tissues in my direction, and I take a few and say, "Thank you."

Mr. Grant then takes the second page from the envelope. "This," he says, "is not technically relevant to this proceeding, but I want to publish it into the record of this inquiry so there's no doubt that it came from the same envelope, and that it was written by the same person." And again he begins to read aloud.

I am Lawrence Page, and by my own hand I am revising my last will and testament. When and if the property on 109th Street is sold, from the part of the proceeds that belongs to my estate, I want enough money to be set aside to pay the entire cost of tuition, room, and board for the college and postgraduate studies of my granddaughter, Gwendolyn Page. If that property is not sold, then the necessary money should be taken from other available assets in my estate.

In addition, immediately upon my death, I want thirty-five thousand dollars taken from my personal funds and given to this same Gwendolyn Page for the purchase of a violin and a violin bow of her choosing.

I also want enough money to be provided from the funds of my estate so my granddaughter Gwendolyn Page can continue her musical studies here in New York without interruption until the end of this current school year.

These three provisions will be administered by my attorney, Kenneth Grant, as part of his duties as the executor of my estate.

Mr. Grant looks up and says, "And this codicil is signed by Lawrence Page and witnessed by Jason Di Renzo, of the same address as the deceased. It's dated on the last day that my client was seen alive."

Robert is smiling and nodding at me, and everyone looks pleased, even Uncle Hank. I'm all weepy again, but what the lawyer said doesn't surprise me. Here's my grampa, an hour or two before he dies, and he's thinking about someone else. It's beginning to fit.

Looking at the detective, Mr. Grant says, "Shall I open and read these other letters?"

The detective shakes his head. "I don't think it's necessary now."

So Mr. Grant reaches to his left and then his right, handing out the remaining letters, one to Uncle Hank and the other to me.

The policeman says, "We've got the preliminary

coroner's report, and as of this moment, this case is pretty much closed."

Mr. Grant raises his eyebrows. "So it's . . . suicide?"

And everyone else around the table winces at the word.

Detective Keenan says, "Actually, no. Mr. Page took a small oxygen bottle into the freezer with him, so he didn't suffocate. And he was all bundled up in his coat and cap and boots, so it wasn't the cold, either. And he'd put a piece of duct tape over the freezer latch, so he could have opened the lid and gotten out anytime he wanted to. The coroner is ninety-five percent certain that this man would have still passed on, no matter where he'd been at the time of his death. He chose a strange place to lie down, but it's accurate to say that he died in his sleep. According to the coroner, Lawrence Page died of natural causes."

Standing up abruptly, the detective walks to the door. "Sorry to rush everybody along, but I've got to ask you to leave now. We'll be in touch as needed."

And then the detective stands there, one hand on the doorknob, as the group files out of the room.

I'm the last one out, and I'm expecting the detective to follow me, but he doesn't. He slams the door shut on my heels, and then three other nonuniformed officers in the hallway line up at the door, knock once, and slip back into the conference room. One of the three men has a big video camera.

Before Daddy, Robert, and I are more than twenty

feet away, I hear shouting from the room, then the sound of furniture banging around.

I hesitate and look back, but Robert says, "C'mon, just keep going. That's got nothing to do with us."

But I stop and then Robert does too, and I look at him. Because it sounds like he's afraid.

Then from behind the closed door of the conference room, someone yells, "Get your *bloody* hands off of me!" It's a man's voice. And he has a British accent.

My heart stops, and I gasp. "Isn't that . . . ?"

But Robert shakes his head and makes a stern face at me. "Let's just go, okay?"

The others are already outside, so we go down the stairs and out of the police station, and then we hurry to catch up with my dad and Uncle Hank. Mr. Grant is already in a cab, and he turns and waves to me out the window. And I smile and wave back.

Then we're walking behind Uncle Hank and Daddy, and I start to say something to Robert, but he whispers, "Not now."

So as we cross Amsterdam Avenue and go downhill toward Broadway, I'm left with my own thoughts.

And I'm thinking that I don't believe what Robert said, that the commotion in the conference room has nothing to do with us.

Because I'm sure Robert's involved in this, right up to his dark brown eyebrows.

And that means I'm involved too. Even if I don't want to be.

chapter 16

COMEUPPANCE

My dad takes us all to a steakhouse for an early supper, so it's over an hour before I get to talk to Robert alone.

The meal feels awkward. There's only one thing on our minds, but none of us wants to talk about what Grampa did, or how the investigation turned out, even though it was as close to a happy ending as anyone could expect.

And those generous gifts to me are almost embarrassing. I feel like I've been picked as the favorite, Grampa's little pet. Even so, I can tell that the others are all happy for me, Uncle Hank included. Three times during the meal my eyes fill up with tears, thinking how sweet Grampa is to take such care of me.

Then Hank and Daddy start telling stories about growing up in Queens with Grampa and Grandmother, about trips to The Bronx Zoo and Coney Island and Jones Beach, and before long all four of us are laughing. And just when I'm starting to feel happy, my dad says,

"I called Veterans Affairs 'fore I left home, and since he's a decorated officer, they're gonna send us a color guard and a bugler, and they'll have a presentation flag too. He'd want you to have that, Hank." And the two men start talking about all the other arrangements for Grampa's funeral.

So I say, "If it's okay, Robert and I are going to walk back to Grampa's."

My dad says, "Sure, sweetheart, but I'd rather you took a cab."

I make a face. "Daddy, I'm a city kid, remember? Besides, it's not even dark yet."

He pushes a twenty-dollar bill into my hand. "Then here, take some money anyway and stop for a treat somewhere. You're pullin' out before dessert."

Robert thanks Daddy for the meal, and then we're outside. Before we're thirty feet from the restaurant, someone calls out, "Gwennie?"

I know that voice. It's Uncle Hank.

Robert says, "I'll wait here for you."

I walk back and when I stand in front of him, he talks fast, like he has to get it all out in one breath. "I feel bad, the way I acted, and about what happened. I wanted you to know that. Said some mean things too. Can't undo anything, but I wanted you to know. The fuel costs hit me, that's all. Couldn't even pay my drivers last week. It just . . . I just . . ."

This is hard for him. He's looking down into my face. "It's okay, Uncle Hank. And what happened, it wasn't your fault. I know Grampa didn't blame you. He even told me not to judge you. And I don't. I think everything's going to be all right, don't you?" Because that's what I hope.

He nods awkwardly, smiles a little. "Well, got to get back inside. See you soon, Gwennie."

"Bye, Uncle Hank."

I've been thinking of questions to ask Robert all during dinner, but we walk north on Broadway without talking. I've just been given a brand-new portrait of my uncle Hank, and I need to let the paint dry a little.

But after ten seconds, my curiosity won't be still. "So that was William, in the police station, right? And you went to the police and turned him in, right? Was that your errand this morning?"

Robert's got his hands stuffed into his jacket pockets. He slips me a sideways glance and half a smile. "I also made an important stop at that Italian bakery."

I ignore his attempt at humor, because this isn't funny, none of it. "But why did you think William would be at the police station?"

Robert shrugs. "Well, for starters he told us yesterday that he would be very interested to see how the case turned out. You remember that, right?"

I nod, and Robert says, "And he also bragged about what a hotshot snooper he is. But most of all, I was pretty sure William would come there to contact me again. I don't think I fooled him last night. At all. He *knows* that I know a lot more than I told him. And two years ago? I can remember how completely desperate *I* was to find out *anything*, to follow up *any* clue, even a tiny one, if it might mean I could get my life back again. And as far as William is concerned, *I* am a *huge* clue—a real break. He could have hung around this house and watched for me, but it's February, and it's cold out there. But he knew that I *had* to be at that police station at three P.M. today. So, was I sure he'd show up? No. But I'd have bet you my trumpet that he would. And he did."

"So . . . what did you tell the detective?"

"Ahh," Robert says. "That was the artistic part: To tell the truth, and nothing but the truth, but not quite the *whole* truth. I told Detective Keenan that there was this crazy guy who had slipped into your grampa's house yesterday during all the confusion, and that he was hiding in the study when everyone was giving their statements."

I nod. "So far, so true."

Robert ignores my commentary. "And then I told the detective that this crazy guy talked to us after everyone left, and that he said he was dying to know how the case would turn out. Also completely true. And then I told him that this man said he'd figured out a way to avoid the most sophisticated security systems, *and* that he'd been acting like a regular Robin Hood at some of the richest stores in Manhattan."

"So that's not *quite* the truth," I say.

"Close enough. And then I said, 'It's almost like this

guy thinks he's invisible or something. Which would make somebody into a pretty great thief.' "

"No! You said that?"

Robert grins. "Sure did. Because that's the big bait. Catching a broad-daylight robber would do a lot for a detective's career. And I also gave him William's juice glass, from the dinner dishes last night. So he could match fingerprints from the crime scenes. Because he had to leave fingerprints all over town. Invisible robbers can't wear gloves."

And standing there with my mouth open, it dawns on me just how far out of my league Robert is. The guy's a plotter. But I want to know the rest.

"So what'd he say—when you said that stuff about how he thinks he's invisible?"

"Well, the detective took this long pause, like a count-to-ten, because now he's not so sure about *me*. And he said, 'So you think he might try to hang around the meeting this afternoon, right in the police station?' And I say, 'This man seems to think he can get away with anything.' Also true, and also great bait for a detective. Then this was the crowning touch. I said, 'If he's so good at hiding himself, I think an infrared camera would probably make him show up plain as day.' "

"Robert!" I stop short on the sidewalk, and he faces me, beaming.

"And that's what they did. They lit up their camera, and they tracked his body heat right there in the room after we left. And it was four guys to one, so I'm thinking William the invisible creep is in jail. Right now."

I reach into my shoulder bag and pull out my cell phone. "Call him."

Robert looks at me like I'm insane.

"I mean Detective Keenan. Call him right now. I want to know, to really know that that man isn't walking around my neighborhood tonight. Because if he's still on the loose, and he wants to find you, he's going to come to Grampa's house again. And I don't want that to happen. Or if it might happen, then I want to be prepared. So call, okay? For me."

Robert takes the phone and calls 411 to get the non-emergency number of the Twenty-fourth Precinct.

"Hello? Could I talk with Detective Keenan? It's Robert Phillips calling."

Robert nods to me and whispers, "He's there."

"Detective? This is Robert. We talked about that crazy guy, remember? I just wanted to know if you got him. . . . Oh, that's too bad."

Robert shoots me a glance, and I gasp and grab his arm. He pulls loose and keeps talking.

"But I really called because I remembered something else he told me yesterday. He said he had an apartment north of Fourteenth Street, a first floor walk-up above an old meat-packing plant. . . . Right, with an electronic keypad instead of a lock. . . . Right. So I thought you should know about that. . . . Well, anyway, good luck." And Robert hangs up.

I'm frantic, and my voice has gone up an octave. "They didn't *get* him? Robert, that's really bad. It's terrible. Because he's not stupid, and he knows the police were looking out for him, and . . . and nobody could have told them but you. Or me. So now . . . now he *knows* that one of *us* tried to turn him in. And . . . and he'll try to do something, he'll—"

Robert waves his hands at me. "Hold it, hold it, hold it—calm down. The detective was lying to me. I'm sure they got him. No doubt at all. So just relax."

I'm stunned. "*Lying*? What do you mean? He's a *policeman*. Why would he lie? Police don't do that."

"Right," says Robert, "*unless* it's in the interest of public safety. If the police have a photo of a dangerous suspect, but the suspect doesn't know that, do they go on TV and say, 'We have no information at this time'? Yes they do, because that *lie* makes the suspect think he can walk around freely, and then the police can spot him and arrest him.

"Do you think that detective, who's got an invisible man in his custody, is going to tell people about it—even me? No way. And about the rest of it, whether William tells him about me being invisible and all that? I don't know what's going to come of that. But for now, I think the police are going to keep a tight lid on this, or maybe they'll make William an offer he can't refuse, make him go to work for them. Who knows? Anyway, I'm sure it was right to get him off the streets. So we've done our civic duty, and we'll have to see how all the rest of it works out. Because that's not our job. So. Where's the ice cream in this city?"

How Robert can think about ice cream right now is beyond my understanding. Of course, I've been on such an emotional seesaw today that everything is beyond my understanding.

But Robert turns on his ice cream radar, which guides us across 105th Street, where we find a sweets shop that's actually selling waffle cones in February, and he orders for both of us, two massive cones with three scoops each, whipped cream, nuts, sprinkles, the works. Then, by carefully decorating his nose with an assortment of toppings, Robert finally gets me to smile.

Even though I'm having a little fun, and even though I'm grateful for the good things that have happened today, I'm still uneasy about the William situation, and always, always, I feel this sadness that won't go away. Because I can't stop thinking about my grampa and that big freezer. About what he did.

And the selfish part of me is still wishing that all the complications would vanish. Because I want to get my story back. *My* story. I just want to be a musician, and suddenly, I know why.

It's because I've been imagining that it's going to be easy. It's because I think I'll be able to lose myself in great sweeps of harmony, and the all-knowing, infallible conductor will always lead the way. And me? I imagine myself gliding seamlessly from one movement to the next, with hardly a rustle as I turn the pages of the score.

Because I want things to work out the way they do when Bach is in charge. Or Paganini. Or Jane Austen. Or even Yeats. Because I'm desperate for a nice, tidy ending, maybe with a pleasant rhyme or two, or that wonderful last burst of symphonic harmony that makes me want to shout "yes!"

But it's not happening that way.

chapter 17

GIFTS

I t's Monday night, and Robert tells me again that I should practice, but I say, "No, it's all right. You go first tonight." And like a gentleman, he goes down to the rehearsal room and leaves me alone.

With Daddy upstairs watching TV, I hide out in my room. I've talked to my mom for half an hour, said hi to both my sisters, and I've talked to both my big brothers. Plus I've had a call from Uncle Belden, and while we were talking, I could hear a West Virginia catbird singing, and I pictured its little throat moving, pictured it sitting in a tree out in front of his crooked front porch. And as he said good-bye, Uncle Belden wished me well on my auditions.

My auditions.

My first audition is at eleven tomorrow morning, but I don't care anymore. I don't want to go. There's a line in a Yeats poem that comes winging up out of my memory, and it slaps me hard:

Things fall apart; the center cannot hold;

And it hurts to feel this way. I'm so used to being Little Miss Organized and Little Miss Punctuality, and I've been a perfectionist for so long that I can't remember any other way to be. I didn't even get to my lesson this afternoon, and I missed my only practice session with the grad student who's doing the piano accompaniment on the Sibelius during my audition. It's like I don't know myself anymore.

I keep thinking about the questions Robert asked me this afternoon, after we'd had our ice cream. He said, "You know, I don't believe that, what your grampa said in his letter. He said, 'I'm at that point in my life where I know what's going to happen next.' And I don't think anybody can know that, do you? I mean, when he climbed into that freezer, like what was he thinking? Because you never know what's going to happen next, not really. You just have to take your best shot and keep hoping things'll work out. Right? Because no matter what the coroner says, I don't really think your grampa died of natural causes. Do you? I hate to say it, but it seems to me like he was kind of bailing out. And didn't he sort of create more problems than he solved? What do you think?"

The worst part is that I just kept shrugging my shoulders. I couldn't answer any of Robert's questions. I still can't. I wanted to say, "Well, if Grampa hadn't done what he did, I probably wouldn't have met you. And that would have been too bad." But I couldn't say that.

It's dark now, and I turn off the lights in my room so the place matches my mood. And I lie across my bed and stare up into nothing, and I think back just five days ago.

Last Wednesday night Grampa was sitting upstairs watching CNN. I'd had a good lesson with Pyotr Melyanovich, and I was down in the practice room making Sibelius smile. My first audition was still almost a week away, but I was going to be ready. I was building up my confidence. I was almost at the peak of my preparation, and soon I would march across the plaza at Lincoln Center, throw open the doors of the Juilliard School, and show those people how a violin ought to sound.

And now I almost want to laugh. Or cry.

What pride. And what ignorance—to think everything was going to just trot along like the pony ride at the state fair in Lewisburg, to think that Lizzy would get to marry Mr. Darcy in real life. And to think that I could keep telling myself my own perfect little story.

Right. Think again.

I know that I'll go and take that audition at Juilliard tomorrow. I'm not a no-show. I'd still go if both my arms were broken.

But I don't kid myself. I know I'm not ready, mentally or musically. So I'll have to muddle my way through.

My cell phone rings, and blue light fills the room.

All these calls. Everybody means well, I know that. And everyone wants to say how sorry they are about Grampa. But I don't want to talk to one more person about him. I don't want to share those memories. I need to keep that part of my story for myself.

It's on the fourth ring now, and I want to whip the thing against the wall.

But like a nice little girl, I flip open the phone.

"Hello?"

"Hi, is this Gwen? This is Alicia. Bobby gave me your number. Is this a good time?"

"Oh—hi . . . sure, this is good. Robert talks about you all the time." Which feels like the right thing to say to a girlfriend when she's there and he's here.

She giggles. "Robert. I keep forgetting that he's trying to use his *professional* name now." Another giggle, and there's a whiff of sarcasm in her voice. I like her.

She says, "Anyway, *Bobby* said it's been a rough couple of days. And I'm so sorry about your grandfather. But that's not why I called. Bobby said if I asked, maybe you'd play a little violin for me. Over the phone. He said I should request the fast caprice."

I can't help smiling. "He's trying to be my big helper, and he's recruited you to cheer me up, right?"

She laughs, a beautiful sound. "That's my Bobby . . . and your Robert. Not very subtle, but sweet. But I wouldn't have called if I didn't really want to hear you play. Bobby says you're a great violinist, and he never exaggerates, at least not about music. So, how about it?"

"It's going to take me a minute or two to get ready. Want to wait?"

"Minutes, hours, days—I'm all ears." Again, that trace of irony.

I toss the phone on the bed, flip on the light, and run upstairs to get my violin.

My dad's in front of the TV, and he says, "Hey there, you gonna play for me now? How 'bout somethin' by Bach?"

"A little later, Daddy," and I'm back down the stairs.

Talking loud toward the phone, I say, "I'm opening the case . . . and this is a quick pluck or two to check the tuning . . . and now I have to get the bow tight, and it needs a little rosin." I pick up the phone, and say, "Could you hear any of that?"

"Loud and clear. And this is by Paganini, right?"

"Right. He's this wild, romantic Italian guy, a real genius, like a violin rock star. And he wrote these twenty-four solo pieces back around 1800, and they're just incredible. And impossible. So here goes. This is caprice number two."

I bring two pillows to the edge of my bed, put the phone on top of them, stand up straight, set my bow, take a deep breath, and begin.

The fast caprice. And it is, because it's all sixteenth notes, and it dips and sweeps and skips all over the fingerboard. It's been over twenty-four hours since I've played, probably the longest break I've had in years, but

I'm hearing and feeling every note, and every hair on the bow is alive and speaking. And the insane double-stops and the nonstop octaves that constantly challenge the melody—it's all flowing, and the music is pouring out.

It's when I'm riding my bow on this wild climb up the fingerboard, and it's when I'm skidding down the other side—that's when I'm suddenly hearing Charlie Daniels, and he's playing "The Devil Went Down to Georgia," the instrumental section in the middle. Because this caprice and that song, they're blood brothers, with the same sizzle and pop and showmanship, except the bearded guy with the leather hat plays *so* much faster.

And when I'm almost to the end, and I'm out there on the edge of the musical universe, and I start trying to re-enter the atmosphere so I can land this song, there's Charlie again, running side by side with Paganini. And I'm thinking that I'd pay a million dollars if just once I could see old Niccolò up there on the stage of *Austin City Limits*, just him and Charlie Daniels, both of them setting their strings on fire.

And when I finally drop into the wrenching, clenching, double-stopped finish of the caprice, I can't quite believe what I've just heard. And felt. Because it's been three minutes of pure beauty. And I played that piece with my whole self, my whole heart.

And I played it with the lights on.

I pick up the phone. But for ten seconds, maybe fifteen, I can't talk. Because something new just happened, something important.

Alicia doesn't talk either.

Finally I clear my throat and say, "So, that was it."

She's quiet another few moments. "That was . . . it was just beautiful. Really. Thank you. Perfect. And Bobby's right about you. I'm sure of it." Then she pauses. "Bobby told me that you know what happened to him. Two years ago."

"Yes, and he told you about the man that showed up here? In the city?"

"Yes, he told me. Scary."

Then I say, "Look, I hope this isn't too personal or anything, but when Robert disappeared for all those weeks—like, afterwards, did he change? From the experience?"

She thinks a second or two, and says, "He didn't do a Jekyll and Hyde or anything, if that's what you mean. But yes, there was a change. Like with music? Before it happened, he liked to play the trumpet, and he was in the jazz band at his school and everything. But then afterwards, it just started to mean more to him. He got serious about music. That's what I think changed—he got more serious, about a lot of things. And he thinks more. We both do."

I don't know what to say next, but she can tell, and she saves me.

"Well, listen, thanks again for my private concert. I

loved it. And I hope we can really meet someday. Because I want to hear you play in person. And I want to talk more, okay?"

"Sure," I say, "I'd like that," and I mean it. "And thanks for calling. And thank *Bobby* for putting you up to it."

We both laugh, and then say good-bye.

Gifts. Moments like this are gifts. A person calls from a thousand miles away, and it feels like a friend, and suddenly there's some light again.

I dig around in my shoulder bag so I can check my list of audition times for the millionth time. And in the bag I see the letter, the one from the envelope Grampa sent to Mr. Grant. I stuffed it in there at the end of the meeting at the police station.

My name's on the front, blue ink in Grampa's shaky writing. It's almost too precious to tear open. And I nearly don't, because, really, what else could Grampa possibly say to me? Or give to me?

But I can't resist, and there's a single sheet of paper with something folded inside. At first I think he's giving me one of Grandmother's necklaces. But I unfold the paper, and his army dog tags drop onto the bed, the ones he wore for six years during World War II.

So far tonight, a blind girl who doesn't complain about her life has made me laugh from a thousand miles away; and now my grampa, who never once complained about anything, has made me cry from somewhere else, somewhere beyond a thousand miles away.

But I dry my eyes, and I pick up my borrowed violin and bow, and I walk down to the basement, and I knock on the rehearsal room door.

And when Robert opens it, I smile and say, "Time's up. I've got an audition tomorrow."

chapter 18

GREATER LOVE

On Tuesday morning I wake up early. I don't touch my violin. I don't even look at it. I shower and dress and go upstairs. I'm not hungry, but I force myself to eat two eggs and a piece of toast anyway. There's not much talk.

After breakfast I get my case, and at the door, Robert gives me a hug, and he says, "I know you'll do great. You will."

And then Daddy and I walk over to Broadway and get a cab.

Ten minutes later we're walking across the plaza at Lincoln Center. Alice Tully Hall, the Metropolitan Opera, Avery Fisher Hall. Some of the best musicians in the world will be rehearsing and performing here all week long.

It makes me feel small.

In the lobby of the school, I check in at the tables along the back wall, and then Daddy and I sit down to wait. My accompanist comes and asks if I want to find a practice room and warm up. It's probably a good idea, but I'd rather be still.

I'm glad my dad is here. This is not his world at all, and he's completely unimpressed. And that helps me. No matter what happens here today, cars will still be expertly repaired at the Pro Shop Garage off Interstate 79 near Elkview, West Virginia. No matter what, life will go on. It's good to remember that.

I reach into the pocket of my jacket, then open my palm in Daddy's direction and say, "Look what Grampa gave me."

He takes the dog tags, squints to read them, and then runs his fingers across the stamped lettering.

"It's not a small thing, to give these up. You know that, right?"

I nod, but I hold back my feelings. It's not the right moment to be getting all emotional.

Then Daddy says, "You find the hidden message yet?"

"What? What message?"

He turns the ID over and taps his thick fingernail against the dull metal above Grampa's name. I take it from him and bring it up close. And I see something, scratched into the stainless steel, maybe by a pin or the point of a knife, years and years ago. There are lots of other small scratches, and the surface is worn so smooth that I have to catch the light just right to see anything at all. Out loud, I say, "J . . . 15 . . . 13, right?"

My dad nods.

"What's it mean?"

He shakes his head, then he taps the middle of his chest and I hear a metallic clink. "Scratched the same thing on my own tags the day I got 'em. Secret code. Soldier stuff. But I'll give y'a clue. That J? It *doesn't* stand for Jesus."

My dad doesn't have a subtle bone in his body, which is one of the reasons I love him so much.

I say, "So it's a Bible verse, right?" Another nod. "And the J stands for . . . Joshua?" Nothing. "Judges?" Nothing. "Job? . . . Jeremiah?"

I know my books of the Bible, and I run through the rest of the J's in order. Nothing, until I say, "John?" And there's a flicker of a smile. "So it's John 15, verse 13, right?"

"Can't say. Secret code. Soldier stuff."

"Come on, Daddy. Tell me. Please?"

But he shakes his head. "Oughta know your Bible better."

I look at the clock, and I've got seventeen minutes. So I grab the tags and I say, "Save my seat."

Because I want to know this. Right now. It feels important. Everything feels important right now.

And there's got to be a Bible somewhere close. Because New York City has everything, even Bibles.

I'm out the door, and as I trot past the fountain at the center of the plaza, I think there has to be a bookstore within a block or two. Then I look up, and I adjust my course, because now I know where I'm going: just across

Columbus, straight toward the fifteen-foot-high red neon letters that say Hotel Empire.

In two minutes I'm at the front desk, and in four minutes a friendly woman in a housekeeper's uniform is handing me a Bible, courtesy of the Gideons.

I sit in a huge red chair and open the book. Matthew, Mark, Luke, John, John 12, John 14, John 15.

And there's verse 13. And it's so simple, one sentence. Soldier stuff.

> Greater love hath no man than this,
> that a man lay down his life for his friends.

Walking back across Columbus Avenue, the tears are streaming down my face. Because now I know.

I know why Grampa tucked himself into that foxhole last Thursday. He did it for me. He knew he was going, and he hid himself so it wouldn't make a commotion. He tried to buy me a few more precious days of harmony and order, peace and quiet. If he could have moved all the mountains of West Virginia and brought them here to shelter me, he would have. But in the end, he hoped that one or two more days in my little practice room would be enough. And it was.

Grampa said the people who loved him and cared for him would understand. And now I do. Because now I have a whole story.

I have my own story, and I love my story, but I know I can't tell it alone, not now. Because stories have centers, but they don't have edges. No boundaries. And I needed to learn that. Thank you, Grampa. And Mama. And Daddy. And Mr. Richards and Pyotr. And Robert, and Alicia too. Even William.

No edges.

Passing the fountain, I slip the chain over my head and tuck Grampa's tags inside my white shirt. A minute later, my eyes wiped dry, I walk back into the lobby of the school. I sit down again next to my dad, and when I take his hand, he turns and smiles at me.

Five minutes later a woman at the registration table calls my name.

I pick up my violin case, and I nod and smile at my accompanist, because she's part of my story too. Together we walk to the elevator, ride to the third floor, then take a right along the corridor to find Room 311.

And I am not afraid. I can play.